What's Wrong with Liberalism?

Critical Political Studies
Edited by Jules Townshend

Published titles in the series:

Capitalism and Democracy in the Third World:
The Doctrine for Political Development
PAUL CAMMACK

Voting Behaviour: A Radical Critique
HELENA CATT

Forthcoming titles in the series:

Analysing Public Policy: A Critique of Key Concepts
PETER JOHN

What's Wrong with Liberalism?

A Radical Critique of Liberal Political Philosophy

Maureen Ramsay

Leicester University Press
London and Washington

LEICESTER UNIVERSITY PRESS
A Cassell Imprint
Wellington House, 125 Strand, London WC2R 0BB
PO Box 605, Herndon, VA 20172
First published in Great Britain 1997

British Library Cataloguing-in-Publication Data
A CIP catalogue record for this book is available from the British Library
ISBN 0-7185-1808-X (hardback)
0-7185-1811-X (paperback)

Library of Congress Cataloguing-in-Publication Data

Ramsay, Maureen, 1948–
    What's wrong with liberalism?: a radical critique of liberal
political philosophy/Maureen Ramsay.
        p.   cm. – (Critical political studies)
    Includes bibliographical references and index.
    ISBN 0-7185-1808-X. – ISBN 0-7185-1811-X (pbk.)
    1. Liberalism.   I. Title.   II. Series.
JC574.R36   1997
320.5′1–dc20   96-34461
                                                                    CIP

Typeset by BookEns Ltd, Royston, Herts.
Printed and Bound in Great Britain by
Creative Print and Design Wales, Ebbw Vale.

Contents

Acknowledgements   vii

Introduction   1
1. Human Nature   7
2. Freedom   38
3. Equality   68
4. Justice   101
5. Rights   143
6. Women's and Children's Rights   166
7. The Public and the Private   191
8. Wants and Needs   222
    Conclusion   253

    Bibliography   255
    Index   265

Acknowledgements

I would like to thank the students in my classes whose contributions, questions and enthusiasm helped to inspire me and to order and clarify the ideas presented here. I am grateful to Valerie Bryson for reading a draft of the chapters devoted to feminist concerns and to Jules Townshend for his constructive suggestions and continuing support. I am particularly indebted to David Beetham for his encouragement, advice and the time he devoted to reading and commenting on the structure and content of this book. Thanks are also due to Alan Sivori and Lorraine Sherriff for their help in preparing the manuscript.

Finally, I am grateful to my family and friends who constantly reminded me that the abstract individual of liberal theory is a fiction, and for this reason, no-one was neglected while I wrote this book and I do not have to thank them for their forbearance or patience, only for their reciprocal care.

For my children –
Rachel, Matthew and Saoirse

Introduction

In our society, liberal ideas dominate ordinary people's thinking and inform the practice of political parties of all hues. It is not an exaggeration to say that the whole of the Western political system was founded on and shaped by liberal principles and values. Some, following Fukuyama, have even claimed that liberal democracy is on the verge of world-wide triumph in both former communist countries and the developing world, demonstrating the superiority of liberal values and heralding the 'end to history'.

Typically, liberal democratic systems claim to respect the intrinsic worth and dignity of each human being and to embody a commitment to the importance of individual freedom. They seek to limit government power and to safeguard civil liberties. They hold dear the rights to freedom of speech, expression, religion and association, the right to vote and to participate in a competitive party system. To varying degrees, they uphold the right to own, use and dispose of property and extol the virtues of free choice, private enterprise and the market. In so far as these systems propagate and embrace these ideas, they draw on and are deeply ingrained with liberal values. So too, is the thinking of most people. Consciously or unconsciously, their political and moral beliefs reflect an acceptance of liberal ideas. Most people do not ask themselves the abstract questions of political philosophy and come up with liberal answers. They do not ask, what is the truth about human nature and how does this determine the form social organization can or should take? What is the meaning of freedom? In what sense are people equal and how can inequality be justified? What is justice? Are there any human rights? What is the role of the state? What is the nature of the good life for human beings? Can there be an adequate moral basis for social and political organization? But, implicitly, most people assume the validity of liberal answers to these questions and their views demonstrate the pervasiveness of liberal ideas. Think about the statement, 'it's only human nature' or that 'you can't change human nature' and how often this is said in a context which is supposed to explain some obvious fact about human behaviour, the consequent state of the world and the need for social policies which accommodate, control, channel and regulate it.

In these everyday discussions, it is taken for granted that people are self-seeking, acquisitive, and greedy, that they always want more, and that competitiveness and conflict are given facts about human nature. Think about how often it is assumed that people are autonomous, rational moral agents, when they are urged to take responsibility for their lives and are praised or blamed for their actions or behaviour. 'It's his own fault.' 'It serves her right.' 'He deserved it.' Think about how inequalities in wealth and income are accepted on the grounds that some people deserve greater rewards because of their superior ability, talent, skill or hard work, or because they need these as incentives to work in important and responsible jobs. Consider the defiant way people say they live in a free country, whenever anyone criticizes their (usually unpopular) views, their choices or their way of life. Consider the condemnation of societies that suppress freedom of speech, fair trials and free elections; the association of tyranny with planned economies and the outrage at invasions of privacy and you will see how far liberal ideas permeate our society.

The main purpose of this book is to explain and criticize liberal concepts and values in order to expose the empirical, theoretical, practical and moral deficiencies at the heart of liberal thought. This is not an original aim, nor are my arguments new. And although these arguments are philosophical and analytic, I also think that the thrust of them is obvious to anyone. I believe that if people considered these arguments they would recognize the bankruptcy of liberalism in theory and in practice, and that this coheres with their actual lived experience in liberal societies. For at the same time as they endorse liberal ideas, if they think about it, they cannot help but recognize that there is something wrong with them. The same people who argue that human beings are self-interested, greedy and competitive, also experience situations where people are unselfish, caring and cooperative, and they would not have survived into adulthood, at home, at work or at play if this were not the case. People believe that it is right to reward merit and that incentives are necessary, but they also think that some of the benefits and burdens in society are undeserved. They are cynical about politicians' excuses for pay differentials and they recognize that vast disparities of wealth and income are unjust and unfair. They believe we live in a free society, but they know that they and others like them do not have the resources to do, to say, to get or to buy what they want. They condemn the planned economies of the former communist states, but they find little to celebrate in the inequalities, the unemployment, the homelessness, the exploitation, the waste and the environmental damage that result from free market operations. They believe people should not be dependent on the state and should be responsible for themselves and their choices, but they deplore the devastating effects on economic and social security, health, welfare and education when public services are eroded and replaced by private concerns. In theory they are proud of their civil liberties and think that 'an Englishman's home is his castle', but in practice, they are indifferent to or attach very little real significance to their formal and legal rights, and they do not find their private lives a source of personal freedom and fulfilment.

The reasons for liberalism's continuing force and appeal and supposedly imminent world-wide triumph cannot be the justice of liberal society. The arguments in this book attempt to show that neither can it be the adequacy of the concepts and beliefs that inform it. And though changing the world does not depend only on changing what people think, in so far as ideas have the capacity to inspire and guide action, challenging the ideas which underpin liberal democracy is a small step towards averting this unhappy ending to history.

Aims and Structure of the Book

This book aims to provide an introduction to and a critical analysis of the key concepts which underpin liberal political theory and practice. It focuses on those concepts which are directly relevant to formulating a theory of a just society and to challenging the validity of liberal political ideals, values, institutions and policies. Each chapter tackles a different concept and, where appropriate, analyses the contribution of representative thinkers in early seventeenth- and eighteenth-century liberal thought and contemporary developments and modifications to classical liberalism. The purpose of each chapter is to critically evaluate the received ideas and current thinking, the political beliefs and practices informed by a liberal understanding of the concepts of human nature, freedom, equality, justice, rights, the public and the private and the sovereignty of individual desires, wants and preferences. This will be done by appraising the concepts, theories, modes of reasoning, problems and issues from a variety of critical perspectives to demonstrate that the sacred tenets of liberal thought are defective.

For analytic purposes, the ideas and values of liberalism have been presented in an abstract, general and schematic way. In practice, liberalism is more complex and diffuse, less one-dimensional and clear cut than this analysis sometimes suggests. This analysis tends to identify liberalism with a package of beliefs informed by a conception of the abstract and asocial individual; that typically conceptualizes freedom as negative liberty; that sees equality as a formal and legal concept and that limits the role of the state to the public sphere, to protecting civil and political rights. These beliefs are of course more properly understood as components of classical liberalism which resurface in aspects of present-day conservatism and libertarian thought. It has not been forgotten that liberalism is a changing doctrine and that in its modern versions has a different understanding of what is necessary for autonomy and what commitment to the equal moral worth of each individual entails. This leads to a more substantive conception of equality and a justification for enlarging the role of the state in order to redistribute wealth and income through taxation and welfare programmes.

It will be argued, however, that modern liberalism cannot fulfil its promise to deliver richer notions of freedom, equality or social justice. First, because liberals take as given the inevitability of capitalist institutions, and second, because all versions of liberalism are individualistic. They all start with the same basic proposition that the good of the individual is the main focus of moral theory and social, economic and political institutions. They all share the view that society is composed of individuals each competing for their fair share of resources. This prioritization of the individual over society provides the moral base for the prioritization of individual liberty and corresponds to the importance attached to civil liberties and the individual's right to pursue their own good in their own way. The re-distributive and quasi-egalitarian aspects of richer, more nuanced versions of liberalism, on the one hand, seem to spring free from the confines of the basic structure of liberal theory. Defences of the welfare state and justifications for redistribution and state interven-tion appear to come into conflict with liberalism's philosophical foundations and fundamental commitment to individual rights and liberties, minimal state intervention and neutrality between competing conceptions of the good.

On the other hand, contemporary liberalism, because it cannot jettison its commitment to the priority of the individual and its particular conception of that individual without ceasing to be liberal, places limits on how freedom, equality, justice and rights can be conceptualized, justified and implemented while remaining within a liberal theoretical framework. This tends to undermine modern liberalism's progressive edge and richer conceptualizations of liberal values tend to collapse back into their original and cruder formulations.

Since the individual is the centrepiece of liberal political philosophy, Chapter 1 will begin by examining the liberal conception of human nature. It is this that determines their commitment to and understanding of the moral and political values that are constitutive of liberalism. Subsequent chapters will examine these, which for analytical purposes have been taken as separate from each other, but which are really interrelated and stand or fall together.

Chapter 2 examines the central moral value of liberalism, the freedom of the individual which is derived from the belief in the intrinsic and ultimate value of each individual. Chapter 3 looks at the concept of equality based on the liberal egalitarian view of human beings in the abstract, and considers various liberal justifications for differentiation between people and departures from the principle of equality. Chapter 4 continues this theme by exploring the conflicting conceptions of justice within the liberal tradition that take as their starting-point the equal moral worth of individuals. Chapter 5 is concerned with the concept of rights, in particular the distinctively liberal preoccupation with and prioritization of civil and political rights which are derived from the general value of the freedom of the individual. Chapter 6 further explores the concept of rights and the assumptions that underpin it in relation to the problem of equal or special rights for women and the denial of rights to children. Chapter 7 addresses the conceptual distinction liberals make between the public area of life in which the state can legitimately interfere to protect individual rights and the private sphere where individuals are to be left alone. The final chapter comes full circle and returns to the starting-point in Chapter 1. It takes as its target of criticism the liberals' insistence on the sovereignty of individual desires and challenges their hostility to attempts to defend the concept of need as the moral basis for politics.

1

Human Nature

The emergence of the liberal tradition in political theory is associated with the breakdown of feudalism in Europe in the mid-seventeenth century and the transition to capitalist or market society. It reflected the interests of the new commercial middle classes and embodied their hostility to all forms of absolute and arbitrary authority. Historically, liberalism was opposed to religious conformity, ascribed status, economic privilege, political absolutism and the tyranny of majority opinion. Liberalism began as an emancipatory project which expressed the radical moral belief in the equal and intrinsic worth of each individual. The developments and diffusion of liberal ideas over three centuries and the different forms liberalism has taken make it difficult to define it as a single, coherent package of beliefs. But common to all variants of liberalism is a distinctive conception of human nature which determines and sets limits on the values, concepts and practices which can properly be thought of as constitutive of liberal thought.

The Abstract Individual

Common to all variants of the liberal tradition is a distinctive conception of human nature. The most important point for liberals about human beings is the fact that they are individuals. In liberal thought the individual is viewed as morally prior to society. In traditional contractarian liberalism, individuals actually exist temporarily before society exists and are bearers of fundamental natural rights which they possess by virtue of being human. Human beings have equal natural rights which are prior to any social organization and which take moral priority over any collective good or group. For Locke, there were three such rights – the rights to life, liberty and property. In Kantian strands of liberalism, the intrinsic dignity and equal worth of human beings are presupposed by his conception of individuals as rational autonomous beings who exist as 'ends in themselves' and not merely as means for another's will. The individual is seen as an objective end, never to be used by other individuals or society as a means to any collective goal.

For utilitarians, the foundation for the moral sovereignty of the individual is in non-moral 'facts' about human nature and psychology. Each person is motivated by their desires and passions, is the best judge of their own interests and uses reason to calculate the best means to satisfy them. Since the individual is the best judge of their own interest, the individual alone and no other social group or collective can determine what is morally right. The good of society is 'the greatest happiness for the greatest number', an aggregate of individual desires in which each person's interests are given equal weight. The equal moral value of the individual is the value of each individual's desires.

In different ways natural rights theorists, Kantians and utilitarians assert and justify the supreme moral value of the individual. Natural rights theorists do this by claiming there are natural rights which are derived from a pre-social, pre-political human nature and which take priority over any collective interest. Kantian justifications assume a transcendental human nature with an autonomous will independent of society, not to be overridden whatever the good consequences for society. Utilitarians appeal to a non-social human nature in taking self-interested desires as natural facts about human beings.

The liberal commitment to this ethical individualism is underpinned by a set of related ontological and methodological theses, involving respectively linked claims about reality and about explanation. These theses are reductionist in that they assert that the compositional units of the whole are ontologically prior to the whole, that is, the units and their properties exist before and are more real than the whole. This means that society itself does not exist, but is in reality only a collection of the individuals that compose it. For Bentham (1967, Ch. 1, para. 10) the concept of society is a fiction: 'the community is a fiction's *body*, composed of the individual persons who are considered as constituting as it were *its members*'. This view surfaces in the more contemporary liberalism of Hayek and Popper. Collective entities such as 'society', 'the economic system', 'capitalism', 'imperialism' and most of the objects of social science are not concrete facts but 'popular abstractions', 'professional theories', 'abstract objects' or 'theoretical constructions' (Hayek, 1955, pp. 37–8; Popper, 1961, p. 135).

Reductionist methodology tries to explain and understand the properties of complex wholes in terms of the units from which they are composed, so that a fundamental understanding of society comes from a study of the individuals that make up that society. Explanations about social phenomena are reduced to explanations in terms of facts about individuals. Hobbes held that 'it is necessary that we know the things that are to be compounded before we can know the whole compound' for 'everything is best understood by its constitute causes'. The causes of the social compound being isolated and atomistic individuals – 'men as if even now spring up out of the earth, and suddenly, like mushrooms, come to full maturity, without all kinds of engagement to each other' (Molesworth, 1839, vol. i, p. 67; vol. ii, pp. xiv, 109). Mill states explicitly the methodological implications of utilitarianism which sees society simply as collections of individuals each seeking to satisfy their own interests: 'the laws of the phenomena of society are, and can be, nothing but the actions and passions of human beings', that is, 'the laws of individual human nature' (Mill, 1875, p. 469). This is reiterated by Hayek (1949, p. 6) who writes that 'there is no other way toward an understanding of social phenomena but through our understanding of individual actions'; and again by Popper (1962, p. 98) 'all social phenomena, and especially the functions of all social institutions, should always be understood as resulting from the decisions, actions, attitudes, etc., of human individuals'.

This reductionist ontology and its methodology are the basis for the moral and political values of liberal individualism. If individuals are more real or fundamental than collective entities which are just hypothetical constructs, then it makes no sense to talk about the public interest. Abstract objects can have no interests. The only interests which exist are the actual interests of real people. If society is simply an aggregate of individuals, then there is no collective good over and above the good of individuals. Any political value that appeals to the social whole is therefore either at best nonsensical, or at worst a totalitarian threat to the interests of the individual.

Because the individual is of ultimate value and is the fundamental unit of explanation, it follows that individual interests are of supreme importance. Individual interests are defined as the given wants and preferences people actually have, and, accordingly, the function of government is to respond to these. Liberals then, explicitly or implicitly, assume that individual wants and preferences are autonomously chosen since they ignore the social context in which these wants are acquired, shaped or moulded. This assumption is known as abstract individualism, that is, a way of conceiving the individual in abstraction from specific social and historical circumstances, whose choices are given and occur in a vacuum. Liberals may not deny that what people want is shaped by their different social experiences, but they will none the less argue that we ought to respond to what people actually want. This claim arises from a commitment to an empiricist epistemology.

Empiricism is a doctrine of the nature of knowledge, that asserts that the raw data of individual experience is all that we can know. This doctrine takes many forms and was originally articulated by Locke, Berkeley and Hume. But liberal–democratic theorists such as the utilitarians, Bentham and Mill, Adam Smith and orthodox non-Marxist economists, many twentieth-century political scientists and defenders of the market economy also subscribe to an empiricist epistemology in so far as they identify felt needs, expressed wants and demands as the sole objects of knowledge. That is, as the only real 'needs' people can be said to have. This is because wants and preferences are directly observable and their existence can be proved. Wants are facts. It is a demonstrable disposition to desire or prefer something. This can be verified by subjective avowals, since people always know what they want. To establish what individuals want we can simply ask them or, alternatively, 'read off' what they actually consume or use. For instance, in the free market, existing wants and preferences are revealed ex-post through the experience of effective demand.

If individual experience is all that can be known, then it follows that the individual will 'know' their own experience better than anyone else. So, in championing the sovereignty of individual felt needs, liberals are asserting the existence of rational individuals who are the best judges of their own interests. This is clearly expressed by Bentham and J.S. Mill. Bentham states: 'generally speaking, there is no-one who knows what is for your interest so well as yourself' (Bentham, 1843, vol. iii, p. 33). Mill concurs:

The popular dictum, that people understand their own business and their own interests better, and care for them more, than the government does, or can be expected to. This maxim holds true throughout the greater part of the business of life, and wherever it is true one ought to condemn every kind of government intervention that conflicts with it. (Mill, 1900, p. 924)

Even though liberals can acknowledge that social determinants influence people's wants and that these are not neutral facts, but embody values, they will still insist that we must accept these existing values as if they were facts, because these are the values people actually can be seen to have. Political policies and practices must serve to satisfy the given wants that people have and these policies and practices should not judge, criticize or presuppose them. If no judgements are made about what is good for individuals over and above their actual choices, then whatever the individual desires is good by virtue of the fact that it is desired by the individual. If what people want is valued simply because they want it, values and choices are subjectively valuable and there can be no objective way of discriminating between the different choices people make. The political and moral significance of this identification of people's interests with what they perceive them to be and thus with what is valuable, is that appeal to the empirical nature of given desires involves no hypothetical claims or value-laden assumptions about what people truly desire or really need. Therefore, there is no danger of coercing people in their best interests of endorsing one way of life over another. This supports the idea of equal respect for the dignity of the individual and their capacity for rational, autonomous choice.

To emphasize real needs or true interests above the actual wants of real people is considered to be the hallmark of the authoritarian. A typical statement of this position is given by Anthony Flew:

An emphasis on needs as opposed to wants, gives purchase to those who see themselves as experts, qualified both to determine what the needs of others are and to prescribe and enforce the means appropriate to the satisfaction of those needs. (Flew, 1977, p. 213)

Those who claim to know what real needs are will feel justified in imposing them on other people's actual needs. Thus 'real need' theories threaten individual freedom. They are dangerous slides down the slippery slope at the end of which there is a 'Platonic Guardian, whose absolute power is warranted by nothing else but a putative expertise consisting precisely and only in alleged privileged access to the objectives that everyone ought to have' (Flew, 1977, p. 220).

The stress on the moral, ontological and epistemic primacy of the individual and their desires and values, supports the liberal idea of the moral autonomy of the individual and is the foundation for liberalism's most cherished value, the freedom of the individual. Liberals may recognize that social determinants influence the formation, experience and satisfaction of an individual's desires. However, the insistence on taking manifestations of desire as the starting-point of theory and practice means these desires are seen as given and independent of social forces and socialized expressions of them. This then amounts to subscribing to an abstract, asocial and ahistorical view of human nature. This abstract individualism is nowhere more apparent than in the liberal theories' account of the content of the human personality and human motivations.

Self-interest and material consumption

The liberal view that human beings are motivated by self-interest, in that each seeks to maximize their own happiness, pleasure or satisfaction, comes from seeing human beings as isolated individuals rather than social beings. Abstracted from any social connections or relationships what else could they be motivated by? Hume in the *Treatise of Human Nature*, Hobbes and Bentham all assumed universal egoism. Hume wrote 'In general, it may be affirmed that there is no such passion in human minds as the love of mankind, merely as such, independent of personal qualities, of services, or of relations to one-self' (Hume, 1888, Book III, pt. 2, section 1). Hobbes agreed that 'of the voluntary acts of every man, the object is some *good to himself*' (Molesworth, 1839, vol. iii, p. 120). Similarly, Locke assumed that in the state of nature, the preservation and protection of 'life, liberty and property' were primary motivations. Bentham took self-interest not only to be self-evident, because it was rooted in human psychology, but also to be morally justified: 'Nature has placed mankind under the governance of two sovereign masters, pain and pleasure. It is for them alone to point out what we ought to do, as well as to determine what we shall do' (Bentham, 1967, p. 125). If all human action and behaviour is motivated by self-interested desires, and those desires are fixed and unalterable, then the only way one can behave and the only rational behaviour is to direct action to their successful satisfaction. For Bentham, to do so was not just rational, but explicitly moral. Actions are morally justified according to the quantity of individual pleasure and pain they produce.

In early liberal thought, not only are individuals motivated by self-interested desires, these desires are also unlimited and are desires for material possessions. Hobbes states explicitly that human beings are motivated by the desire for gain. 'Men from their very birth, and naturally, scramble for everything they covet, and would have all the world if they could, to fear and obey them.' They are driven relentlessly from desire to desire, by 'a perpetual and restless desire of power after power that ceaseth only in death' (Molesworth, 1839, vol. vii, p. 73; vol. iii, p. 85). C.B. Macpherson (1964, 1973) characterizes the individual of classical liberal theory as essentially an infinite desirer and consumer of utilities. He emphasizes the connection between this conception and the growth and defence of capitalist wealth accumulation, consumption and the new individualistic morality. He argues that implicit in Locke is the assumption of the rational and moral acceptability of unlimited desire, and explicit in Bentham is the concept of the human essence as the desire to maximize utilities; the notion of the human good as an indefinite increase of the aggregate of material goods and the criterion of a good society as the maximization of utilities. Infinite desire is seen as part of human nature, and therefore justifies unlimited appropriation and consumption. The assumption of infinite desire together with the assumption of scarce resources means that individuals will be motivated by the desire to secure for themselves as large a proportion of these as possible and that this therefore will be rationally and morally justifiable.

There is a strand of liberalism exemplified by Mill who reacted against and rejected the Benthamite notion of man as consumer of utilities. Mill was concerned to make a distinction between 'higher' and 'lower pleasures' which were quantitively the same in calculations of utility. 'Higher' pleasures are those which benefit our nature as human beings in that they utilize intellectual, moral and aesthetic capacities rather than the capacity for material and physical gratification. Therefore, Mill argued that the utilitarian criterion of social good as the maximization of the provision of material goods should be replaced by the maximization of man's capacity for self-development and for the use of these human capacities. Mill believed that a full development of capacities would generate these higher desires and steer people away from material consumption.

MacPherson (1973, pp. 31–3) argues that despite Mill's and other liberals' attempts to redefine the human away from a Lockean and Benthamite conception of man as infinite consumer or appropriator, it has been impossible for liberalism to dispense with this latter conception or to combine it with other conceptions which emphasize self-development. The concept cannot be dispensed with because it is necessary to provide a justification for the right to appropriate as an incentive for material production and to justify the power relations of a capitalist market economy. The concept of man as a consumer of utilities cannot be combined with other self development conceptions of human nature, because maximizing utility necessarily prevents the effective exercise of the right of the individual to exert, enjoy or to develop his capacities. Contemporary liberals still operate with the conception of man as consumer of utilities in so far as they demand the freedom of the individual to use his capacities and resources to maximize material utility, and in so far as they defend the right to appropriate as an incentive. Similarly, the notion of human beings as utility maximizers bent on material acquisition remains the basic assumption of orthodox economic theory.

The public good

If all desires are self-interested, and rationality and even morality are regarded as means to the satisfaction of the desires already specified, then it becomes difficult to see how any theory of the public good can be formulated. If human nature is basically self-interested, how can it be answerable to any moral rules which aim at the good of all? Moreover, how can the good of all or, indeed, the good of very many be achieved if all individuals are relentlessly pursuing their own interests? Bentham thought this was relatively unproblematic because the general good was simply an aggregate of each individual's interests. The notorious problem here, however, is that in aggregating utility, the interests of the individual are frequently overridden. A liberalism based on universal egoism and utilitarian calculation destroys the principle of equal respect for the individuals which liberals claim to endorse. Where each individual is related to others as a means of maximizing utility, individuals are necessarily treated as means to ends rather than as ends in themselves.

In trying to address this problem, other liberals have modified the assumption of universal egoism or the conclusions which seem to result from such an assumption. A popular eighteenth-century solution was to claim that social harmony was possible because human nature is only partly egoistic. Benevolence is also the product of natural instincts. For example, J.S. Mill thought that utilitarianism required that individual actions should be aimed at the general happiness, whether or not this increased the individual's own happiness. He suggests that one reason why this could be done is because there is 'a natural basis of sentiment' in 'the social feelings of mankind' which make it impossible to totally disregard other people's interests. (Mill, 1962, p. 284). Here he offers a psychological explanation rather than a rational justification for how it is possible to disregard one's own interests and act to increase the general happiness.

Another solution to the problem of reconciling individual self-interest with the general interest was to proclaim that by a happy coincidence, harmony between the two just happens. Mandeville in *The Fable of the Bees* (1705) argues that the pursuit of individual private self-interested desires will produce public virtues. Adam Smith's 'hidden hand' of the market restates the same idea that individuals pursuing their own interests will create automatic harmony and be conducive to the general good without anyone necessarily intending this. The notion that each person's materially self-interested actions will promote economic progress, prosperity and well-being is the assumption behind classical economic theory and is still very much alive in current defences of the free market.

Reason

The final solution to the problems of taking self-interest to be the central motivating force has been to modify and control self-interest by the use of reason. Hume, Hobbes and Bentham considered reason to be a calculative tool, as a prudential and instrumental capacity. For Hume, human beings were motivated by their passions and these were unamenable to reason. Reason could only inform the passions as to the most effective and efficient means to satisfy them. So for Hume, it is not contrary to reason to prefer the destruction of the whole world to the scratching of my finger because 'reason is, and ought only to be the slave of the passions and can never pretend to any other office than to serve and obey them' (Hume, 1888, Book II, pt. 3, section 3). Hobbes makes reason subordinate to the demands of the appetites and aversions to ensure self-preservation. Bentham, too, sees desires as given and beyond the scope of rationality. Reason is the capacity to calculate the best means to individual self-interest.

Other liberals give rationality a different emphasis, associating it with the capacity to formulate general and impartial principles of morality. Kant believed that we can use reason to escape the tyranny of our inclinations and to guide desire. As rational beings we are able to universalize our conception of ourselves and treat other human beings as rational beings like ourselves. Rationality requires us to respect other people as ends in themselves and therefore we should respect other people's pursuit of their own interests. Rationality also requires us to universalize our actions impartially. This means that when we act we do not discriminate in our own favour, we escape the bias of our own desires and respect the interests of others. This is conducive to the general progress and happiness. Mill, too, thought people were able to act on the moral principle of impartiality by reasoning from the fact that each person desires and pursues his own happiness, and each person's happiness is equally desirable, to the conclusion that therefore everyone ought to aim at the happiness of everyone. More contemporary liberals like Rawls believe that reason is not just a capacity to act in self-interest but also involves impartiality. It is, however, the former conception which predominates. Rawls assumes that people in the original position, who are ignorant of their own special interests, will act impartially when deciding principles of justice. However, he also assumes that people in the original position are 'mutually disinterested' and that they will be motivated by the desire to secure for themselves as large a share of resources as possible. They will therefore act rationally by choosing those principles of justice which minimize their own risk of being worst off in society.

Although some liberals associate rationality with impartiality, most tend towards identifying rationality with self-interest, even when this can be constrained by moral considerations. All liberals, however, stress the importance of rationality and conceive of it as a mental capacity concerned with thinking, calculating, weighing and deliberating. All see it as the property of an abstract individual thinking in isolation from their social roles, relationships, groups or cultural norms. All see reason as a natural potential possessed equally by all individuals, and whether reason is conceptualized, as prudential or moral, it is considered to be indispensable to individual freedom.

Freedom

The freedom of the individual is the most important liberal value. It is a consequence of liberalism's central belief in the intrinsic dignity and equal worth of each individual. If individuals are of equal value, because of their universal capacity for rational autonomous action, then freedom is both an intrinsic good, essential to a truly human life, and an instrumental value necessary for individuals to pursue their own ends and purposes. Limitations on freedom by other individuals or by society will use people as means to ends, rather than treat them as 'ends-in-themselves'. If each individual is valuable by virtue of their rational capacity to judge what is in their own interests and to calculate the best means to satisfy them, then freedom is the means by which the rational individual can pursue and satisfy their own interests. Any imposition on the individual is against their essential nature as rational and independent beings.

In early liberal thought, freedom is defined negatively as freedom from interference. Negative liberty is concerned with the areas in which the individual should be left alone. Hobbes defined freedom thus: 'By LIBERTY, is understood, according to the proper signification of the word, the absence of external impediments: which impediments, may oft take away part of man's power to do what he would' (Molesworth, 1839, vol. iii, p. 116). Locke also, understands freedom as the right of non-interference. In the *Second Treatise*, he asserts the natural right to freedom from the arbitrary power of others. Freedom for individuals is 'Freedom to order their actions, and dispose of their possessions and persons as they think fit, within the bounds of The Law of Nature, without asking leave, or depending on the will of any other men' (Locke, 1967, p. 269).

Mill held a negative conception of liberty, portraying freedom as the absence of restrictions upon an individual's 'self-regarding' actions. 'The only part of the conduct of anyone, for which he is amenable to society is that which concerns others. In the part which merely concerns himself, over his own body and mind, the individual is sovereign.' The only justification for interference with individual liberty, is self-protection. 'That the only purpose for which power can be rightfully exercised over any member of a civilised community, against his will, is to prevent harm to others'

(Mill, 1962, p. 135). Contemporary writers such as Hayek, Friedman, Nozick and Berlin defend a negative conception of liberty. In Isaiah Berlin's definition, negative liberty is the freedom from actions of others or from having actions limited. 'Political liberty ... is simply the area within which a man can act unobstructed by others.' Freedom is the absence of coercion, 'coercion implies the deliberate interference of other human beings within the area in which I could otherwise act' (Berlin, 1969, p. 122).

Freedom defined negatively makes no judgements about what ends or interests individuals should have. Freedom is freedom from impediments to pursue individual interests and therefore, for the state to protect freedom, it must remain neutral between different individuals' conceptions of their own good. Because each person is of intrinsic value, everyone must have an equal opportunity to enjoy liberty. That is, each person must have equal freedom to pursue their own interests, provided that by so doing they do not infringe the rights of others. This equality, however, is understood as a formal, procedural equality, as a set of constitutional laws and practices which give people an equal opportunity to pursue their different and competing versions of the good. Any more substantive views of social or economic equality are ruled out by the distinction negative libertarians make between being free and being able to do something, so that freedom is the absence of restraint rather than the power, abilities or resources to do something.

Liberal theory then, *formally* equates individuals and this abstract equality masks the *actual* inequalities in power, wealth, resources and abilities which exist between real individuals in liberal society. Freedom from interference typically means freedom from constraints by the state. Therefore, liberals who operate with this conception of freedom will be committed to a view of the role of the state as negative and protective, and to distinguishing between the public and private realm. The public realm is the area of life within which the state can legitimately interfere, and the private realm is that area of life within which the state has no legitimate business.

Early liberals were committed to a minimal view of the state. The task of the state was essentially protective, to secure internal order and external defence. Interference was only justified to protect individual rights or to generate civil liberties: the right to own property, to be represented in government, to travel, to form associations, to worship and to publish opinions. Negative liberty was associated with limited intervention in the economic field to protect persons and property against fraud or force. State planning and welfare policies were thought to interfere with the freedom of the individual to keep what they legitimately own and to define their own interests. This 'nightwatchman' view of the state limited only by side-constraints of natural rights has been restated and defended in recent times by Nozick (1974) and was reflected in the free-market conservatism of the 1970s and 1980s.

In contrast to conservative views, however, liberals believe that in the area of social or personal life, individual liberty is sacrosanct. The only justification for state interference here is to prevent harm to others. The importance of the absence of restriction in the private sphere is a consequence of the negative view of freedom as being left alone, together with the assumption that if left to their own devices, individuals who know their own interests will successfully pursue them. This itself is a consequence of the view of the abstract individual who is separated and self-sufficient, independent of social ties and not constituted by them or by any group identity. Such are these asocial individuals' desires that they cannot be fulfilled in social or collective activity, but require a separate private sphere for their exercise and satisfaction.

However, Mill also had a less negative view of freedom which was informed by Kant's idea of freedom as autonomy or individual self-determination. Freedom as autonomy in this sense was used by Mill in defence of limited government and to advocate freedom from social pressures to allow the individual to develop their capacities to the full. This idea was taken further by liberals such as Green and Hobhouse who saw that freedom as self-direction and self-development clearly implied government interference. In the economic sphere, inequalities in wealth, social power and education affected the individual's ability to take advantage of political and legal rights and their opportunities for self-development. This led these and twentieth-century liberals to advocate state provision of welfare, education and a minimum standard of living as the means of promoting individual liberty by guaranteeing that everyone has an equal opportunity to enjoy it. The most systematic liberal theoretical justification for the provision of welfare in the present day is given by John Rawls (1971) in his *A Theory of Justice*.

Although such defences enlarge the area in which the state is justified in intervening, the values and goals which underpin such justification remain the freedom of the individual and the successful pursuit of their own goals. What is different about welfare liberalism is the means to achieve them. And, generally, freedom of the individual from interference remains the conception of freedom at the core of liberal thought. This is most obvious in liberals' continued commitment to limited intervention in the private sphere, and whether or not they advocate welfare provision, in their emphasis on the primary importance of the protection of civil liberties and individual rights.

The liberal conceptions of freedom, equality, justice, rights and the notion of the private sphere which are derived from their concept of human nature are the subjects of subsequent chapters. But, first, I will outline three influential challenges to the concept of the abstract individual and suggest that they variously have the effect of undermining this basic premise of liberal theory and thus, the rationale for the beliefs, values and commitments that follow from it.

Marxist Challenges

Marxist approaches challenge the epistemological inadequacy of the concept of the abstract individual at the heart of liberal thought and stress instead the social and historical nature of human beings:

Man is no abstract being squatting outside the world. Man is the world of man, the State and Society ... the human essence is no abstraction inherent in each single individual. In its reality it is the ensemble of social relations. (Marx, 1968, p. 29)

Marx echoed Aristotle who drew attention to the social, political nature of human beings:

man is by nature a political animal: it is his nature to live in a State. He who by his nature and not simply by ill-luck has no city, no state, is either too bad or too good, either sub-human or super-human — sub-human like the war-mad man condemned in Homer's words 'having no family, no morals, no home'; for such a person is by nature mad on war, he is a non-co-operator like an isolated piece in a game of draughts. But it is not simply a matter of co-operation, for obviously man is a political animal in a sense in which a bee is not, or any gregarious animal. Nature, as we say, does nothing without some purpose; and for the purpose of making man a political animal she has endowed him among the animals with the power of reasoned speech. (Aristotle, 1962, p. 28)

In *The Grundrisse*, Marx reiterates this point as a direct challenge to the eighteenth-century view of the isolated individual for whom society is 'a mere means to his private ends':

The human being is in the most literal sense a *zoon politicon*, not merely a gregarious animal, but an animal which can individuate itself only in the midst of society. Production by an isolated individual outside society is a rare exception which may well occur when a civilised person in whom the social forces are already tyrannically present is cast by accident into the wilderness – is as much an absurdity as in the development of language without individuals living together and talking to each other. (Marx, 1973, p. 84).

Real living individuals always exist in some specific social context and it is to this that we must refer in order to understand the nature of human beings already formed in society. The social nature of human beings arises from the biological fact that human beings need food, clothing and shelter in order to survive. Unlike animals, they have to produce to meet their needs. They do not just use nature to meet their needs, but must consciously and purposively transform nature in order to do so. This conscious production to meet needs is the distinctive feature of human beings. Production is not an isolated activity, but a social activity which requires co-operation. Producers are not independent, self-sufficient atoms, but interdependent. Productive activity is intrinsically social since it depends on knowledge, skills and experience which are a social product. Even Robinson Crusoe who epitomizes the isolated individual and who displays all the virtues of liberal individualism, could not have survived on his island-grown food, caught animals, made pots, built barricades or canoes without drawing on the social activity of others.

For Marxists, the key to understanding historical development and human nature is productive activity. The first historical act of production was production to meet needs.

Men must be in a position to live in order to 'make history'. But life involves before everything else eating and drinking, a habitation, clothing and many other things. The first historical act is thus production of the means to satisfy these needs, the production of material life itself. (Marx, 1968, p. 48)

It is this, the way production is organized in any particular society that conditions social, political and intellectual life. If we want to understand politics, social institutions, human beings, their beliefs, wants and preferences, we must look not at collections of individuals, or at what the autonomous individual believes or chooses, but at the economic system they live in. 'The mode of production of material life conditions the social, political and intellectual life process in general. It is not the consciousness of men that determines their being, but, on the contrary, their social being that determines their consciousness' (Marx, 1968, p. 29). So human nature is not given, it is a historical product. Human beings are determined by their material conditions and human nature cannot be investigated in abstraction from the social, historical and material circumstances that give rise to human needs and desires, beliefs and interests. This historical materialist method of investigating human nature is the foundation for a critique of liberal assumptions about the abstract individual.

Investigating human nature under capitalism means that account must be taken of the way work is divided, that is, the social relations of production. Under capitalism, the way production is organized requires the division of society into two distinct classes. The dominant or capitalist class, who own and control the productive forces and the subservient or working class, the direct producers. Each have opposing interests, aims and aspirations which result from their respective economic positions and their similar social conditions and experiences. Human interests are not defined subjectively by the autonomous individual, but are determined by the individual's position in the reproduction of social relations and are defined objectively in class terms. The division of society in this way itself presupposes a conflict between individual and collective interests. This view of class antagonisms directly contradicts the economic and political theories of liberalism which conceptualize society as an aggregate of individual interests and assume a harmony between these and the common good.

Marxism also claims that individuals as members of classes do not always know or pursue their own interests in the rational way that liberal theory implies. People may be mistaken about their interests or may be systematically misled as to their true nature. This is because the ruling class, in addition to its economic dominance, maintains its power through the control of the beliefs, values and ideas of the working class. These ideas may be expressed through politics, law, religion, science, morality or culture, but the function of this ideological superstructure is to maintain and legitimate the social and economic dominance of the owning class. For Marx (1968, p. 39) 'the ideas of the ruling class are in every epoch the ruling ideas', that is, they serve the interests of the ruling class. People are conditioned into believing these ideas and the distortion of human nature and reality they embody. They take these partial interests to represent universal interests. In so doing, they accept as natural and inevitable relations of domination and exploitation, inequalities in wealth, status and power, and accounts of human nature as self-interested, acquisitive and competitive. The working class suffer from 'false consciousness' when they identify their own interests with those of the ruling class. Far from being the best judges of their own interests, individuals can be systematically mistaken about them.

It is not an illusion, however, that people behave like isolated individuals and in competitive, acquisitive and self-interested ways under capitalism. But, they are determined by their material conditions to behave in such ways; and this behaviour represents a distortion and restriction of human nature rather than an expression of it. In his early writings, *The Economic and Philosophic Manuscripts* of 1844, Marx uses the concept of alienation to sum up what is wrong with human nature under capitalism. Alienation is the idea that human beings have forfeited to someone or something else, something that is essential to their own nature. According to Marx, human beings are alienated from their true essence, from themselves and from each other. This is caused by the division of labour, the private control of industry, the specialization of work and the lack of community in capitalist society.

Workers are alienated because they work for someone else who owns and controls what is produced and because of the way in which production is organized. They are alienated from the product of their labour. Moreover, what is produced is determined by profit, not need. The worker is alienated in the process of production. Work is not satisfying in itself, but is just a means to existence. The worker is alienated from the distinctive human potentialities and creative powers that are underdeveloped under capitalism. Capitalism alienates workers from each other and obscures the way they are interrelated. Individuals compete with each other, seeing themselves as isolated individuals rather than social beings with common interests.

Marx believed that the features of the liberal abstract individual are in fact a social product. Conflict is not endemic to human nature but is an inevitable result of the division of society into classes who have diametrically opposed interests. Egoism and competitiveness are not intrinsic facts about human nature, but are produced by a system which endorses and rewards the pursuit of individual self-interest and which requires workers to compete for wages and jobs, and capitalists to compete for markets. Human beings are not infinite consumers, but consumerism is a product of capitalist social relations which generate the need to have, to possess, to consume and to accumulate in increasing quantities. Human beings are not utility-maximizers but are encouraged to act like this by the operation of the capitalist market geared to the pursuit of profit. Characteristics that are thought to be natural are a reflection of a particular set of social relationships and a response to the capitalist mode of production.

Marxism's insistence on the social and historical nature of human beings provides a challenge to the liberal idea of the abstract individual with universal capacities and characteristics. If human beings are naturally social and mutually interdependent, then co-operation rather than competition is a natural relationship and a basis for social organization. If human nature is socially determined and human beliefs, desires and motivations are relative to forms of society and characteristic of particular social relations, then egoism and acquisitiveness are not given features of human beings. The placing of human nature in a historical context means that the possibility to change or develop aspects of human nature can only come about by changing the material conditions on which they are based. Furthermore, if human desires are socially produced in ways which mean that individuals can be mistaken or deceived about their true interests, then the rationality, autonomy and sovereignty of the individual's expressed desires must be called into question as the starting-point of political theory and as the basis of liberal values.

Communitarian Challenges

Like Marxism, communitarian criticism of liberalism focuses on the conception of the individual as asocial, atomised, solitary and self-seeking. Communitarian approaches are not new; they may be said to date from at least the time of Aristotle, for whom the individual was necessarily social.In Aristotle's *Ethics* and *Politics* individuals are conceived of in relation to their social roles, so that individual responsibilities and commitments are derived from their place in the nexus of social relationships. Moral questions and political arrangements are not individual matters but are derived from the social relationships in which individuals stand. Moral behaviour and justifiable social arrangements depend on the social conditions which make them possible. That is, a shared form of social life which gives rise to common interests and purposes.

Other writers, such as Hegel, T.H. Green and R.P. Wolff have appealed to the idea of community within which moral action takes place to combat the individualistic premises and conclusions of liberal theory. More recently, Sandel (1982), Taylor (1990), Waltzer (1983) and MacIntyre (1981, 1988, 1990) have systematically attacked the liberal idea of the independent individual detached from all social roles and attachments. They stress in different ways the individual's dependence on community, how community is both part of the individual's identity, and a condition for attaining certain kinds of human goods which are precluded by liberalism (see Mulhall and Swift, 1992). Communitarians reject the concept of the abstract individual or what they variously call the 'unencumbered self' or the 'antecedently individuated self' of liberal theory.

They argue that liberal theory assumes the priority of the self over its ends, values or conceptions of the good. For instance, utilitarians portray the self as the sum of its self-seeking, self-generating rational desires. Kantians portray the self as rational and autonomous, independent of desires and particular purposes. These conceptions of the self take people's desires and goals as already formed, or, as autonomously chosen independent of or prior to society. In doing so, they give an account of the self as separate from its embodiment in any particular society and ignore the way society shapes human desires, values and purposes.

This is not just a claim about the effects of the socialization process which, if true, would show the idea of the abstract individual to be empirically false. Communitarians also claim that the notion of the 'unencumbered self' is conceptually incoherent. This idea is not peculiar to communitarians, but has its roots in Wittgenstein's arguments about the impossibility of a private language. According to Wittgenstein in the *Philosophical Investigations* (1958), it would be impossible to learn a language or to conceptualize experience in the absence of other people. Language and thought are necessarily social. For language to be intelligible there has to be a link between the individual's experience and belonging to a society of shared meanings. It is impossible to conceive of an individual having experiences, beliefs, desires or emotions without presupposing a social context which interprets and gives meaning to the raw data of experience. For example, individual desires are not only socially conditioned, but the very fact of wanting or preferring presupposes a social context to make that want intelligible. Desires do not just spontaneously occur within the individual, and any purely individual explanation would not account for any desire. To explain a desire we have to specify what the wanted object is for. We must specify ends and purposes, and the context in which it occurs. The goals, ends or purposes for which things are wanted are called 'desirability characteristics' by Anscombe (1957, p. 37). And according to Richard Norman, the 'desirability characteristics' of the end or goal themselves presuppose publicly acceptable standards or norms. He argues 'the intelligibility of a want is essentially a matter of its relationship to public, supra-individual standards or norms' (1971, p. 55). Reference to the 'desirability characteristics' of the end or goal is meaningful only in a social context, and has to be made in order to make the want claim intelligible. Conceptually, as well as empirically then, the idea of the abstract individual is false. Human desires, interests and goals can only be acquired and understood in a social context.

According to communitarians, liberals also make a substantial error about the content of an individual's desires and interests. They suppose society is simply an association of private individuals who come together to advance their pre-social and separate interests. This precludes any conception of the good which arises from seeing that social relationships are valuable in themselves, not just as means to the individual's own good. The existence of social bonds means that individuals share interests and ends in common, and define themselves not as separate from others but inter-subjectively. The individual is not detached from others, but is partly constituted and defined by their social identities and attachments. Individuals are variously citizens of a society, members of families, nations, parties, movements and have commitments to social groups and causes. These shared identities merge the individual's interests, ends or purposes with those which are characteristic of their community. Implicit in this line of thought is the view that community itself is something to be valued, and that good is found in community rather than in the fulfilment of individual interests.

If individual meanings, identities and interests are inherently communal, then it follows that there can be no trans-historical or cross-cultural political theory. Liberal claims and values cannot apply universally because different cultures embody different values and different standards of rationality. Therefore, it is not possible to develop an account of the public good by using the concept of impartial reason or by aggregating the preferences of abstract individuals. What counts as rational, what is in the individual's interests, what is thought to be valuable, will be relative and internal to particular communities and their social practices. According to communitarians, there is no standard of rationality which is external to or outside of particular communities.

Communitarians claim that the liberal state itself embodies a particular conception of the good despite its alleged neutrality. Utilitarians argue that the state should not judge preferences, but aggregate them. Rights-based approaches see the state as providing a framework of basic rights and liberties within which individuals can choose their own values and conceptions of the good without adjudicating between them. However, communitarians argue that this supposed neutrality disguises the fact that by protecting the individual's capacity to make choices about how to live their lives, liberal thought endorses one way of life over another, that is, the one that is autonomously chosen. And this presupposes a conception of a person as a rational and autonomous chooser. It necessarily excludes different conceptions of the good based on the social and communal nature of human beings. Since the liberal conception of the person is neither neutral, empirically accurate or conceptually coherent, the autonomous individual cannot be a valid starting-point for political theorizing.

Radical Feminist Challenges

Feminism is not a unified body of thought, but its many strands have in common the idea that the relationship between the sexes is unequal and oppressive. Liberal feminism and traditional Marxist feminism adapted the principles of their respective political theories and their conceptions of human nature to consider the question of women's subordination and emancipation. Mill, in his classical statement of liberal feminism *On the Subjection of Women*, argued that women, like men, have an equal capacity for reason and therefore they must have equal opportunities to pursue whatever interests they have. Modern liberal feminists are committed to the same central belief that women as individuals are capable of reason and, by virtue of this, are entitled to full human rights. Women must be free from interference to choose their roles and explore their potential in equal competition with men. Traditional Marxist analysis investigates women's oppression in its historical context, identifying the material causes of and solutions to sexual inequality in the way production is organized and the social relations which result. In this analysis questions of gender are subsumed under questions of class inequality.

There are many different strands to radical feminist analysis, but all are agreed on the inadequacy of the liberal idea of the abstract individual with universal characteristics and many reject the equation of class and gender oppression in Marxist theory. For radical feminists women's oppression is the most fundamental form of oppression and women share common interests in ending it. Gender is the most basic social division and this division is political, rather than natural. This view is premised on the idea that distinctions of gender structure every aspect of public and private existence and is expressed as a theory of patriarchy (see Millett, 1985, Ch. 2).

Patriarchy is understood as a social system based on male power and female subordination. In all societies the relationship between the sexes has been based on male power and is therefore political. Men dominate every arena. Male interests are embodied in traditional power structures like the state and are maintained by the economic dependency of women in the home and the economic exploitation of women at work. However, the patriarchal power of men over women extends beyond the political and economic sphere: it permeates every aspect of cultural, social and personal life. According to many feminists, the family is a central part of the power structure. Different theorists focus on the different ways in which the family sustains and reproduces patriarchal power in public life and is a source of oppression in private life. Some (for instance, Delphy, 1980) concentrate on how domestic labour is exploited within the family. Others focus analysis on the family as an oppressive structure where women have the monopoly of child care, where sexuality is defined and abused, where oppressive gender roles are learnt and patriarchal values are internalized. These analyses show how the family functions to sustain women's oppression and highlight aspects of the family as political issues. For many radical feminists it is women's role as reproducers that is the natural or social cause of oppression, the basis of patriarchal power and the site of struggle for overcoming it (Firestone, 1979). Patriarchy, however, also rests on the use or threat of force. Sexuality is based on male violence and control and is bound up with male power. Radical feminists like Rich (1980) view heterosexuality itself as a political institution. It is a manifestation of male power which defines female sexuality and which ensures that women serve men domestically, emotionally and sexually. Patriarchal power relations are reflected in all forms of sexual violence, and in rape, pornography and prostitution. Patriarchal ideas are also reinforced by the male control of knowledge, language, morality, religion and culture which structures attitudes and beliefs about what is normal, natural, superior or important.

These analyses pose a fundamental challenge to liberal and to traditional political theory because women are no longer marginal to theorizing, but at the centre of analysis. Radical feminists show that women are oppressed in both the public and private spheres. The state is not a neutral arbiter between individual interests, it embodies partial interests and is systematically biased against women. Power structures are interrelated so that, contrary to liberal assumptions, there is no room for a private area of life free from power and political interference. Liberal theory obscures how questions of the family, sexuality, gender, housework, reproduction, knowledge and language are political questions.

A unifying thread running through radical feminist analysis is an account of the imposition of male interests through the many institutions of patriarchy. Male control in every arena shapes men and women's perceptions of reality and of themselves. It forms their sexual and gender identities, moulds their needs and wants and limits their aims, expectations and opportunities. If patriarchal interests dominate in this way, then the liberal idea of the abstract or pre-social individual independent of social determinations is again called into question. So, too, is the notion of the autonomous individual as the best judge of their own interests. If male dominance is so pervasive, then patriarchal conceptions and assumptions will be internalized and accepted as natural. This will be contrary to the real interests women have in ending oppression. The idea that women as a group have shared gender interests, and require collective action to realize them, conflicts with the liberal idea of the isolated individual acting to maximize their own interests or to achieve their own good in their own way.

Radical feminist analysis also criticizes the male bias in liberal accounts of human nature as rational, independent and self-interested. They stress the differences between male and female nature, though they disagree as to whether these differences are rooted in biology or whether they are the result of social experiences and practices. Radical feminists argue that whether reason is viewed as prudential or moral, both these liberal conceptions are expressions of male dominance. The emphasis on technical calculation in instrumental accounts of reason, and on impartial, impersonal and objective reasoning in moralized accounts is not only false to the experience of women, but also devalues female ways of thinking, moralizing and reasoning. These accounts of rationality assume the existence of competing self-interested or independent autonomous individuals. This may describe male behaviour, but this description is not universal since it does not account for women's experience of co-operation, altruism, nurturing, empathy, care and mutual support. Not only is it a fact that women are motivated to act thus and do behave in this way, it is also appropriate and necessary that they do. Rational calculation and impartial reasoning are inappropriate responses in relationships with friends, families, children and lovers. Co-operation and interdependence are essential for the organization and reproduction of society and social relationships.

Some feminists believe that these qualities of 'female nature' are in fact natural qualities. It is not uncommon within eco-feminism to find the view that, because women are closer to nature, they are less aggressive, more gentle, caring and co-operative than men. Rich (1977) argues that because of their bodily experience women have greater connectedness and relatedness to the world. Women can 'think through the body' in more active, fluid, creative ways, and can express the unconscious, the subjective and the emotional as well as the structural, the rational and the intellectual typical of male thought. Daly (1978) also argues that it is women's experience of connectedness that allows them to move away from one-dimensional male thinking. Post-modernist and French feminist thought develops these ideas, arguing that by articulating the pleasure of the female body, based on women's multi-faceted diffuse experience of sexual pleasure, women can defy the confines of male logic and restricted categorizing (see Cixous 1981; Kristeva, 1981; Irigaray

1991). For other radical feminists, female ways of knowing and reasoning arise not from biological or bodily differences but from social practices and spheres of activity which have been regarded as female.

Gilligan (1982) argues that as a matter of fact men and women reason differently about moral issues. These differences arise because of the differences in the moral development of girls and boys. According to Gilligan, men's moral orientation is based on impartiality, impersonality, rationality and universalizability and is constituted by obligation and rights, appeal to rules, principles and the fairness of procedures. This arises from their early experience of abstraction and separation. Girls, from their early experience of nurturance and connectedness, pay attention to responsibility, context and relationships. This results in a moral orientation with an imperative to care. Noddings (1984) argues similarly that a morality based on rules or principles does not capture what is distinctive or typical about female thinking. Both Gilligan and Noddings agree that women are less likely to justify moral decisions by appeal to rules and principles, impartiality and universality because they consider the kinds of specific situations and contexts involved.

Chodorow (1978) and Dinnerstein (1987) attribute male and female ways of thinking to child-rearing practices. Mothers treat daughters and sons in different ways. Daughters are seen as a reflection of themselves and they identify with the mother. This bonding gives girls a sense of relatedness and an emphasis on close, personal relationships. This in turn gives rise to features of a feminine approach to knowing that is less rational than male thought, more intuitive, empathetic, co-operative and caring. The mother treats the son as the Other. Consequently, the boy has an early sense of separateness and establishes his male identity as distinct from the mother and the female, modelling himself on the absent father. This sense of individualism, autonomy and separateness inclines towards objectivity and impersonality, features typical of a masculine approach.

Other feminists suggest that it is the social practice of women's responsibility for childcare that generates the different social priorities and values that women have. Ruddick (1990) argues that the distinctive ways of thinking arise from good maternal practice and that these values and priorities are the basis of a critique of the male values of self-interest, competitiveness and aggression.

The various radical feminist approaches reject the liberal idea of the abstract individual and the liberal account of human nature and motivation. They highlight the differences between men and women that, whether social or natural, suggest that liberal theory, in treating male nature as the norm and as universal, has an inadequate understanding of human motivation and behaviour. Liberal theory imposes particular goals and values, which deny women's experience and ways of thinking. It also denies the reality of human interdependence and the importance of the fact that human beings have bodies and are sexual beings so that questions of sexuality, gender, reproduction are ignored as politically insignificant.

Conclusion: The Inadequacy of the Abstract Individual

It is not necessary to accept the whole of Marxist, communitarian or radical feminist thought to see that separately and together they present a powerful challenge to liberal political theory and the view of human nature and the human individual on which it is based. All point to the inadequacy of the concept of the abstract individual as the starting-point for political explanation and analysis. If this concept can be undermined, then so too can the values and the justifications for political and social organization that follow from it. The assumption of the asocial, atomistic, solitary and self-sufficient individual has been shown to be unrealistic and implausible, given the facts of human biology. The practical necessities of survival and reproduction require co-operation, nurture, support, interdependence and interrelatedness. The idea that the relevant features of individuals, their wants, purposes and interests are given, in abstraction from any social or historical context, denies how social relationships effect, determine or partly constitute individual identities.

For Marxists, individuals are shaped and moulded by class society; for communitarians, individuals cannot be separated from their social bonds and attachments and for radical feminists, it is gender relations which structure the nature of the individual. Whether or not class, community or gender are the primary or the only determinants is not relevant here. What these analyses show in keeping with sociological, psychological and anthropological empirical research is that the liberal picture of individuals independent of society and as sole generators of their wants and preferences is simplistic and mistaken. Taken together, they point to the various ways in which individuals depend on and are determined by their social relationships. They reveal how beliefs, motivations and interests are conditioned by social, economic, political, patriarchal, commercial and cultural forces and how these are reinforced by the agencies of socialization and social control ranging from the family unit and the education system to the beliefs and value systems of society in general. This recognition of the socially interdependent and socially constructed nature of the individual erodes the foundation for the construction and justification of liberal political theory. It has several implications.

First, it undercuts the idea that individuals are the best judges of their own interests. If individual interests are socially determined, then the individual can be mistaken about, ignorant of or even misled, regarding the true value of their own interests. This means that it is not necessarily rational for individuals to act to maximize their perceived interests, and may even be irrational for them to do so. People's interests are not given, but socially produced. If these rest on false or superficial beliefs about what is worth desiring, then they are contrary to reason. A false belief that something is worth desiring does not give rational grounds for its positive evaluation or provide reasons for acting to pursue that desire. A true belief that something is worth desiring does give grounds for its positive evaluation and provides reasons for action, but not simply because it is desired, but what it is in virtue of that it is worth desiring. Moreover, if it is possible to explain why a society produces false beliefs, then it is possible to evaluate negatively the kind of social relations and conditions that make that false belief necessary and then evaluate positive action to change them.

In addition to showing that it is not necessarily rational to pursue given desires, this analysis also reveals that reason itself is inadequately conceptualized when it is relegated to a calculating role in informing desires as to the best means to achieve their object. Because people's desires are produced by beliefs, some of which may be false or inadequate, then the evaluative and practical judgements to which they give rise can be criticized. Hence, reason is not just a technical tool, but has an explanatory, critical, evaluative and educative role. Not only does this analysis call into question the rationality of expressed interests and the equation of rationality with means—end calculation, but if individuals are not always the best judges of their own interests, because these interests are socially produced, then it also makes problematic the concept of autonomy and the value liberals place on the sovereignty of individual desires and the freedom from interference to pursue them.

Second, the notion of the social individual challenges the idea that society is a collection of isolated individuals each striving separately to satisfy their competing interests. The existence of group identities, shared class or gender identities means that individuals can have intersubjective interests and ends in common which can only be realized collectively. What it is rational to do to realize them will be objectively defined by and relative to group norms and values, rather than subjectively defined by individuals or arrived at by the use of reason as a trans-historical and universal category.

Third, an account of the public good cannot be derived by aggregating the sum of individual interests or by impartial reason. If interests are not individual and private, but are relative to groups, and the dominant group imposes its interests on others, then presenting the common good as an aggregate of individual interests, or arriving at it through a process of impartial reasoning, forgoes any analysis in terms of power relations which belie the existence of common interests. As such, the notion of the public good is an ideological device which endorses partial interests which it represents as general interests.

Fourth, the idea that individuals cannot be abstracted from their social context has methodological implications. It means that, contrary to the assumptions of utilitarianism, political individualism and economic theory, social phenomena cannot be explained in terms of facts about individuals. This is because the individual is irreducibly social and no account can be given of individual experiences, beliefs, desires or purposes without presupposing a social context, and without taking account of the historical, social, economic and cultural forces which have real effects on, and which make intelligible, individuals' experience and behaviour. Human action presupposes the pre-existence and reality of society and makes no sense without it. Analysis which excludes explanation in terms of social phenomena, social forces, structural features of society and institutional factors is both limited and implausible. This analysis is challenged not just by Marxists and feminists, but also by sociologists and by most ordinary explanations given in daily life.

Fifth, the idea of the social nature of the individual calls into question the liberal assumption of the abstract individual as rational, calculating, utility-maximizing and non-altruistic. For Marxists, self-interested utility-maximizing behaviour represents a distortion of human nature which is a reflection of and a response to capitalist social relations. Not only are co-operation and interdependence necessary for production to meet needs, but these are capacities that can be developed and encouraged by different relations of production. Communitarians reject the egoistic model of human nature because it cannot account for the values intrinsic to particular communities which are by definition intersubjective. Radical feminists see rational self-interest as describing the behaviour of men and false to the experience of women, for whom self-sacrifice, nurturing, sympathy, emotion and care are not irrational. The liberal notion of human nature, then, is at best a partial and therefore an inadequate account of human motivations and behaviour. In different ways, these analyses illustrate that taking a particular set of motivations and behaviour to be universal and characteristically human ignores the fact that different social conditions and social relationships promote and develop other characteristics and qualities. And to ignore this amounts to ideological legitimation for a particular view of human nature and the relationship between the individual and society.

Sixth, the idea that social bonds create identification with others and it is this that gives rise to co-operative and altruistic behaviour cannot be acknowledged by liberals who can only see that the object of the individual's actions is their own benefit, not other individuals or society. This creates the problem of how to reconcile self-interest with any notion of a collective good, for why should individuals do other than act in their own interest? A natural harmony or a coincidence between the interests of egoistic individuals is an implausible solution, with the possibility of conflict remaining a permanent problem. The idea that individuals will co-operate and act in the general interest because they too will ultimately benefit, ignores the problem of the free-rider who is paradigmatically the free rational utility-maximizer. The postulation of an alternative psychology of limited benevolence by some eighteenth-century thinkers on its own cannot help to bridge the gap between consideration of the individuals' own interests and those of others.

This account assumes that benevolent dispositions will benefit particular interests and general interests. However, benevolent dispositions are defined in terms of individual psychology and there are no explanations of the social relations which produce this sentiment or the social conditions under which the particular and the general interest will coincide. Nor can moralized accounts of the impartiality of reason help. In utilitarian versions, the claim that it is rational to treat our own interests as no more important than others, is not reinforced by any social or psychological theory as to why or when we might desire to act in others' interests. Individuals who are motivated by self-interest or by limited benevolence are unlikely to take an impartial viewpoint. Kantian versions of rationality break the link between the interests of the individual and their moral responsibility, by insisting on the primacy of the rational status of duty over the interests and inclinations of the individual. Once duty and desire are separated in this way, however, it becomes difficult to see how impartial reason could motivate this trans-social individual to act in the general interest, without there being any psychological or social basis for interest in what reason prescribes. All these solutions to how individuals can act in the interests of others cannot solve the problem because they take as their starting-point the abstract individual whose commitments are made without reference to their social identities, and forms of social organization where interests are shared are not recognized as preconditions for moral activity. Hence, there can only be abstract reasons for acting in the general interest. The real possibility of this is bound up with the social nature of human existence. Commitments to other people and social groups are not something that is separate from, hostile or external to the self, but part of and intrinsic to the social individual's identity.

The seventh and final problem is linked to the notion of rationality and autonomy. Kant's idea of rational autonomous agents as ends in themselves and the utilitarian conception of rational individuals as best judges of their own interests support the value of autonomy which requires that each individual should have the greatest amount of freedom to pursue their own ends and purposes. For this reason liberals believe that political institutions should be designed to be neutral between competing conceptions of the good. This precludes any substantive account of what is good for human beings other than what the individual believes to be good or freely chooses. It has been shown, however, that autonomy is a problematic concept if individual desires and purposes cannot be said to be freely determined and if they rest on false or superficial beliefs about what is in their interests. This calls into question the value of freedom to maximize and pursue given desires which may be contrary to the agent's best interests. It may be irrational to be sceptical about people's real needs and interests and to accept the authority of the individual's self-definition. If this is so, then a political philosophy informed by the sovereignty of individual desire and neutral between competing conceptions of the good is misdirected from the start.

2

Freedom

The liberal concept of human nature is at the heart of liberal political philosophy. It constitutes the grounds for the celebration of individual freedom, liberalism's fundamental moral and political value. Because liberals believe in the intrinsic and ultimate value of each individual, they emphasize the value of individual autonomy, respect for individual judgement and the importance of individuals pursuing their own self-interested desires as they define them. In order to protect the individual's dignity and worth, liberals believe that social institutions should be neutral between competing conceptions of the good and designed to allow each individual maximum freedom to pursue their own interests.

The traditional liberal concept of freedom defended by Hobbes and Bentham, the classical liberal thinkers Locke, Kant, Smith and Mill, and more recently by Berlin, Hayek, Friedman and Nozick is predominantly a negative one. Modern revisionary liberals and socialists defend a more positive conception.

The distinction between negative and positive conceptions of liberty was elaborated by Isaiah Berlin in his *Two Concepts of Liberty*. According to Berlin, negative liberty is involved in answering the question, 'what is the area within which the subject – a person or group of persons – is or should be left to do, or be what he is able to do, or be, without interference by other persons?' Positive liberty is involved in answering the question, 'what, or who, is the source of control or interference that can determine someone to do, or be, this rather than that?' (Berlin, 1969, p. 121–2). Negative liberty is concerned with non-interference, with what rules restrict my actions. Positive liberty is concerned with self-government, the extent to which 'I am my own master'. Berlin claims that although the freedom of non-interference and the freedom which consists in self-mastery seem to be positive and negative ways of saying the same thing, historically these concepts have become diametrically opposed and have led to 'the great clash of ideologies'.

Berlin wants to defend negative liberty which he sees as being part of the intellectual tradition of classical liberalism, and to demonstrate that positive liberty represents at times 'no better than a specious disguise for brutal tyranny' (Berlin, 1969, p. 131). This is because if freedom is characterized as self-mastery, it suggests the self divided against itself, between the 'real or rational self' and 'the actual self'. This in turn can be used to justify imposition of people's 'real selves' over their 'actual selves' in order to enhance their freedom.

The terms negative and positive liberty have often been used by Berlin and others to make the following comparisons and to show the advantage of the former over the latter. Negative libertarians, concerned as they are with freedom from constraints, seek to establish and defend an area where the individual is free from interference by the state, society and other individuals. This implies a negative view of the role of the state, limited to securing a framework for mutual non-coercion and to protecting individual rights and civil liberties. Negative liberty has also been closely connected with the doctrine of *laissez-faire* which advocates that the coercive or proscriptive actions of government in the economy should be restricted to the minimum necessary to allow it to function. Government intervention is justified only to maintain private property and guarantee free competition and trade, which give free scope to private enterprise and free choice. Commitment to negative liberty, then, implies endorsement of the institution of private property and the free market. Private property is seen to embody basic liberties in a material form and is the guarantor of individual autonomy. The free market is both non-coercive and maximizes individual freedom of choice. State regulation of industry and more than a minimum of collective welfare provision are seen as impediments to liberty. In social and personal life, the concept of negative liberty and the restriction it puts on government actions entail a large sphere of private life within which an individual can act without interference, as long as by doing so, no harm is caused to others. Because the negative view of liberty concentrates on freedom from external constraints, it does not specify any ends or purposes that the individual should be free to pursue. Therefore, it is thought to be a value-free notion. The political outcome of such a notion is associated with a tolerant, pluralistic and democratic society.

In contrast to this, the idea of positive liberty, because it is concerned with identifying the abilities, powers, capacities, opportunities and resources necessary for self-determination, is associated with an interventionist government and a wider role for the state in both public and private life. Critics of positive liberty claim this could lead to a denial of liberty in the sense that, by interfering in this way, the actual desires and interests of the individual are overridden in the name of their best interests or for the collective good of society which the goals and principles of the state are said to embody. The notion of positive liberty is thought to be value-laden, because in making distinctions between ends and what is in people's 'real' or 'rational' interests, it gives a normative account both of these and the means necessary to achieve them. Because this can license the state to impose 'real' interests over people's actual desires, positive liberty is associated with an intolerant, monist and even totalitarian society, where individual liberty is denied. According to Charles Taylor (1991, p. 178), negative liberty theorists are prone to embrace a crude and stringent version of their own theory in order to make sure that the dangers of positive liberty are avoided. This is obvious from the account of negative liberty given by Isaiah Berlin.

Negative Liberty

The key feature of Berlin's definition of negative liberty is that it is freedom from interference by others: 'Political liberty is simply the arena in which a man can act unobstructed by others.' If someone is prevented by others from doing what they would otherwise do, they are coerced. Freedom, therefore, is the absence of coercion: 'To coerce a man is to deprive him of his freedom.' The term coercion, however, does not cover every inability to do something. 'Coercion implies the deliberate interference of other human beings within the area in which I could otherwise act. You lack political liberty or freedom only if you are prevented from attaining a goal by human beings' (Berlin, 1969, p. 122). The plausibility of defending negative liberty depends upon accepting that the meaning of freedom can be divorced from the value of freedom; a sharp distinction between freedom and ability; between freedom and its conditions and a stringent definition of coercion. Defenders of negative liberty insist upon separating the definition of the meaning of freedom from the value of freedom. Oppenheim, for example, argues that 'Being free to do what one cannot do is usually of no value to the actor; but having a freedom is not the same as valuing a freedom one has' (Oppenheim, 1980, p. 67). According to this view, it makes sense to say that a tramp is free to dine at the Ritz, even though this freedom is of no value to him. Separating freedom from what it is valuable for is significant, since if this is possible, freedom can be defined in value-free terms. It can be described and measured empirically. If the value of freedom is included in the definition, then this involves value judgements about the worth of liberty in terms of human interests, needs and purposes. Since these judgements are subjective definitions of freedom which embody values, they cannot provide objective criteria for what it means to be free. Defining freedom as the absence of interference can be an objective criterion, since in principle it is possible to empirically identify obstacles to freedom and this does not involve judgements about which interests, ends and purposes people should realize in order to be free.

Strict negative libertarians make a sharp distinction between being free and being able to do something, so that freedom is the absence of coercion, rather than the power, the ability, resources or opportunities to do something. They argue that freedom and ability are not the same thing. According to Hayek (1991, p. 83) this would mean that we could only be free when we are able to do whatever we want. Freedom would be the power to satisfy desires such as the desire to fly like a bird, be released from gravity or alter the environment to our liking. This identification of freedom with power or ability equates freedom with omnipotence and this should not be confused with the kind of freedom any social order can secure. It would be absurd to say that the inability to fly or defy gravity are restrictions on freedom, because they are not the result of, nor are they alterable by, human action. Underlying this view is the assumption that only human beings can restrict freedom. If there are no conceptual or logical connections between freedom and ability, then the question of what resources and opportunities are open to people is not relevant to their freedom. If freedom is concerned with the effective power to do things, then equating freedom would require the redistribution of resources. Recognizing this, and perhaps because of this, Hayek argues that liberty and power are different things.

The confusion of liberty as power with liberty in its original meaning inevitably leads to the identification of liberty with wealth; and this makes it possible to exploit all the appeal which the word 'liberty' carries in the support for a demand for the distribution of wealth. Yet, though freedom and wealth are both good things which most of us desire and though we often need both to obtain what we wish, they still remain different. Whether or not I am my own master and can follow my own choice and whether the possibilities from which I must choose are many or few are thus entirely different questions. (Hayek, 1991, p. 87)

Abilities and powers on this view are not relevant to freedom. The only inability that is relevant is that which results from deliberate interference. The poor are free, if they are free from deliberate interference to get what they want. The fact that they are unable to get what they want because of lack of wealth is only an infringement of their freedom, if and when, this inability is related to the coercive power of another. What matters for freedom is the absence of coercion. Coercion is narrowly defined as deliberate interference, when someone is prevented from doing something by the intentional action of another. Because coercion relates to actions of other individual human beings, it rules out structural coercion as an impediment to liberty. Because coercion relates to intention, the unintended, but foreseeable, consequences of human activity cannot be said to infringe liberty.

Can the meaning of freedom be separated from the value of freedom?

If freedom is defined simply as the absence of impediments, then it seems that negative libertarians are narrowly concerned with what takes liberty away. Being free simply means to be without interference and no account is given of what the agent is prevented from doing. It is difficult to see how we can make sense of freedom as non-interference, without being able to say what we are free to do or what we want to be free to do, for otherwise what would be the point of being left alone? The reason we do not want to be interfered with is precisely because it will enable us to do something else. If freedom is not defined in relation to what we are free to do, then freedom has no connection with human desires, interests and purposes. It is not bound up with what people want to do or with what is worthwhile doing, that is, with their actual, their significant or their 'real' interests. This is thought to be the advantage of the concept of negative liberty by some of its defenders. According to

Oppenheim (1973, p. 56), Day (1970, 1977) and Parent (1974a), the judgement that X is free to do Y neither entails nor presupposes any judgement about what it is right to do, what it is in X's real interests to do, or that such an action is part of a good or praiseworthy way of life. This view is also defended by Steiner:

> To ask whether an individual is free to do A, is not to ask a moral question. It is, rather, to ask a factual question, the answer to which is logically prior to any more questions about his doing A ... It follows from these considerations that statements to the effect that 'X is free to do A' do not imply or presuppose statements to the effect that 'X wants to do A' or that 'X has no obligation to do or not to do A'. Nor therefore do they imply or presuppose statements about what X 'really' wants or about what is in his 'real' interests to do or have done to him. (Steiner, 1974, p. 35)

Freedom, then, is a descriptive term and the question of whether or not an individual is free is an empirical one to which there is a right answer. Freedom has no logical or conceptual link to human desires or purposes, what makes life worthwhile or what makes freedom valuable. This seems counter-intuitive. If freedom has no connection with what we are free to do, in terms of human desires, interests and purposes, then freedom is a restrictive notion which seems to equate being free with being left alone *per se*. Although there are occasions when we want to be left alone because we don't want to do anything, for instance, when we are depressed, tired or harassed, this is not what we ordinarily mean by being free. Nor is it why we regard freedom as important, for this would amount to valuing solitary confinement for its own sake, and not valuing the point of being free. If I am in a situation, where there are no restrictions on my activity, but I don't want to do anything I can do or, conversely, if I cannot fulfil any of my desires or purposes, then it seems perverse to call this state freedom. Even by liberal theories' own standards there is a link between negative liberty and what makes freedom valuable.

Market society is often justified precisely because people are free to do what they want and to make their own choices. This makes freedom valuable as a means to satisfy wants. It is claimed that no value judgements are made here. The wants people happen to have are simply accepted as facts. However, this position cannot avoid the connection between freedom and its value. It amounts to positively evaluating the existing patterns of wants. If what people want is accepted simply because they want it by virtue of the fact that it is desired, then the normative nature of this acceptance cannot be evaded. The unquestioned premise is that it is good for people to have what they want, so that here the connection between freedom and its value is preserved. Other aspects of liberal thought also do not separate the meaning and nature of liberty from its value or worth. The reason why liberals argue for negative liberty is that it provides the opportunity for uncoerced choice, the ability to live an autonomous life shaped by a person's own purposes and values. Here, what it means to be free is inextricably bound up with what gives liberty its worth and this can only be explained in terms of human desires and interests. Acting to achieve our own interests and realize our own ends and purposes is both what it means to be free and an explanation of why freedom in the liberal tradition is valued as the absence of interference. Furthermore, it is only when we know what we are free to do that certain kinds of obstacles can be identified as restrictions on freedom. The value and importance of freedom follow from the identification of which factors are relevant to acting to achieve what we want to be free to do. To describe a free action is also to evaluate its worth. Charles Taylor illustrates the point that we cannot make judgements about freedom without reference to judgements about what it is important to do.

> Even when we think of freedom as the absence of external obstacles, it is not the absence of such obstacles *simpliciter*. For we make discriminations between obstacles as representing more or less serious infringements of freedom. And we do this, because we deploy the concept against a background understanding that certain goals and activities are more significant than others. (Taylor, 1991, p. 149)

Taylor argues that my freedom is restricted if the local authority puts up traffic lights near my house and if there is a law which prevents me from worshipping according to my beliefs. The former, however, is not thought of as a significant restriction on freedom and the latter is. This is to do with judgements about the importance of the activities and purposes that are hindered by each of these restrictions. If we can see this to be so, then:

> Freedom is no longer just the absence of external obstacles *tout court*, but the absence of external obstacles to significant action, to what is important to man. There are discriminations to be made; some restrictions are more

serious than others, some are utterly trivial. About many, there is of course controversy. But what the judgments turn on is some sense of what is significant for human life. Restricting the expression of people's religions and ethical convictions is more significant than restricting their movement around uninhabited parts of the country; and both are more significant than the trivia of traffic control. (Taylor, 1991, p. 150)

If judgements, ascriptions and descriptions of freedom depend on evaluating the worth of what we are free to do, then it is unclear how negative liberty can be a value-free notion, how it can be unconnected to human desires and purposes or how the meaning and value of freedom can be thought to be separate issues.

Freedom and Ability

If it is recognized that freedom and its value are connected, then it is difficult to deny the connection between freedom and ability that this involves. Negative libertarians have argued that there is no logical or conceptual connection between freedom and ability. But if negative liberty is valuable as a means to doing what we want, or to achieving our ends and purposes, then the ability to achieve them may also require the opportunities, resources and capacities to secure the goals that are the point of being free from interference to achieve. If the absence of coercion is valued, it is because we value the ability to do something else. Being left alone cannot secure this. In order to be free to do something, we must be able to do it, and the ability to do something may depend on more than the absence of interference. It may require the presence of positive conditions. Freedom from interference is useless and valueless for those unable to do what they want to do because they lack the necessary abilities and conditions. Negative libertarians are able to hold this distinction between freedom and ability or freedom and the conditions of its exercise because they claim the only inability that is relevant to freedom is that which results from the coercive power of other human beings. Some negative libertarians interpret this to mean that the impediment must actually prevent action in order to make that action unfree.

Must the impediment prevent action?

Parent (1974b, pp. 433–4) and Steiner (1974, p. 33) argue that the restraint must make an action physically impossible to count as a restriction. Steiner writes, 'An individual is unfree if and only if his doing of any action is rendered impossible by the action of another person. That is the unfree individual is so because the particular desire in question is prevented by another.' This would mean that a person is only unfree when they are physically forced or prevented from doing or not doing something. That is, when they are subject to direct occurrent force. When someone directly and forcibly controls another person's behaviour as it occurs (by physical violence) and when the agent has literally no control or choice but to do what the coercer makes them do, only then are they unfree. This would rule out dispositional force as being coercive. For example, if someone *can* control another's behaviour by coercive means, by making threats or offers, because the threat may deter, but need not prevent another person performing an action, the agent is not unfree to do so. So, according to Day (1970, p. 260), in the 'your money or your life' situation, the agent is not unfree to keep his money because he has not been forced to hand it over. He may not *want* to hand it over, but he can keep it. According to this strict account of coercion, as that which makes an action physically impossible, if coercion is defined relative to the agent's desires, then freedom will be relative to individual desires and therefore will depend on subjective values. In order to maintain freedom as a non-normative notion and be able to describe freedom objectively, it must be defined as the absence of physical constraints. This account of coercion refers to facts, observable physical constraints and not the agents' or other people's goals, interests, values or desires.

The attempt to define coercion in factual terms in order to maintain a non-evaluative account of negative liberty, suffers from the problem of making the notion of coercion, and hence freedom too narrow. An action has to be literally impossible to be unfree, and many of the restraints that we take to be coercive do not fit this definition. When a person is threatened, we normally describe the threat as coercive and describe that person as being unfree to do what they want to do. According to Parent and Steiner this is not the case. If a person succumbs to the highwayman's threat and decides to hand over the money, he is doing what he wants to do. He has merely altered the pattern of his desires. Before the threat was issued, he wanted to keep the money, after the threat, he no longer wanted to. So, handing over the money is not a case of unfreedom. Steiner writes, 'Interventions of an offering or a threatening kind effect changes in individual's relative desires to do certain actions.

But neither the making of threats or offers constitutes a diminution of personal liberty' (Steiner, 1974, p. 43). This seems disingenuous. There is a difference between the 'before' and 'after' desires, which lies precisely in the fact that the former is uncoerced and the latter is not autonomously chosen. At the issue of the threat, the agent wants to hand over the money and in this sense the agent's behaviour is chosen and desired by him at the moment of performance and so is voluntary. But the desire and the action have an irreducibly unfree component in that the choice the agent had to make was a compulsory choice between alternatives that were neither chosen, controlled, nor desired by him. Feinberg makes a similar point:

When the highwayman sticks his gun in one's ribs and says 'your money or your life', he allows one the option of giving or not giving one's money, and the option of staying or not staying alive, but he closes the option of keeping *both* one's money *and* one's life. (Feinberg, 1980, pp. 37-8)

The person threatened has not changed his desire to keep his money and his life and now only desires to keep his life. He still desires to keep both, but now cannot do so because he is prevented from doing so. He must make a choice and whatever choice he makes, this involves some significant loss or penalty. As Feinberg says elsewhere:

In cases of coercion via threat, there is a sense in which the victim is left with a choice. He can comply or he can suffer the (probable) consequences. But if the alternative to compliance is some unthinkable disaster – such as the death of a child – then there is really no choice but to comply. In intermediate cases, between the extremes of overwhelmingly coercive threats and mere attractive offers, the threat, in effect, puts a price tag on non-compliance and leaves it up to the threatened person to decide whether the price is worth paying. The higher the price of non-compliance, the less eligible it will seem for his choice. For this intermediate range, threats are like burdens on a man's back, rather than shackles, or bonds, or bayonets. They make one of his alternatives more difficult, but not impossible. This is the way in which taxes on socially undesirable conduct can be said to be coercive. Although they discourage without actually prohibiting, they can quite effectively prevent. (Feinberg, 1973, pp. 7–8)

Threats are coercive when they close an option that was previously open; when they prevent an agent from doing what he would otherwise do; when the agent can no longer perform an action without penalty and when the price of non-compliance is high. This means, first, that freedom cannot stop short at the absence of external physical constraints that make action impossible, and, second, freedom must involve for its elucidation and intelligibility some reference to what makes freedom worthwhile, such as the availability of options, choices or some sense of fundamental human desires or interests which it would be difficult for the agent to abandon and which therefore are relevant to freedom.

Do impediments have to be deliberately imposed?

To qualify as an inability relevant to freedom, then, coercion does not have to relate only to the physical impossibilities of performing an action in order to make that action unfree. Does, however, the person imposing the impediment have to do so deliberately to be said to be restricting the agent's freedom? Negative libertarians argue that they do. Berlin (1969, p. 122) states 'coercion implies the deliberate interference of other human beings within the area in which I would otherwise act'. Freedom can only be restricted by an identifiable person who acts to deliberately do so. This means that inabilities which arise from unintentional acts and which are the indirect results of social arrangements are not restrictions on political liberty. Dyer (1964, p. 447), for example, argues that if a person is unintentionally impeded by another, he is unable but not unfree to perform an action. He is only unfree if it was the coercer's intention to make it impossible for him to act. Hayek argues that market outcomes do not infringe the liberty of those who end up with the least resources and who are therefore unable to get what they want, since these outcomes are the unintended consequences of individual actions and not foreseeable for particular individuals. But the fact that the consequences of an action are unintentional and not foreseeable is not sufficient to show that these consequences do not limit the freedom of those who suffer from them. Plant argues:

Given that ... property rights are distributed very unequally then the critic of the market would argue that those who enter the market with least will end up with least. Given the existing structure of property rights, this is one of the more obviously foreseeable effects of markets. Clearly this outcome is not intended, but is this sufficient to make it non-coercive to the worst off? It is arguable that the answer is no, for the following reason. In our individual lives we can be held responsible for the unintended but foreseeable consequences of our action. If this were not so there would be no crime of manslaughter. In this sense, therefore, the idea of individual coercive action needs to be broadened to include non-intentional action but whose consequences for others can be seen. If, therefore, like Hayek we support the spread of markets against the background of unequal property rights, and if the consequences of this are as I have suggested, then we bear responsibility for those outcomes, even if they are unintended. On this view, an action, whether performed by an individual or by an organisation like a market, can be coercive if its foreseeable even if unintended effect is to make it practically impossible for people to do what they would have been able to do had the intervention not taken place or had been different. (Plant, 1991, pp. 234-5)

The criterion of intentionality cannot provide an adequate defence for the view that unintentional actions should not be classed as coercive. An action, whether intentional or not, which has the consequence of limiting or restricting another person or persons, where the likelihood of that consequence occurring was known, must be regarded as an act of coercion whatever the aims of the perpetrator. This is partly because the effects of the action on the subject of action are both knowable and are the same, whatever the intention. It would be absurd to claim that patients who wait in hospital queues are free if this is an unintended consequence of government's privatization policies, and not free, if this was the result of a policy intended to kill off some sick people. Similarly, if the government cuts old age pensions with the intention of letting some people die of hypothermia or simply because it wants to save money, it does not make sense to say that in the former case they are not free and in the latter they are. The irrelevance of intentionality is also to do with the fact that although the coercive action may not have been intended, the inability which results does not absolve the agent of responsibility for the consequences. Miller (1983/4, p. 81) argues that moral responsibility, not intentionality, is the criterion for judging whether or not an action is coercive. He argues that only those impediments (intentional or not) for which moral responsibility can be attributed are impediments. They are coercive, not because they are intentional, but because the inabilities which result are the moral responsibility of society since they are within its power to prevent.

Defining freedom as the absence of deliberate and intentional interference neglects the possibly unintended but nevertheless inevitable and foreseeable effects of social arrangements and capitalist property relations and removes them from critical scrutiny with respect to freedom. By calling poverty, hunger, disease and ignorance unintended consequences, negative libertarians can suggest that these are beyond human control and alteration, and that they are effects for which human beings are not responsible. And sometimes negative libertarians seem to suggest that this is the case. By insisting that the absence of freedom is a matter of direct and deliberate human intervention, they talk as if the indirect and unintended results of social arrangements were not the result of other people's actions at all. When Berlin argues that lack of resources for the poor, for 'men' who are half-naked, illiterate, underfed, or diseased, is not a lack of freedom, because no individual through direct interference has deprived them of resources, he implies that these inabilities were some kind of natural inability and not the result of human social arrangements. This is because he wants to separate freedom from ability, from the conditions of its exercise and from its value. He acknowledges that political rights and formal freedom from state intervention are no use to those without resources, and that without conditions for the exercise of freedom, they are valueless. However, he claims that those who escape from poverty and deprivation and those who are given or acquire resources are not increasing their freedom. 'Everything is what it is: liberty is liberty, not equality or fairness, or justice or culture, or human happiness or a quiet conscience' (Berlin, 1969, p. 125). They may be acquiring the conditions for the exercise of freedom, but not freedom itself. He defends the distinction between freedom and its exercise in the Introduction to his *Four Essays on Liberty*

This is not a mere pedantic distinction, for if it is ignored, the meaning and value of freedom of choice are apt to be downgraded. In their zeal to create social and economic conditions in which alone freedom is of genuine value, men tend to forget freedom itself; and if it is remembered, it is liable to be pushed aside to make room for those other values with which the reformers or revolutionaries have become preoccupied. (Berlin, 1969, p. 110).

What can it mean, however, to say that I have freedom, but not the conditions of its exercise? If I cannot exercise freedom because I lack the resources to do so, how can I be said to have it? How can it make sense to say that the half-naked, the illiterate, the underfed and diseased are free to be clothed, be educated, to eat or be treated, but they lack the conditions? Surely it is the distinction between freedom and its conditions which downgrades the meaning and value of freedom, and not vice versa? The problem seems to stem not from the liberal insistence that freedom and its conditions are separate and different issues, but from a selective use of *which* conditions are the result of the actions of human beings, and so from a restricted understanding of the conditions which are relevant to freedom. Surely the negative act of non-interference is both a part of liberty and a condition of liberty? It is a condition for making choices, but it is only one condition. If there is no law that prevents the poor from sending their children to private schools, then they have the legal conditions necessary for freedom. But if they have no money, then they lack the financial conditions. The fact that laws are deliberate constraints and financial ones are not is irrelevant, since both are necessary conditions for the exercise of freedom. If I lack one of these, I lack liberty. Both conditions, if they are the result of human social arrangements are restrictions on liberty. Berlin, by denying this, implies that it is questionable whether poverty and lack of material resources are a consequence of other people's actions at all. Berlin writes:

If my poverty were a kind of disease, which prevented me from buying bread, or paying for a journey round the world or getting my case heard, as lameness prevents me from running, this inability would not naturally be described as a lack of freedom, least of all political freedom. It is only because I believe that my inability to get a given thing is due to the fact that other human beings have made arrangements whereby I am, whereas others are not, prevented from having enough money with which to pay for it, that I think myself a victim of coercion or slavery. In other words, this use of the term depends on a particular social and economic theory about the causes of my poverty or weakness. If my lack of material means is due to my lack of mental or physical capacity, then I begin to speak of being deprived of freedom (and not simply about poverty) only if I accept the theory. If, in addition, I believe I am being kept in want by a specific arrangement which I consider unjust or unfair, I speak of economic slavery or oppression. (Berlin, 1969, p. 122)

Berlin seems to be suggesting here that poverty is a natural inability like lameness, and therefore not a lack of freedom. Poverty can only be described as a lack of freedom if we accept a particular social and economic theory that attributes the causes of poverty to arrangements made by other human beings. In a footnote he mentions

Marxist, Christian, utilitarian and all socialist doctrines as examples of theories which do this. He implies that there are other plausible theories which do not. However, people who believe that there is a causal relationship between social arrangements and poverty do not do so because they are committed to a particular theory, but because this relationship can be substantiated, the theories in question are making factual claims about social arrangements and their effects which can be verified empirically. Moreover, there are no credible theories that claim poverty is a natural rather than a social fact. Macpherson points out that it is only vulgar free enterprise theories which have suggested that the poverty of the poor is their own fault, and that even free enterprise theories of any significance from Smith and Bentham to Mill and Green have recognized that it is arrangements made by other human beings which determine the distribution of resources. He adds:

However, we need not rest on the views of the classical economists, we may simply point out, as an evident general proposition, that the distribution of access to the means of labour is a matter of social institution: land and labour may, at the decision of a society, or those who control it, be held in common, or owned individually, or held in any combination of these ways; and property in land and capital may be subject to any or no limits on amounts and ways of acquisition. It is surely equally clear that the difference between individuals' access to the means of labour is an important determinant of their incomes ... And of course it is not differences in income alone that are in question ... differences in access are at least as important in determining what I can do and what I can get. On these grounds we may conclude that the unequal access to the means of life and labour inherent in capitalism is, regardless of what particular social and economic theory is invoked, an impediment to the freedom of those with little or no access. (Macpherson, 1973, p. 101)

To leave out lack of access to opportunities and resources from the category of coercive impediments to liberty because they are not the result of deliberate and intentional interference and to remove these inequalities to the category of conditions of liberty, is to give an inadequate and limited definition of freedom. Liberty is infringed by direct coercion. Political power can involve domination and force of this kind, but this is not the only, nor the most common, nor even necessarily the most effective way of preventing people from doing something they want to do. Inequalities in power, wealth and material resources are just as surely preventative causes. They can only be classed as diminishing the conditions of liberty rather than liberty itself, by defining impediments so as to leave them out, that is, by denying that they are preventative causes. A definition of liberty that takes no account of these and denies that those with unequal access suffer an impediment to liberty, neglects as sources of unfreedom the possibly unintended, but nevertheless inevitable and foreseeable effects of capitalist property relations, and implausibly suggests that these inequalities are not the results of social arrangements made, maintained and alterable by other human beings.

Internal Obstacles to Freedom

So far, it has been argued that freedom cannot just mean the absence of external obstacles which are directly and deliberately imposed, but must also include the absence of unintentional and indirect impediments which are the result of modifiable social arrangements. Another major area of criticism of the view of freedom as the absence of external obstacles is that this overlooks the significance of internal obstacles to freedom. Charles Taylor in his article 'What's Wrong with Negative Liberty' (1991) argues the definitive case for showing how freedom can be restricted by internal factors as well as external ones. We have seen how Taylor argues that freedom cannot just be the absence of external obstacles to satisfy any old end or to achieve any old purpose. It must be the absence of external obstacles to do what is important. This is because, even this notion of freedom:

requires a background conception of what is significant, according to which some restrictions are seen to be without relevance to freedom altogether, and others are judged as being of greater and lesser importance. So some discrimination among motivation seems essential to our concept of freedom. A moment's reflection shows why this must be so. Freedom is important to us because we are purposive beings. But then there must be distinctions in the significance of different kinds of freedom based on the distinction in the significance of different purposes. (Taylor, 1991, p. 151)

According to Taylor, those who insist that freedom is purely freedom from external obstacles without acknowledging that the application of the concept of freedom requires reference to significant purposes, ignore why we value freedom. They also rule out one of the most powerful motives for the defence of freedom offered by liberal theorists from Kant to Mill. The point of being free from interference is that it allows individuals to be self-determining, to pursue their own good in their own way. If this is recognized, then it is clear that freedom can be thwarted by internal obstacles as well as external ones. Our important purposes, our ability to be self-determining can be frustrated by our desires. If we are the subject of neurotic impulses, cravings, obsessions and compulsions, we may be acting on our desires without being free. In so doing, we may defeat our significant purposes. Similarly, if we suffer from weakness of will, inhibitions, inner fears or are slaves to conventional norms, then we can be prevented by these from doing what we have set ourselves to do. Freedom involves making qualitative distinctions between which desires and motivations are important to us. In many cases we are able to do this by distinguishing between our first-order desires and second-order desires (desires about desires). If we have an irrational fear that prevents us from doing something that we want to do, then we experience that desire as an obstacle, as an internal inhibitor to the fulfilment of our ends. Such desires are obstacles to our purposes and so to our freedom to achieve them. Their absence would not only make their fulfilment possible, but also could be sustained without any regret or loss as to who we are.

Thus we can experience some desires as fetters, because we can experience them as not ours. And we experience them as not ours because we see them as incorporating a quite erroneous appreciation of our situation and of what matters to us. (Taylor, 1991, p. 158)

Feinberg makes a similar point:

If we are prevented by some internal element – an impulse, a craving, a weakened condition, an intense but illicit desire, a neurotic compulsion – from doing that which we think is the best thing to do, then the internal inhibitor is treated as an alien force, a kind of 'enemy within'. On the other hand, when the inhibitor is some higher-ranked desire and that which is frustrated is a desire of lesser importance albeit greater momentary intensity, we identify with the desire that is higher in our personal hierarchy, and consider ourselves to be the subject rather than the object of constraint. When the desire to do that which is forbidden is constrained by conscience, by the 'internalized authority' of the prohibiting rules themselves, we identify with our consciences, and repel the threat to our personal integrity posed by the refractory lower desire which we 'disown' no matter how 'internal' it may be. (Feinberg, 1973, p. 14)

Internal motivational conditions, then, are necessary for freedom. We must be able to discriminate between desires and exercise a capacity to evaluate wants, not just satisfy them. Freedom cannot just be the absence of external obstacles, but also involves the absence of internal obstacles to achieve significant purposes. Freedom to act on significant purposes, however, may also fail because what we take to be important may be the product of social forces which operate in such a way as to determine our desires and to limit what we believe to be a feasible set of options. Here we may be subject to internal constraints of which we are unaware. We may be acting upon our desires without being free. We may have misidentified our most significant purposes. In this case, ignorance of the social conditioning and its consequence and ignorance of the alternatives available mean that we are not exercising free choice.

Behaviour motivated by the desires is determined in ways we cannot control, and is insufficiently purposive, intentional and self-directing to be called freely chosen. Freedom here involves the ability to identify our most important purposes. Freedom can be curbed by means other than direct coercion. An adequate account of freedom must acknowledge the abilities, opportunities and resources that are relevant to freedom. Freedom must include internal factors to significant actions as well as direct and indirect external ones. That is, it must include states of mind and capacities, some self-awareness, self-understanding, moral discrimination and self-control and some ability to discriminate, evaluate and identify our significant purposes, because we can fail to be free when these internal conditions are not realized and these capacities are unexercised.

Positive Liberty

Berlin begins his characterization of negative liberty with what sounds like an eloquent statement in its defence.

The 'positive' sense of the word 'liberty' derives from the wish on the part of the individual to be his own master. I wish my life and decisions to depend on myself, not on external forces of whatever kind. I wish to be the instrument of my own, not of other men's acts of will. I wish to be a subject, not an object; to be moved by reason, by conscious purposes, which are my own, not by causes which affect me, as it were, from outside. I wish to be somebody, not nobody; a doer – deciding, not being decided for, self-directed and not acted upon by external nature or by other men as if I were a thing, or an animal, or a slave incapable of playing a human role, that is, of conceiving goals and policies of my own and realizing them. This is at least part of what I mean when I say that I am rational, and that it is my reason that distinguishes me as a human being from the rest of the world. I wish, above all, to be conscious of myself as a thinking, willing, active being, bearing responsibility for my choices and able to explain them by reference to my own ideas and purposes. I am free to the degree that I believe this to be true, and enslaved to the degree that I am unable to realize that it is not. (Berlin, 1969, p. 131)

He goes on to show how the notion of self-mastery is a dangerous one and can lead to monstrous denials of liberty. This is because freedom as self-determination and self-mastery suggests a distinction between the 'real' and the 'empirical' or 'actual' self. The 'real self' has as its goal rational self-control. Advocates of positive liberty feel justified in imposing on 'everyday' selves the ends they perceive to be the fulfilment of people's real selves. Their 'real self' is identified with the social whole of which the individual is part, and this organic whole is taken to embody all the real selves of these individuals. Their 'real' interests are associated with collective interests and are embodied in certain kinds of society. In imposing the organic will on individuals, the society is said to achieve a higher liberty for all its members. Those who resist imposition of these ends are mistaken about the nature of their real goals and hence, are justifiably constrained. Berlin concludes:

Once I take this view, I am in a position to ignore the actual wishes of men or societies, to bully, oppress, torture them in the name, and on behalf of their 'real' selves, in the secure knowledge that whatever is the true goal of man (happiness, performance of duty, wisdom, a just society, self-fulfilment) must be identical with his freedom – the free choice of his 'time' albeit often submerged and inarticulate self. (Berlin, 1969, p. 131)

Berlin's point is that all theories of rational self-direction generate the paradoxical notion that people can 'be forced to be free'. There are theories of positive liberty originating from Rousseau in which freedom as rational self-direction can only be realized in the collective control of the common life. For Rousseau (1975, p. 177) the enforcement of the 'general' or 'real' will over the 'particular' will is the condition of freedom. 'Whosoever refuses to obey the general will shall be compelled to do so by the whole body. This means nothing less than that he will be forced to be free.' But as so many commentators have pointed out (notably Charles Taylor (1991) and C.B. Macpherson (1973)) this is a distortion and a caricature of positive liberty. Positive liberty is a cluster of concepts, at the heart of which is the notion that self-rule or self-determination is valuable in itself. This notion has no necessary connection with collective control, a prescribed form of life or forcing people to be free. The ability to act in accordance with our own conscious purposes is in fact antithetical to the idea of freedom as coercion by the fully rational, by those who have mastered the self. Berlin's criticism would only hold if it could be shown that self-rule in itself is part of the false ideal of freedom, as he claims, and that the notion of self-rule inevitably leads to coercion and imposition.

Is self-rule part of the false idea of freedom?

The idea that autonomy or self-rule is valuable in itself is not just a premise of would-be totalitarians, but is a key notion of the liberal tradition and a value that is central to liberal democracy. When discussing negative liberty, it was argued that the reason people want to be free from interference is because they want to be or to do something else. This is not necessarily that which is in accordance with their higher or rational self, but with any old self. The meaning of freedom cannot be separated from the value of freedom to be, to have or to choose something, and this is part of the liberal rationale for having a larger sphere of negative liberty within which an individual can act, free from interference. The reason negative liberty is valuable for both Kant and Mill is that it promotes autonomy. If people were incapable of rational self-direction or self-determination was unimportant, then there would be no need for liberals to be concerned with the extent to which the state interfered with or controlled their actions. It is because liberals think of human beings as capable of rational and autonomous action and because they attach importance to this capacity, that they value negative liberty.

Kantian liberalism is premised on the assumption of equal respect for individuals because they each have a rational will. Therefore, they should be treated as having goals and projects of their own, as ends-in-themselves. The idea of freedom as the autonomy of the individual informs Mill's view that 'the only freedom which deserves the name, is that of pursuing our own good in our own way' (Mill, 1962a, p. 138). It was for this reason that individuals should be free from interference to pursue their own interests and their own conceptions of the good. The only reason for denying people the freedom to make their own decisions is when this harms others or when they are not fully rational. By this Mill's means 'unless he is a child, or delirious, or in some state of excitement or absorption incompatible with the full use of the reflecting faculty' (Mill, 1962a, p. 229).

The notion of self-determination, then, is not part of the false ideal of freedom. It is central to both Kant and Mill and to the liberal justification of freedom as non-interference. Thus *both* advocates of negative and positive liberty endorse the value of freedom as autonomy or self-rule. The crucial difference between liberal views and those of positive libertarians do not rest on differences in opinion about the importance and value of self-determination, but on what it means to be a self-determining autonomous agent, and what being an autonomous agent requires.

Autonomous agents

Unless agency is not fully developed (as in children) or is impaired (the delirious, etc.), for liberals self-determination is pursuing one's own good in one's own way. Because individuals are the best judges of their own interests, expressed desires represent their autonomous interests. It was argued by Charles Taylor that expressed desires may not be compatible with autonomy because, to be self-determining, an agent has to be free from internal obstacles to significant action. If an individual acts because of impulse, obsessions or compulsions; through domination of lower-order desires or weakness of will or if their beliefs are the result of ignorance, misunderstanding or the failure of critical rationality, then they are not acting autonomously. That individual is in insufficient control over their life to be called autonomous, to be said to be ruling themselves. For this reason, positive libertarians argue that autonomous agency requires the absence of internal impediments as well as the absence of coercion.

Positive libertarians also complain that the liberal view of what it means to be a self-determining autonomous agent ignores external obstacles to the development and exercise of autonomy. Their view of the isolated, abstract individual ignores the social, economic, political, patriarchal, cultural and commercial forces which influence the individual's perceptions of their interests. This means that expressed preferences are not autonomously chosen, nor do they necessarily reflect their real interests, in the way that liberal theory supposes. If the dominant ideas in any society are the ideas of those who control material production, then people's expressed interests are moulded by power relations to serve the economic interests of the producing and owning class. People can make factual errors about the means to achieve their interests through ignorance or through mistaken beliefs about what will achieve or satisfy them. But, more fundamentally, they can mistake their interests by identifying them with those of the ruling class. They may make mistakes about the desirability and possibility of alternative social arrangements and ways of life, by accepting the *status quo* as normal, natural and inevitable.

The explanation of how expressed interests are constrained and conditioned by social forces, and of the social function this conditioning serves, is an argument against the liberal view that they are autonomously chosen. They are unfree in the sense that they are not self-determined. If what people perceive to be in their interests results from power relations, then the satisfactions available and the availability of satisfactions are restricted in ways over which the agent has little control, and function to serve the interests of those who determine them. If an agent has no control over the formation and development of wants, then action motivated by them cannot be free activity, even if the agent is free from external impediments to pursue the wants so formed and developed. If the agent has an inadequate understanding of the position they are in, and the possibilities of political change, then this is an obstacle to their interests and incompatible with their autonomy. The individual whom liberal theory supposes is autonomous, is not a self-determining moral agent if their significant desires are fettered by internal obstacles and if their expressed desires are the product of social conditions over which they have no control.

The requirements for autonomous agency

The second crucial difference between liberal notions of autonomy and notions of positive liberty following on from the above is the belief that an autonomous agent requires more than the absence of external obstacles. Being an autonomous agent requires intellectual and mental capacities, self-awareness, self-control, discrimination between motivations and critical appraisal of socially conditioned beliefs, circumstances and possibilities. The fact that people's desires, beliefs and expectations are socially determined and that they may be mistaken about their interests reduces the value liberals place on individual autonomy to pursue given desires. Absolute autonomy is impossible because people's desires and actions are causally determined by their personality and environment. This is inevitable, whatever that environment happens to be. However, politics has some bearing on the degree to which people can be autonomous. Autonomy requires the ability to evaluate and revise our ideas, desires and beliefs; it requires the ability to achieve critical distance from our social determinations and social situations. Political and social organization can help minimize restraints and maximize opportunities for the development of the critical and self-critical capacities which are essential for the possibility of autonomous life. Autonomy also requires the absence of those external obstacles, the inequalities of power, which hinder the development of self-determined desires. Moreover, positive libertarians claim that it is these inequalities which prevent people from exercising autonomy. People are unable to satisfy even their expressed desires, never mind their true interests, due to inequalities in access to income, wealth, material and non-material resources which result from inequalities of power.

Thus, it can be concluded that autonomy or self-rule is not part of the false ideal of freedom as Berlin claims, but this notion is central to both liberal and positive libertarian views on the value of freedom. The difference between these views rest on whether or not the actual desires or expressed preferences of the agent are self-determined, and on what is required for the exercise of autonomy. Positive libertarians argue that the development and exercise of autonomy require more than freedom from deliberate interference. They require freedom from direct and indirect, internal and external constraints, and the presence of positive conditions — mental capacities and abilities, opportunities and resources.

Does the internal logic of the notion of autonomy or self-rule inevitably lead to coercion and imposition?

It remains to answer Berlin's charge that the notion of positive liberty as self-rule or self-mastery lends itself to coercion and legitimizes politics which do not respect autonomy.

The emphasis on the social conditioning of people's expressed preferences does not imply that these are not real or rational, or that they should be coerced in the name of their real interests. People's beliefs about their interests are informed by their own reasons and intentions, and their expressed preferences are 'really' their own. However, it is possible to criticize the social structures and relations which condition their beliefs about their interests, and the social function and consequences of these beliefs. This account provides people with reasons for criticizing and changing a system that channels and limits the expression and satisfaction of their interests, and which requires for its reproduction, the efficacy of mistaken beliefs. The process of desire formation can be condemned independently of an appeal to a self divided between the 'actual' and 'the real'. Showing that people are not self-determined, that their choices and preferences are not autonomous and that the development of autonomy is not compatible with unequal power relations in society, does not involve forcing people to be self-determining. People can only emancipate themselves.

However, Berlin argues that the transformation of the idea of rational self-direction into a totalitarian doctrine is the result of the faulty premises of the positive libertarian argument and of the assumptions they make.

first, that all men have one true purpose, and one only, that of rational self-direction; second, that the ends of all rational beings must of necessity fit into a single, harmonious pattern, which some men may be able to discern more clearly than others; third, that all conflict, and consequently, all tragedy, is due solely to the clash of reason with their rational or the insufficiently rational – the immature and undeveloped elements in life – whether individual or communal, and that such clashes are, in principle avoidable, and for wholly rational beings impossible; finally, that when all men have been made rational, they will obey the rational laws of their own natures, which are one and the same in them all, and so be at once wholly law-abiding and wholly free. (Berlin, 1969, p. 154)

Macpherson (1973, pp. 111–13) disputes that all these assumptions are inherent in any concept of positive liberty. The first assumption is an inaccurate characterization of positive liberty. Advocates of positive liberty believe that rational self-direction is valuable to pursue any purposes a person may have. As we have seen, this is also an assumption of liberal thought. To say that positive libertarians think this is 'the one and only true purpose of man' is seriously misleading. Macpherson argues that assumptions 2, 3 and 4 do not follow from the core idea of the value of rational self-direction, because in them 'rational' no longer means simply the pursuit of (multifarious) conscious purposes, but means conformity to a pre-ordained cosmic order. An advocate of positive liberty need not assume that if people were self-determining, their autonomous interests would fit a single harmonious pattern – that all people must conform to or that human beings have a specific set of purposes that are 'one and the same in them all'. Rather, they believe that when the chief impediments to self-direction are removed, there would emerge not a pattern, but a proliferation of views, goals and ways of life, given that human diversity would have full scope to flourish. They do believe, however, that they would not necessarily conflict. This is not because people's values or ends would be the same, or because they would dovetail into one true purpose, but because they believe that in a society where freedom is realized, the major sources of conflict, the inequalities in power and resources, will be removed.

These arguments refute the idea that inherent in the concept of positive liberty as rational self-determination are assumptions that lead to coercion. It is true that advocates of positive liberty do give some account of the necessary conditions, resources and opportunities that are necessary for people to be free, and that they must make some judgements about what human needs, capacities and interests are of basic importance. However, this does not commit them to any specific conception of the ends and values human beings must pursue or any prescribed notion of what human fulfilment really consists in. Neither does it justify the idea that the state is an embodiment of real interests, nor that it should coerce people in order to make them free. Rational self-determination depends on the possibility of creating the conditions necessary for the development and exercise of autonomy.

There are collectivists and paternalistic elements in all government action. Governments do contravene people's expressed preferences in order to promote their interests or aggregate freedom. Laws and policies on defence, law and order, pay, pensions, national insurance, taxation, health, education and drugs are all interferences that are justified precisely because they are thought to be in people's long term interests and because they contribute to a collective good. The underlying assumptions are that people do not necessarily know their interests in the immediate and rational way that liberal theory assumes, and that there can be valid judgements made about which human interests are of fundamental importance. It is these which justify interference. Such policies recognize that autonomy requires interference. Positive libertarians seek to extend this interference in order to facilitate access to the conditions which enable people to be self-determining and to pursue their own ends.

One Concept or Two?

Freedom as a negative concept, as merely freedom from something, undermines why we value freedom. We want to be free from interference so that we can do or be something else. Whether or not this is identified with what we want to do, what we choose to do, what would be in our real interest to do or what we must do in order to be self-determining, the question of the value of freedom cannot be separated from its meaning. Freedom as deliberate interference is too narrow a definition of what counts as an impediment to liberty. This is a purely physicalist concept imported from Newtonian classical mechanics to politics, where the causal power of one billiard ball hitting another is equated with the political power of one person bullying, coercing or deliberately interfering with another. This leaves everything apart from this kind of direct coercion outside the realm of freedom. However, it has been argued, non-deliberate interference, the lack of resources, abilities and opportunities which are the result of inequalities in political, economic and social power are also external obstacles to freedom, and that freedom therefore requires the presence of positive conditions. Because freedom can fail to be achieved, as a result of internal obstacles, freedom must also include the absence of internal impediments and the presence of internal states and capacities.

If we cannot detach the meaning of freedom from what makes it valuable and therefore from abilities, resources, opportunities and capacities, then two things follow. First, if freedom is conceived in this way, then it is explicitly an evaluative notion. Second, the distinction Berlin makes between negative and positive liberty is not so clear. The first point holds because freedom is now concerned with judgements about what is valuable, what are important purposes and interests, as well as what desires, resources, opportunities and capacities are relevant to freedom. This presupposes some theory of human nature and human needs from which such conclusions can be drawn. It does not, however, involve advocates of such views in assumptions about the true goals and purposes which human beings must pursue, nor does it justify imposition in the name of their true interests.

The second point, that the distinction between negative and positive liberty becomes blurred, arises because freedom involves both the absence of constraints, direct and indirect, internal and external and the presence of positive conditions and capacities. Many critics of Berlin's division of liberty have argued that he fails to show that 'freedom from' (negative liberty) and 'freedom to' (positive liberty) are two distinct concepts. Any kind of liberty can be expressed in terms of both freedom from and freedom to. Feinberg (1973, p. 11) writes, 'In the typical case, then, "freedom from" and "freedom to" are two sides of the same coin, each involved with the other, and not two radically distinct kinds of freedom.' He argues that conceptually elliptical statements about freedom will take the form ' – is free from – to do (or omit, or be, or have) – '. Similarly MacCallum argues that freedom is a triadic relation. Every statement about freedom may be expressed in the form, 'X is free from Y to do Z'.

Whenever the freedom of some agent or agents is in question, it is always freedom from some constraints, restriction, interference with, or barriers to doing, not doing, becoming or not becoming something. Such freedom is thus always *of* something, an agent or agents, *from* something, *to do*, not do, become or not become something; it is a triadic relation. Taking the former 'X is (is not) free from Y to do (not do, become, not become) Z', X ranges over agents, Y ranges over 'preventing conditions', and Z ranges over actions or conditions of character or circumstance. (MacCallum, 1991, p. 102)

According to this view, disputes arise, not about what freedom means, but about different interpretations of what counts as agents, constraints and objectives and their relevance to freedom. The dispute between advocates of negative and positive liberty then may be over, whether the agent is the actual, empirical self or the real, the rational self; the self-determined self, the self-aware, self-critical and discriminating self; whether the obstacles are external impediments deliberately imposed by other human beings, or whether impediments to freedom include non-deliberate external impediments, the lack of opportunities and resources as well as internal and psychological constraints; whether the objective is some action or desire satisfaction, or whether it is some conditions of character or circumstance the agent wants to achieve, or values.

The idea that there is only one concept of freedom, but different conceptions according to what or who is identified as an agent, a constraint and an objective clarifies the formal meaning of freedom. It does not help resolve conceptual issues at the heart of debates about freedom. There still remains controversy over the substantive meaning of freedom which arises from different conceptions in each category. The plausibility of accepting the conceptions associated with negative liberty and characteristic of liberal thought depend on whether the notion of the rational autonomous agent is defensible, on whether the satisfaction of given desires and the absence of external constraints adequately capture what it means to be free. This chapter has demonstrated that these conceptions and understandings are fundamentally flawed.

Conclusion

It has been argued that negative liberty is characteristic of the liberal tradition and it is this conception that is the target of criticism in this chapter. Early liberals certainly adopted a negative concept of freedom and this persists in libertarian thinking and in present-day conservatism which sees government intervention as a threat to freedom. It is true that twentieth-century welfare liberals attempted to modify the classical liberal conception of freedom and as a result, grant the state a wider interventionist role. Modern liberals accept some of the criticisms directed at a narrow conception of liberty as freedom from deliberate interference, recognizing that inequalities of wealth and resources affect the ability to take advantage of legal and formal rights, and they advocate state intervention for redistributive and welfare purposes.

In one sense, the revision of classical liberalism is a logical extension of liberal principles. The recognition of the necessity for economic redistribution if individuals are to pursue their own interests is, like classical liberalism, underpinned by a commitment to enhancing individual autonomy. However, this very recognition creates an uneasy tension between welfare liberalism, basic liberal principles and assumptions. Since both forms of liberalism accept and endorse private ownership and the right to accumulate property, economic redistribution will inevitably infringe particular individual rights to liberty. State intervention will involve a reduction of the kind of personal liberty liberalism celebrates. If welfare liberals claim that increasing autonomy and self-fulfilment require redistribution, rather than simply rights against coercion, then this contradicts the central liberal belief in moral neutrality. The state, in providing a range of collective public goods and services, is not neutral, but makes judgements about what is necessary for humans to flourish and what is intrinsically valuable beyond the satisfaction of subjective desires. This, in turn, challenges the individualistic premises of liberal theory and the sovereignty of individual desires.

Advocating welfare undermines liberal emphasis on individual preferences because the provision of public goods cannot be based on expressed desires. Given the assumptions of the liberal tradition, the expressed wants of the individual are sovereign and policies which do not correspond to these are illiberal in that they endorse a particular conception of the good and impose a particular set of values. Provision may both override individual preferences and involve coercive methods to make everyone contribute to the collective welfare.

For these reasons, the conception of freedom as negative liberty is more consistent with liberalism's philosophical foundations and basic assumptions. Not only is the provision of welfare advocated by revisionary liberals at odds with basic liberal assumptions, but genuine positive liberty as the capacities, abilities, opportunities and resources necessary to pursue our own ends and purposes is incompatible with private ownership, the market economy and the capitalist freedoms these liberals want to endorse.

Welfare liberalism accepts as given substantial inequalities in the initial distribution of material resources and human capacities, and seeks by rearguard action to reduce the consequent inequalities in market outcomes through taxation and welfare policies. It does not confront or attempt to alter inequalities in the underlying distribution of property, capital and wealth or the means of producing or acquiring them that generate the inequalities in the first place. Moreover, welfare liberalism does not go beyond advocating minimum provision for very basic social needs. It is not concerned with eliminating inequality or with equalizing access to social power, consumption or productive resources. It does not seek to ensure that each person has the capacities, abilities, opportunities and resources that positive liberty demands.

The tension between welfare liberalism and traditional liberal assumptions and the acceptance of the market is manifest in the tendency of all forms of liberalism, even the most egalitarian of Rawls and Dworkin, to fall back onto defending negative conceptions of liberty, to distinguishing between liberty and its worth and to prioritizing civil and political liberty over economic equality and welfare provision. Any substantive notion of equality which would give people equal freedom to pursue their own interests has always been a problem within liberalism, even though a commitment to treating people equally is at the moral base of liberal theory. The next chapter will assess the different liberal justifications for inequalities in social power, wealth, income and status.

3

Equality

Equality is a fundamental presumption of liberal political and moral theory and is rooted in the idea that since each individual is regarded as being of equal moral worth, they are entitled to the same rights and respect. The view of the equal moral worth of individuals originally rested on the classical liberal claim that all individuals are endowed with natural rights, which they possess by virtue of being human. These natural or human rights are not restricted to any particular group of people, but apply equally to all 'men'. For Hobbes and Locke all men in the state of nature had natural freedom and equality. Every man had the right to be free since all were born free and equal. Liberals in the seventeenth and eighteenth centuries, in the name of natural rights, fought against the feudal premise of natural subordination to seek wider opportunities for more people. However, for liberals the premise of the fundamental equal worth of individuals need not be based on equality in the state of nature or be supported by a doctrine of natural rights. It might be couched in utilitarian terms, that everyone is to count for one and nobody for more than one, or more usually in Kantian terms where the equal moral worth of each individual is presupposed by the notion that they all possess a rational autonomous will.

This largely abstract understanding of the equal value of each individual does not lead to any idea of substantive equality or equal treatment for individuals. The notion that individuals are equal in this abstract sense is compatible with the idea that because people differ in certain ways, they ought to be treated differently. Though individuals at an abstract level may be of equal worth, real people are obviously unequal in the sense that they have different abilities, capacities, characteristics, skills and different degrees of need. Aristotle, to whom the formal principle of distributive justice is attributed, argued that, 'Equals should be treated equally and unequals unequally according to their relevant differences.' If a person is equal to another in the relevant respects, then they should be treated equally. This formal principle requires equality of consideration. It also requires that justice be seen to be done, that is, conflicts should be settled by mutually agreed principles. Most importantly, it requires impartiality. Inequalities of treatment cannot be arbitrary, but must be judged on the basis of relevant inequalities. This means for every difference in the way people are treated, a relevant reason must be given. Aristotle's principle is only a formal principle. It has no substantial content. It does not tell us what are the relevant inequalities that justify treating people differently or that justify choosing some people rather than others to have a larger share of resources.

Inequality and Desert

Liberals reject race, sex or class as relevant criteria, but typically argue that what is relevant when treating people differently is their desert or merit. Desert-based theories may take a number of forms: they may make assumptions about the personal qualities or characteristics of people that are meritorious and therefore deserving of reward; they may involve making judgements about the moral or social worth of an individual, taking into account their personal virtues, their willingness to work, their talents and skills, whether they perform a socially useful role or make a significant contribution to society. However, the central motivating idea behind these theories is that it is just and fair if inequalities in social power, wealth, income or prestige are earned and deserved by virtue of an individual's superior merit, skills, ability or contribution. Unequal outcomes are only unjust if they are the result of undeserved differences between people, such as their gender, skin colour or social circumstances.

Historically, the idea of the equal moral worth of individuals led classical liberals to oppose the feudal premise of natural subordination and to promote the idea of abstract formal equality between people. This was progressively reflected in the call for equal political and legal rights for all citizens, regardless of gender, race, creed or social background, and in economic equality, understood as the freedom to compete on an equal footing in the market. They believed that these freedoms ensured that each individual had an equal opportunity to rise and fall according to their own ability and to pursue their own interests, provided that in doing so, they did not infringe on the rights of others to do the same. Modern welfare liberals argue for more than equal political and legal rights and market freedom in order to ensure that everyone has an equal chance to be free. They accept the need for state intervention to produce equal opportunities by providing universal health care, state education and other welfare measures to help the naturally disadvantaged. Though this extends the idea of what it means to be free and what equal opportunities might involve, the dominant idea in the liberal justification for inequalities is that these are justified if they are deserved. Discrimination on the basis of race, gender, religion or other irrelevant factors is undeserved and therefore unjust. Discrimination according to desert or merit is a relevant reason for inequalities and is not only justifiable, but it is also just.

The equality to which liberals subscribe is equality of opportunity. Because people possess different talents and skills, it is right to reward merit and ability and willingness to work. However, the competition for scarce resources must take place in the context of fair equality of opportunity, with the most meritorious gaining the rewards. The equal opportunities liberals advocate are contrary to any substantive idea of equality because these are opportunities which lead to unequal outcomes. The principle of equal opportunities emphasizes the fairness of procedures rather than outcomes. It is in accordance with the liberal idea that individuals are the basic unit of society and that the purpose of social arrangements is to allow individuals to satisfy their own interests. Since individuals are the best judge of these, the system of justice should not specify any particular distribution. It should establish rules so that each individual can fairly compete and pursue their own diverse desires and interests.

A theory of justice based on desert or merit distinguishes between people and justifies differential rewards. It is a non-egalitarian criterion for just distribution, for even with the assumption of equal opportunities, if goods are distributed according to desert, the outcome is an unequal distribution. In historical terms, the idea that justice is a matter of people getting what they deserve is the most common and tenacious theory of justice. Indeed, the connection between justice and desert is often thought to be part of the very concept of justice itself.

There are two broad categories of desert-based theories – merit theories and contribution theories. Several kinds of characteristics are thought to be meritorious and therefore deserving of reward, such as an individual's ability, talent or skills and their moral worth, intrinsic virtues or personal characteristics. Contribution theories argue that rewards should be linked to an individual's contribution to society. Here, desert is getting back what you have earned, the value of your contribution to society. The idea of social justice as merit or desert together with an assumption of equal opportunities is the mainstay of a liberal theory of justice. Everyone is to have an equal chance to use their abilities or to work hard and make a contribution and to deserve a reward.

Natural abilities and responsibility

According to merit-/desert-based theories, justice requires us to treat people as responsible for their actions and therefore to praise, blame or reward them according to their conduct or character in so far as these are the outcome of their free choices, actions or efforts. If they choose to exercise their ability or choose socially useful activity, or if they work hard, they deserve to be rewarded. This view highlights the centrality of human agency in thinking about justice. Here, justice is closely associated with the liberal ideas of respect for persons, their autonomy and self-determination. Respect for persons is given when they are seen as initiators of their own conduct and responsible for their own actions. If people were not thought to be responsible for their actions, then ideas of desert and of rewarding or punishing them would be inappropriate. The merit theory of justice combines the idea of individual autonomy and responsibility with evaluating choices and actions, because rewards are linked to past events and to the individual's responsibility for them.

Morally, the idea of getting what we deserve assumes that people are autonomous initiators of their own conduct and that they are responsible for their own actions. This raises the more general problem of free will and determinism. The idea that anyone deserves anything because of their intrinsic virtues, their natural abilities or their actual behaviour is threatened by the controversy over how far an individual's conduct or aptitude is the outcome of an autonomous free will and how far they are the product of hereditary and environmental determinations. No-one can be said to deserve credit or blame for characteristics or aptitudes, whose possession or lack thereof they are not responsible for. Just as people cannot take the credit for being white, male or coming from a wealthy background, people cannot take the credit for being born talented or able or hard-working, when these are not the product of individual choice. The combination of hereditary and environmental determinations makes it difficult to have an accurate estimate of the extent to which a person can be said to be fully responsible for, and therefore take genuine credit for, their actions and to be deserving of reward. If and when this is so, then giving differential rewards on the basis of natural talent, ability or capacity for hard work is arbitrary from a moral point of view. These are not differences which are relevant when treating people differently. These issues are taken up by modern liberal egalitarians such as Rawls and Dworkin, in relation to these natural assets.

The old egalitarianism of classical liberalism aimed to establish equal political and legal rights and to eliminate social differences, in order to ensure equal opportunities for individuals to compete according to their different talents and abilities. Unequal outcomes are justified when people are rewarded on the basis of these natural abilities and talents. But, for Rawls, these natural assets are as arbitrary and as irrelevant a criterion for different rewards as are the effects of social circumstances and chance, accident or luck.

The existing distribution of income and wealth, say, is the cumulative effect of prior distribution of natural assets — that is, natural talents and abilities — as these have been developed or left unrealised, and their use favoured or disfavoured by social circumstances and such chance contingencies as accident and good fortune. Intuitively, the most obvious injustice of the system of natural liberty is that it permits distributive shares to be improperly influenced by these factors so arbitrary from a moral point of view. (Rawls, 1971, p. 72)

Rawls is claiming that the inequalities of natural assets are as undeserved as inequalities in social circumstances. If distribution based on the latter is unjust, then so too, is distribution based on the former. Both are a matter of luck and people's moral claims should not be based on contingencies for which no-one can deserve praise or blame.

Perhaps some will think that the person with greater natural endowments deserves those assets and the superior character that make their development possible. Because he is more worthy in this sense, he deserves the greater advantage that he could achieve with them. This view, however, is surely incorrect. It seems to be one of the fixed points of our considered judgements that no one deserves his place in the distribution of native endowments any more than one deserves one's initial starting place in society ... Character depends in large part upon fortunate family and social circumstances. (Rawls, 1971, p. 74)

The undeserved nature of natural assets makes the existing view of equal opportunities 'unstable' according to Rawls (1971, p. 74), and 'fraudulent' according to Dworkin (1985, p. 207). The idea of equal opportunities to receive society's rewards commensurate with ability suggests that these abilities are deserved and are the product of individual's voluntary actions or choices. However, those with less natural ability will not enjoy equal opportunities and this is not a product of their choices, but is pre-determined in ways which they cannot control.

Effort

It may be conceded that to reward ability *per se*, is unjust since no-one is morally responsible or can determine or choose the amount of natural ability they have. However, it might be argued that people do deserve rewards for what it is in their power to do, that is, for their voluntary actions for which they are responsible. Those who work hard deserve rewards over those who are lazy or who choose to make no special effort. But, as Rawls points out, the ability to work hard and to make an effort may not be the product of autonomous choices. The character a person has that enables them to make the effort may be due to circumstances beyond their control. He says, 'even the willingness to make an effort is itself dependent upon happy family and social circumstances' (Rawls, 1971, p. 74). Thus, just as natural ability is problematic as the basis of desert, so too is the claim that 'a man deserves the superior character that enables him to make the effort to cultivate his ability' (Rawls, 1971, pp. 103-4).

Taken to its extreme, the logical consequence of arguments which claim that ability and effort are determined by factors beyond our control, is that it negates the idea of moral responsibility, and undermines any notion of individuals being able to exercise autonomous choice. If even an individual's ability to use their talents is pre-determined, then it is unclear how they could be said to be responsible for anything at all. This is a criticism frequently made of Rawls. Nozick (1974, p. 214), for instance, argues that if almost everything noteworthy about an individual is explained in terms of nature and nurture, then the role of the autonomous agent central to liberal thought becomes deeply problematic.

However, even if it were the case that there are some abilities and efforts that are voluntarily acquired, that are the product of people's choices rather than being fully determined, this still would not necessarily justify differential rewards for several reasons. First, because even those who advocate that effort ought to be rewarded do not usually mean effort *per se*, they mean effort that leads to achievement. The fact that someone has tried hard and worked conscientiously, but has accomplished little or nothing, might be an occasion for praise or for commiseration, but is not a reason for deserving a reward. In the same way, advocates of reward according to ability do not mean ability that is not used, they mean ability that leads to accomplishment. Even on these theories' own terms, it is not ability or effort alone, not simply being able or talented or 'doing your best' that counts, but being successful. This means, in effect, that it is actual achievement that guarantees reward, not ability or merit, whether natural or acquired. Even if we agree that acquired ability and effort are deserving of reward, it is clear that desert in this sense does not always correlate with reward. A man may deserve to win a race because of his superior ability and the effort he has put into training, but he may fail to win and therefore is not rewarded. It is quite sensible to say that A won the race, but did not deserve to, or that B deserved to win, but didn't. If ability and effort are characteristics that are to be rewarded, then maybe we should question the emphasis on competition and achievement as ways of identifying who is deserving because of their effort or ability. The fact of winning or being successful is not a guarantee that the person who is deserving gets a reward. This only guarantees that achievement is rewarded, and this may be undeserved.

The second set of problems with the view that voluntary efforts justify differential rewards arises when we consider the logical consequence of claiming that abilities and efforts that are the product of voluntary choices should be the basis of desert. Abilities and efforts for which the individual is not responsible because they are dependent on genetic endowment or fortunate social circumstances are thereby ruled out as deserving. Abilities alone and efforts alone without achievement may be thought to be deserving, but not deserving of reward. If achievement is to be deserving of reward, it must be because of effort and ability. Can, then, voluntary ability and effort which lead to achievement be the basis of desert? There are two difficulties here. One is practical. Such a principle would be impossible to apply since it would involve complex interpersonal comparisons and judgements between different attainments and how they were achieved in order to determine their relative merit. It would involve being able to separate abilities and capacities for effort that were innate or that were the result of fortunate social circumstances from those abilities and efforts that were voluntarily acquired. This kind of judgement would be difficult enough between people and would be an impossible calculation even when applied to a single person's achievement.

Any single action or achievement is likely to be a combination of innate ability, good fortune, conducive social circumstances, effort and acquired ability, not to mention the help and support of other people. Rewards would have to be proportional, not just between individuals and their achievements, but in proportion to an individual's own voluntary actions which were not dependent on advantages for which that individual was not personally responsible. And this is simply not calculable. If it is not possible to solve the practical problem of disentangling the different contributions of hereditary, society and individual choice, then it is not possible to justify reward according to merit. This is because we cannot determine which actions can be credited to voluntary acts and therefore we cannot determine who is deserving.

The second difficulty is this. Even if it was possible to determine which abilities and efforts were the product of voluntary actions, and that those who use both to achieve their objectives are thereby deserving, this does not entail that it is just to distribute social and economic benefits as a reward for desert. It may just be that they deserve their success, they deserve the satisfaction of doing their job well, or that they deserve praise and recognition. It is not clear that justice demands that they get paid more because of this, or that they should have more power and influence because of it. We often think others' voluntary actions are praiseworthy and that the people who perform them are deserving. As well as talent, ability and effort, we admire voluntary acts of kindness, generosity, honesty, altruism and empathy. But for the people who perform these, 'virtue is its own reward'. Odd that!

Contribution

Many liberals justify differential rewards in terms of the value of an individual's contribution to social welfare. Not all these justifications are based on desert. Some are essentially utilitarian in character and these additional arguments will be considered later. Traditionally, justifications for reward according to contribution are premised on the claim that every person has a right to the whole product of his labour. Justice requires that each worker gets back or retains the proportion of wealth they have created. But this kind of return on contribution argument is not really a principle of desert. For here, the justification is *not* that contribution deserves a reward, but that rewards are returns to the worker of their own property, that is, the product of their labour. And this argument depends on whether or not people ought to be rewarded for the outcome of their natural assets, and on whether labour creates ownership of the product of labour in a way that gives rise to or establishes entitlement or property rights. This kind of argument will be examined in relation to Nozick's entitlement theory of justice in Chapter 4.

Strictly speaking, to be said to deserve a reward for making a contribution means that the individual merits or earns a reward for the value of their contribution, rather than the idea that the individual has a right to what they produce because they own it. And this notion of deserving rewards for contributions runs into the same difficulties as the notion of deserving a reward for ability or effort. It assumes that a person can make a contribution and that contributions are the product of the autonomous will of the individual. The extent to which a person can make a contribution and therefore the extent to which they deserve a reward for it depends on morally irrelevant factors for which the individual is not responsible. It may depend on natural and innate ability or skill, family background and education, fortuitous social circumstances, and so on. To justify rewarding contribution *because* of desert, it would have to be the case that each person's contribution was measured in terms of the part their own voluntary efforts and abilities played in enabling them to make that contribution. And, as we have seen, there are insuperable difficulties in separating voluntary efforts and abilities from innate abilities and other extraneous factors for which the individual can claim no personal credit.

But two other difficulties arise with the notion of contributions to social welfare. Both are to do with problems in assessing the value of an individual's contribution to society. The first is the problem of measuring in any objective way the value to society of different jobs or activities. Some people will use the principle of contribution to defend inequalities in the *status quo* by arguing that capitalist entrepreneurs who provide money and business entrepreneurs who invest money contribute most to produce wealth. Others will argue that it is labour that makes the most important contribution. There will be different views reflecting different beliefs and values about who contributes the most in society – a brain surgeon or a refuse collector, a coal miner or a cabinet minister, a primary school teacher or a university lecturer, a housewife or a stockbroker, an artist or an advertising agent, a social worker or a footballer? There seems to be no way of deciding which is the more important contribution without resorting to subjective and questionable assumptions about the value of different roles and activities.

Defenders of differential rewards according to contribution often claim that it is the market which measures and decides this objectively. That is, the market operates in such a way as to ensure that each person gets back from the economy the value of their contribution to it and it effectively allocates rewards according to desert without any human intervention. However, relying on market mechanisms cannot resolve the problem of assessing the value of a person's contribution. Demand is a poor guide to the contributions people value, because some of the things people value do not register as demands on the market, because the market does not supply them (they are not marketable); and because people can be manipulated into demanding things which bring them little benefit. The market does not measure a person's contribution. It merely reflects how much that contribution can be sold for. The reason why a brain surgeon is paid more than a refuse collector is not that the former makes a greater contribution to health, but that his skill is in short supply and therefore can be sold at a higher price. The reason why a stockbroker is financially rewarded and a housewife is not, has nothing to do with the respective value of the contribution, or because one exercises effort and the other does not. It is because housework has no market value.

The second problem in measuring the value of an individual's contribution is the difficulty of estimating an individual's contribution to a joint product. The individual is never producing in a vacuum. It is perhaps because liberals think of individuals as abstract, isolated and self-sufficient, that they can make sense of the separating out of an individual's unique contribution. In practice, any person's contributions depend on past and present knowledge and skills of others, their labour, ideas, help, support and co-operation. An individual's contribution depends not just on other people's labour directly, but also depends on social conditions to which others have contributed, on uncreated natural resources, on technological developments, on the fluctuations of the market and an element of luck or chance.

Desert cannot justify inequality

It is a persistent liberal theory that those who receive the most rewards somehow deserve to do so. However, this cannot be justified in theory, nor is it evident that in practice most existing inequalities are deserved. To be deserved, in this way, it would have to be the case that the people at the top are somehow better than those at the bottom, that they are more industrious and hard-working, or more skilled, or that they make a more important contribution or deliver a more important service. But a cursory glance at differentials in pay show that this is not so. It is not demonstrable that the most able, virtuous, talented or hard-working members of society are those who occupy the most well-paid roles. Nor is it obvious that those on low incomes are the laziest workers, the least skilled, those who make trivial contributions to society or provide a superfluous service.

Whether or not existing distribution reflects desert, any justification of distribution according to desert is fraught with theoretical, practical and moral problems. It is philosophically dubious, in the sense that there is no necessary or *a priori* connection between moral virtue, talent, ability, social worth or contribution and the amount of resources anyone should be given. Even if these were criteria for desert, then there is no correlation between deserving and receiving rewards in terms of vast differences in wealth, income and power. Practically, there are no objective standards by which to judge any of these criteria.

Any list ranking people's personal characteristics, abilities, talents or contributions would be arbitrary and subjective. Judgements vary about what kinds of social roles and what kinds of conduct are important or morally deserving. Such judgements reflect the abilities, characteristics, jobs and roles which a particular society has selected to merit reward. Even if such standards could be established, defended and agreed upon, their application in practice would be difficult. It is unlikely that we would have enough information to assess which actions were the result of an individual choosing to use or develop their innate ability and which actions were the result of individual effort. Judgements about the moral worth of people's whole lives or even the motivation behind their individual actions would require us to have discrete knowledge of their intentions and the inner workings of their mind to assess the worth of their conduct. Similarly, assessing an individual's contribution to society presupposes that it is possible in practice to single out exactly what an individual's contribution has been, and what proportion of their contribution can be properly attributed to their own voluntary efforts.

Morally, it is objectionable to accept that differences in talent, ability and effort are valid criteria for distinguishing between people. These are characteristics which are arbitrary from a moral point of view and are not relevant to treating people differently. To differentiate people in this way and thus to justify unequal rewards is not to treat people impartially or with equal concern and respect. It undermines and contradicts the original liberal notion that people are of equal worth by reducing people to a bundle of abilities and allowing their actual worth to be dependent on these.

Similarly, using social or moral worth as criteria for unequal distribution reduces people's moral claims to equal consideration and respect for their socially valued roles and behaviour. They too are being treated unequally because of an irrelevant characteristic or quality that they may not be wholly responsible for, and if so, they cannot be said to take the credit or blame for it, or to deserve any rewards accruing from it. Justifying inequalities because some people do not deserve rewards assumes that people should be paid back for intentionally being stupid or untalented, or for purposely choosing social roles or jobs that no-one values. It amounts to retributive justice and to justifying retribution for those who do not have the abilities or skills that a particular society has chosen to reward; for those whose character, motivations or morality do not fit the norms decreed by that society; and for those whose social roles, skills and abilities are not valued or have no market value. These people then are doubly punished, since they are already likely to belong to underprivileged groups. Using ability, effort, social or moral worth to sanction further inequalities of treatment is based on fallible judgements about who and what is deserving, and does not give equal consideration to each person's interests and fails to treat people as equally morally worthy.

Given that the abilities and efforts an individual has or can make are largely a product of their social, historical and economic circumstances, i.e., their family, their upbringing and education as well as their genetic inheritance, the notion that people deserve to be rewarded for these, is deeply problematic. And even if we reject the view that people's behaviour is totally determined, and accept that there are choices and actions for which people are responsible, the impossibility of isolating these makes it difficult to give an accurate estimate of the extent to which people can take credit for them, and only in theory, but not in practice, can we make judgements about who and what is deserving.

These considerations could lead us to reject desert as the criterion for treating people differently. If this does not happen and we still hold to the view that it is right to treat people according to their desert, then we can conclude that neither liberal political theorists nor any existing liberal–democratic societies take this seriously. If people are to be treated as they deserve, only those aspects of their behaviour for which they are responsible are relevant to their treatment. Desert only applies to acts which are dependent on an individual's will and the voluntary use they make of their abilities. This much must be acknowledged for responsibility is a prerequisite of deserving. It should follow, then, that society ought to be organized so as to provide the conditions necessary for people to exercise these responsibilities and to make these choices. This would involve more than equal opportunities to compete according to natural ability, but would involve reducing the inequalities in property, wealth, power, resources, education and employment, so that each person had a real chance to display merit appropriate to their given abilities.

The Usefulness of Inequality: Utilitarian Arguments

Other advocates of unequal rewards defend them not by appeal to desert or by denying the equal moral worth of each individual, but by asserting the usefulness of inequality in society when it benefits everyone. One variation of the argument that inequality is socially useful is Davis and Moore's 'functionalist theory of stratification'.

Davis and Moore (1967) argue that inequalities are functionally necessary for any society. They claim that certain positions in any society are more functionally important than others. In order to ensure that the 'right' people are recruited to these important positions, it is necessary to induce those with talents to do the appropriate training, to attract them to these positions and to motivate them to perform these roles adequately. To do this, a system of differential reward is needed and this results in social inequality. 'Social inequality is thus an unconsciously evolved device by which societies insure that the most important positions are conscientiously filled by the most qualified persons' (Davis and Moore, 1967, p. 47). Some objections to the claim that it is necessary to reward people in functionally important positions are similar to those objections to theories which claim that it is just (rather than necessary or efficient) to reward superior contributions to society. Functionalist arguments are thought to be justified in terms of utility, and contributions arguments in terms of desert. The common problems are these. The first problem is the difficulty of identifying in any objective way which contributions or positions are important as opposed to those a particular society values. The second problem is, even if it could be established that incentives were needed for efficiency or that certain contributions were deserving, this does not imply that rewards for them should constitute a system of structural inequality with vast differences of wealth, status and power. The third problem is actual inequalities are not plausibly explained in either a functional manner or by reference to the superior ability or contribution of those at the top. The fact that someone is well paid or is the head of a prestigious institution is not proof that they are the most able or the most deserving. This is an obvious tautology. And it cannot be demonstrated that bankers, miners, tax lawyers, film stars, social workers, nurses or stockbrokers get paid differentially *because* they do more functionally important jobs or because they make a greater contribution to society. The fourth problem is just as desert-based justifications for inequality undermine the moral equality of people by reducing them to their abilities or socially valued roles, so too do functionalist theories by implicitly valuing people for their usefulness.

Criticisms levelled at functionalist theories differ from contribution theories over the issue of desert versus incentive, although some contribution arguments appeal to both to justify different rewards. Functionalist arguments justify rewards not because they are deserved, but because they act as incentives for individuals to develop their talents and to perform functionally important jobs. Similarly, other utilitarian arguments justify unequal rewards as incentives to motivate people to do socially useful work which benefits others. Inequality is justified by its future benefits rather than as just desert.

If the justification for rewarding individuals is because this acts as an incentive, then, strictly speaking, this would mean that only those who would not have developed their talents or made a contribution, if there was no prospect of reward, should be rewarded. There would be no point or justification on this criterion for rewarding those people who would have performed a socially useful function, in the absence of reward. This would require us to distinguish between people on the basis of their motivations in order to determine whether or not they would require a reward. Those who were likely to be motivated to perform socially useful roles by altruism or by a desire for the common good should not be rewarded. Rewards should only go to people who undertake socially useful functions for prudential rather than moral reasons. Thus, those with a commitment to better themselves rather than others, those who are motivated by greed, ambition and self-interest are those who, because they would not work without a reward, should receive one.

It seems counter-intuitive and morally paradoxical to penalize those who act for moral reasons and to reward those who are avaricious and self-seeking, whatever its social utility. And it is questionable how socially useful it would be to reward such people. If the only reason why people wanted to be doctors, lawyers and politicians was the material advantage these jobs bring, then they are hardly likely to be the 'best' people for the job. They are more likely to be corrupted by these rewards, rather than perform any socially useful function.

It is an empirical question whether incentives do actually encourage people to work better and so benefit everybody. Incentive arguments assume that unequal rewards are the only way of motivating people to fill functionally important or socially useful positions. They imply that any work which requires training or responsibility or effort of a special kind would not be done without the prospect of material gain. However, especially when we consider the kinds of work that do actually receive high rewards, this seems incredibly unlikely. It is completely ridiculous to suggest that there is a danger of prospective bankers, lawyers, company directors and consultants being tempted by bricklaying or serving in a supermarket, if they were not highly paid. They do the jobs they do for a variety of reasons, because they are more interesting, more intrinsically worthwhile and satisfying, because they enjoy using their knowledge, developing their skills and exercising their responsibility. They may even be motivated by a desire to help and inform other people or by a sense of social responsibility. And people do unpaid work in the home, as members of clubs, societies, voluntary agencies and political parties for much the same reasons.

It is not obviously the case that the incentive of material rewards is necessary to attract people with ability to do certain already highly paid, socially useful jobs. It is more plausible to suggest that people need incentives to do boring, unpleasant, tiring, dangerous and dirty jobs rather than the jobs that are intrinsically satisfying and rewarding. If this were the case, then current pay differentials would be reversed. Refuse collectors, sewage workers, people who work with toxic substances, miners, fire fighters, bricklayers, typists, cleaners, shop assistants and assembly line workers would be better paid than professional workers. It is often argued by egalitarians that this reversal of pay differentials would be justified as compensation and this is compatible with egalitarian justice (see Miller, 1976, pp. 110–12; Baker, 1987, p. 55; Norman, 1987, p. 86; Feinberg, 1987, p. 86). For instance, Feinberg writes:

The principle that unpleasant, onerous and hazardous jobs deserve economic compensation, unlike the claim that superior ability deserves economic reward, is an egalitarian one, for it says that deprivation for which there is no good reason should be compensated to the point where the deprived one is again brought back to a position of equality with his fellow. It is not that compensation gives him more than others (considering everything), but only that it allows him to catch up. (Feinberg, 1970, p. 93)

This is informed by the egalitarian belief that benefits and burdens should be equally shared. If someone suffers because their jobs involve special costs, then they should be compensated for their extra burden in order to restore equality. However, there are some reasons for doubting whether these compensation arguments are consistent with egalitarian ideals. If differential rewards are merely compensating, and incentives are needed to do certain jobs, then people would have no incentive to choose one kind of work rather than another. In order to get people to do boring, dangerous and dirty jobs, the incentive would have to be more than compensatory. This would create inequalities again. It merely reverses who gets the rewards and gives a different justification for them. Moreover, there is the difficulty of matching the benefit to the burden. Those who defend the idea of compensation imply that there is some direct equivalence or correspondence between benefits and burdens, i.e., that extra money directly compensates for the burdens. However, there are some things that money cannot compensate for. It can compensate for loss of earnings as a result of disease, injury or accident contracted on the job, but it cannot compensate for the loss of life or disabilities which result. It is not clear that giving an equal amount of benefit equivalent to the suffering caused restores and leads to an equal amount of satisfaction, because there is no sense in which the suffering is annulled by the benefit. Giving someone extra money does not cancel out the fact that the work is still dangerous, dirty or boring.

All this suggests that if we are concerned about equality, rather than compensating for the costs of these jobs, we should consider how job structures could be changed so that the costs are not incurred in the first place. Work that is monotonous could be improved by job enrichment programmes, diversifying tasks, increasing control over work and participation in decision-making. Jobs that are dangerous and dirty could be improved by better equipment, conditions of work and more stringent health and safety regulations. We might want to consider whether there are some jobs that are so hazardous that they ought not to be done at all. If they are so socially useful that they must be done, then an alternative to compensation to equalize satisfaction, could be job rotation, so that the costs are equally shared. These solutions are more in keeping with the ideal of equality and would also address the problem of incentives. If there are some jobs that are so awful that nobody would want to do them, why not change the nature of those jobs so that people are motivated to do them because they are more satisfying and less dangerous, or, because people are inspired by notions of co-operation, shared responsibility, collective goals and the common good? This would seem to be a more egalitarian approach than compensatory rewards which entrench the aliena-tion that money cannot compensate for or remove.

And, anyway, the fact is that, now, people do do the kinds of jobs we are considering *without* extra compensation. This itself reflects the fact that people are already motivated to do these by considerations other than the incentives of material rewards. They may be proud of working in an important industry or of providing a public service. They may gain self-esteem from the courage and endurance they have to display. However, of course the fact that people do work in these same jobs without substantial financial remuneration also reflects the fact that they have not had the education or the opportunities to develop the abilities and skills to do anything else.

The fact that large numbers of people cannot do anything else and the only motivation they have to do these jobs is to earn a living is itself a symptom of an underlying inequality of opportunity. Rather than ignore this by rewarding them for the work they can or have to do, attention should be paid to removing the pre-existing inequalities. This would also be a solution to the problem of the scarcity of talent and ability that supposedly justifies the liberal notion that differential rewards are necessary as incentives to inspire the talented few to fill socially important roles which benefit everyone. If scarcity of talent is the problem, then the solution should be to enlarge the supply by expanding educational and occupational opportunities so that more people have the knowledge, abilities and skills that would enable them to do socially useful tasks.

The egalitarian arguments which justify reversing the current structure of rewards as compensation fail to show that compensation is compatible with our concern for substantive equality. Like liberal arguments, they also fail to show that material rewards are the means necessary to motivate people to work. If the liberal justification for unequal rewards as incentives which ultimately benefit everyone is to have any credibility, then first it must be shown that material rewards are the best way of motivating people and this is highly questionable, especially for those jobs that are highly rewarded. Second, it must be shown that these inequalities are actually socially useful, in that they benefit the rest of society. Both these difficulties are apparent in the work of Rawls who offers a different version of liberal equality from the traditional approaches we have considered so far.

Inequalities to Benefit the Least Advantaged: Rawls

Traditionally, liberal political theorists have argued for the equality of various political and legal rights and advocated the elimination of social differences in order to ensure equal opportunities. They justify inequalities in income, wealth, resources, power and authority. These are viewed as fair outcomes, as just deserts or rewards for differences in ability, skill or effort, within the framework of a competitive market. More recently, liberals have added the need for some forms of welfare provision to provide equal opportunities for fair compensation. Inequalities have also been justified by a utilitarian appeal to incentives which produce overall benefits.

Modern liberals, such as Rawls and Dworkin, reject merit and desert as criteria for justifying inequality. They advocate an equality of consideration and respect for individuals which acknowledges their equal moral worth, regardless of differences in merit or ability. This equality of consideration and respect is based on a conception of a moral capacity, the fact that human beings are capable of making choices, forming life plans and of giving justice (Rawls, 1971, p. 511; Dworkin, 1977, pp. 171–7). Rawls rejects the distribution of rewards according to ability or effort because these criteria are morally arbitrary. No-one deserves to be rewarded for characteristics they are not responsible for. Consequently, Rawls claims, to merely advocate equal opportunities is not enough to show each person equal consideration and respect. Equal opportunities amount to an 'equal chance to leave the less fortunate behind in a personal quest for influence and social position' (Rawls, 1971, pp. 107–8). Since the inequalities of the less fortunate are undeserved accidents of birth or natural endowment, they call for redress in the direction of equality of condition or equality of result. This means that justice requires that 'all social primary goods ... liberties and opportunities, income and wealth, and the bases of self-respect are to be distributed equally unless an unequal distribution of any or all of these goods is to the advantage of the least fortunate' (Rawls, 1971, p. 303). No-one should lose or gain because of their undeserved natural capacities without giving or receiving compensating advantages in return. Though no-one deserves the differences in their natural abilities, these abilities should be treated as a social asset, so that the 'basic structure of society can be arranged so that these contingencies work to the good of the least fortunate' (Rawls, 1971, p. 102). The so-called difference principle according to Rawls is the best principle for ensuring that natural assets do not have an unfair advantage. The difference principle states that 'Social and economic inequalities are to be arranged so that they are both (a) to the greatest benefit of the least advantaged and (b) attached to offices and positions open to all under condition of fair equality of opportunity' (Rawls, 1971, p. 83). Rawls identifies differential incentives as a form of inequality which would be justified by the difference principle. He accepts the need for people to have differential rewards as an incentive to work, but they are justified only if they benefit the least advantaged. Otherwise, social justice requires a presumption in favour of equality. This implies government intervention to implement substantial political, social and economic equality and policies which redistribute wealth in the form of taxation and welfare provision for the benefit of the worst off. Rawls's principles seem to be strongly egalitarian, in contrast to traditional liberal notions of equal political rights and equal opportunities. They stipulate that liberty should be shared equally by all, that there should be equal opportunities and that other goods should be distributed equally unless the worst off would benefit from unequal distribution. Inequalities are to be judged against whether the worst off will benefit from their inequality. Unequal rewards for abilities are not justified on the basis of desert, but only as incentives, so that they will be used to serve the worst off.

Rawls's argument suffers from the difficulties discussed earlier in relation to utilitarian arguments. His argument for incentives justifies rewarding only those whose work will benefit the worst off, but who would not work if they were not rewarded. The logical consequence of this is that those who work hard, for moral rather than prudential reasons or whose work will not benefit the worst off, should not be rewarded. But this problem should not really arise, if we accept the premises of incentive arguments. If it is true that people need incentives to work in particular jobs, they will need them whether or not their work will benefit anyone but themselves. Therefore, it is inevitable that in an incentive system inequalities would emerge that did not benefit the worst off. However, the assumption that incentives are the best way of motivating people to work has been challenged and found to be an inadequate explanation of why people work, especially in most jobs where people are well paid. If this is so, then the argument for incentives cannot justify inequality.

Rawls's justification of incentives as unequal rewards when they benefit the worst off is supposed to be a safeguard against allowing natural assets to be an unfair advantage in determining who gets what. He rejects the traditional liberal justification of desert as a criterion for the distribution of resources. His difference principle is introduced to ensure that those who are well endowed do not receive more and those who are handicapped do not receive less because of these arbitrary factors. But Rawls's notion of just distribution does not manage to eliminate reward according to ability. He is opposed to the idea that differences in abilities and effort should lead to differences in income, but his own principles endorse just that. These undeserved differences lead to material inequality because, in a free market incentive system, the well endowed get higher rewards. The issue here is whether the difference principle can justify these inequalities because they have beneficial effects on the worst off groups. Now it is an empirical question whether or not unequal rewards would actually benefit the worst off, as Rawls (1971, p. 78) himself acknowledges. And there are some reasons for thinking this might not be so. First, to come back to the point made earlier, if people need different rewards to do different jobs, they will need to have them regardless of their benefit to the worst off, otherwise they would not work. Second, even if a system of unequal rewards produced more material wealth which benefited the worst off, it is not obvious that this would make them better off in all respects. This is because inequalities of material wealth tend to produce inequalities of social power. As Norman (1982, p. 19) points out, social power is not a commodity that can simply be distributed in different proportions while retaining the same character. Power is a relation between people and there is a balance between the extent to which some people have power, others will lack it. It is contradictory to say that inequalities of power can make the worst off better off if they have less power. Third, it is questionable whether a system of unequal rewards is the system most likely to benefit the worst off. If we do not accept that incentives are the only means to encourage people to work, then prosperity that could benefit all could be achieved by means other than unequal rewards.

Fourth, though unequal rewards could benefit the worst off, in practice, this could sanction large disparities in income. Those who are highly rewarded could justify their increase in wealth because it marginally benefits the worst off. Consequently, in a Rawlsian system, undeserved differences in ability, talent and skill do lead to material inequality just as they do in meritocratic systems, and his arguments fail to demonstrate that these inequalities would substantially benefit the worst off. These problems are compounded when we examine those whom Rawls identifies as the worst off. Kymlicka (1990, pp. 71–3) and Campbell (1988, pp. 92–5) claim that Rawls defines the worst off in terms of their possession of social primary goods, especially economic and material resources, and not in terms of their natural primary goods, their level of health, intelligence, their physical and mental capacities. This means that inequalities are justified which will benefit the materially worst off rather than those who are worst off because they are untalented or physically or mentally disabled. The difference principle allows the naturally well endowed to benefit from their ability and the redistribution of resources to the worst off may not target the worst off groups in terms of their condition. Those with talents and abilities will be advantaged in two ways. They will be able to use their talents and abilities to gain higher material rewards than those who do not have this natural advantage. And, they already have the intrinsic benefit of their natural ability, which those without this undeservedly lack.

Rawls is often criticized because his rejection of desert does not allow people to be deservedly rewarded for their autonomous choices and for their voluntarily acquired abilities and efforts (see Kymlicka, 1990, p. 85), but, ultimately this is not so. The consequences of his position are that those with *both* undeserved and voluntarily acquired ability will be rewarded (as they are in a meritocratic system). Opportunities will be open to those with natural ability and choices will be available to those who can make use of them. The consequence of this is that the undeservedly disadvantaged will not be adequately compensated.

Inequalities that Reflect Choices: Dworkin

Dworkin, like Rawls, seeks to establish that a liberal commitment to equality will involve more than equality of opportunity to compete according to ability. It will require some redistribution and welfare policies to compensate for morally arbitrary and irrelevant features of individuals such as undeserved differences in natural abilities, luck, chance or inheritance. He writes, 'It is obviously obnoxious to the liberal conception; for example, that someone should have none of what the community as a whole has to distribute because he or his father had superior skill or luck' (Dworkin, 1985, p. 195).

Egalitarian redistribution should not be 'endowment sensitive' and reward or penalize people simply because they are more or less talented, because these are assets for which people cannot be held responsible and they cannot be said to deserve any benefit accruing from them. However, fair distribution should allow for the effects of the choices that people make, the use they make of their talents and abilities, and so should be 'ambition sensitive', even though this may result in inequalities. Fair distribution must identify 'which aspects of any person's economic position flow from his choices and which from advantages and disadvantages that were not a matter of choice' (Dworkin, 1985, p. 208).

Dworkin's complex and convoluted theory laid out in *A Matter of Principle* which advocates redistribution policies for the naturally disadvantaged and rewards for those who choose to make use of their abilities, involves a mixture of hypothetical auctions and insurance schemes, market mechanisms and taxation policies. He illustrates his idea of equality via a hypothetical situation in which shipwrecked survivors on a desert island, who do not know their natural abilities are given equal amounts of resources, that is, currency in the form of clam shells. At an imaginary auction they can bid and choose the bundle of goods which will best allow them to pursue their own ends and purposes.

Dworkin argues that in this situation, rational informed individuals would take out insurance cover to safeguard against risks of future handicap or disadvantages. The amounts people would agree to pay in such a situation could be translated into a taxation scheme which would be a way of collecting insurance premiums from the naturally advantaged, and would be channelled into welfare schemes which would 'pay out coverage' by redistributing resources to the naturally disadvantaged. This would compensate for inabilities which were undeserved and would be an attempt to equalize circumstances. However, because Dworkin's scheme is to be 'ambition sensitive' too, this would not lead to an equality of outcome. Those who choose to make use of their abilities would receive greater rewards. This scheme is supposedly in accordance with the idea of equal consideration and respect since it is the result of a fair procedure which embodies what people would have chosen in a hypothetical situation of equality. It treats people as equals by excluding undeserved advantages. It tries to ensure that different rewards are the outcome of the different choices that people make, which themselves reflect their different preferences and values.

Mapel (1989) and Carens (1985) claim that, given the complexity and abstraction of Dworkins' hypothetical situation, it is difficult to see how Dworkins' scheme could be translated into practice. Dworkin has rejected the criterion of desert and has advocated taxation to compensate for some undeserved differences in natural assets. Any unequal outcomes are to be determined by the choices people make from an equal starting-point, where people have an equal amount of resources. But the first major difficulty is how this equal starting-point would possibly be arrived at in reality. What mechanisms and policies could lead to an approximation of an equality of resources and the results of the original hypothetical auction? It would require at least some initial radical redistribution before any unequal subsequent outcomes could begin to be justified and how is this to be achieved? (Krouse and McPherson, 1988, p. 103).

Even if an initial redistribution were practically and politically realizable, it would still be impossible to fully equalize circumstances and to mitigate the effects of natural advantages and disadvantages. For this reason, it is inevitable that unequal outcomes would be the result of unfair natural advantages and not totally the result of people's choices. And this problem is compounded by the further practical difficulty of being able to separate out which actions and achievements are the result of natural ability and which are the result of choices. Thus, it is not possible to identify which unequal rewards are justified, because we cannot identify which accrue from ambitions rather than endowments. Therefore, some of the problems which result from justifying inequality by appeal to desert have not been circumvented. Some inequalities are unjustified because they are rewards for undeserved natural advantages or penalties for unfortunate circumstances. Furthermore, in Dworkins' scheme, those who are rich because of their choices rather than their abilities, will get less than they deserve because they will be taxed to subsidise those who are poor for their lack of effort, rather than their lack of ability.

These outcomes do not seem to differ very much from those which occur under existing welfare state capitalism. This system allegedly combines freedom of choice via the market with welfare provision for the undeservedly disadvantaged. Like other apologists for this system, Dworkin still promotes the central liberal idea that the individual and their choices are sacrosanct. He is less disingenuous than straightforwardly meritocratic liberals because he recognizes that market outcomes are not simply a reflection of the choices that people make, but that they embody pre-existing inequalities which are undeserved. However, he believes that if we remove unfair advantage and compensate for the lack of ability to make choices, then making choices is still what counts. Market freedoms are only to be limited when they penalize people for reasons other than their choices. Welfare provision is justified when redistribution compensates for natural disadvantage, not choice. It is still in the name of equalizing opportunity to make choices that both the welfare state and market freedoms are endorsed.

The version of liberal equality provided by Rawls and Dworkin commits them to advocating welfare provision because both recognize the arbitrariness of natural assets in determining just distribution. However, neither Rawls nor Dworkin eliminate reward according to ability or the emergence of undeserved inequalities. Rawls's acceptance of incentives and his difference principle allow inequalities which are due to different talents or undeserved differences in need. And because neither markets, nor governments, can distinguish natural abilities from the choices people make, Dworkin's proposals have the same effect.

Equality Threatens Freedom: Nozick

Given that the freedom of the individual is the prime liberal value, liberals in general are suspicious of any advocacy of substantial equality, considering it to be a threat to freedom. Many classical liberals argued against the pursuit of social and economic equality on the grounds that it would undermine market freedom and would inevitably lead to coercion by the state (see Acton, 1971, p. 71). More contemporary proponents of the view that equality is incompatible with freedom are Hayek (1960, 1976), Friedman (1962) and Nozick (1974). For Nozick, the liberal egalitarian principles of Rawls and Dworkin are a threat to freedom because they require redistributive policies which violate the rights of individuals to keep what they have justly acquired. Any liberal commitment to welfare provision to enlarge equality or opportunity, according to Nozick, requires interference with individual freedom in order to improve the situation of others.

Even those liberals who defend state interference and welfare provision, in order to achieve equal opportunities to compete, reject any stronger notion of equality on the grounds that it would threaten individual freedom and choice. For these liberals, equal opportunities is the only concept of equality consistent with individual freedom, the prevention of harm and the proper limits of state interference. Given the natural inequality of talent and ability, any system of equal treatment will require authoritarian repression to limit the development of individual talents and capacities. Equal opportunities give people the chance to be rewarded for their talents, efforts or choices; equality of welfare will prevent people getting their just reward for the use they have made of their ability. Equality of welfare could only be achieved by massive state intervention. It would require a political system which imposes government restraint to restrict the freedom of economically dominant groups, of those with social power, and of those social and occupational groups, who by virtue of their skills, ability and effort would otherwise receive a greater share of resources. This can lead to abuses of civil and political freedoms and means continual state interference in every aspect of economic, social and personal life, to ensure the forcible redistribution of resources needed to maintain equality.

The radical egalitarian response to these arguments is to attack both the liberal notion of equal opportunities and the essentially negative view of liberty upon which the arguments for the incompatibility of freedom and equality depend. Radical egalitarians claim that the premises of liberal equality, the idea that human beings are of equal worth, that they are owed equal consideration and respect, are not taken seriously by merely promoting political and legal rights and equal opportunities. If we are concerned with the equal worth of persons, then we must also be concerned with promoting greater equality in the condition of life, that is, an equality of power, privilege, wealth, income and resources. The idea of equal opportunities as an opportunity to compete for scarce rewards is a limited and conservative notion which reproduces inequality. It focuses on differentiating, grading and sorting people and each person is valued not for their intrinsic worth, but for their abilities, their capacity to perform socially valued functions, or for their contributions, which then are measured in terms of their market value. According to Schaar,

The doctrine of equality of opportunity is the product of a competitive and fragmented society, a divided society, a society in which individualism in Tocqueville's sense of the word, is the reigning ethical principle. It is a precise symbolic expression of the liberal–bourgeois model of society, for it extends the market-place mentality to all the spheres of life. It views the whole of human relations as a contest in which each man competes with his fellows for scarce goods, a contest in which there is never enough for everybody and where one man's gain is usually another's loss. (Schaar, 1967, p. 237)

Equality of opportunity, then, not only fails to give people equality of respect but undermines the self-respect of those who turn out to be losers, as many must in the competitive struggle. This undermining of self-respect is compounded by the problem that meritocratic equality of opportunity can lead to a justification of an anti-democratic, paternalist and elitist society, where those at the top, because of their supposedly superior abilities deserve their privileges, power and control, and those at the bottom are denied autonomy, because it is the best who should rule.

The doctrine of competitive equal opportunities whereby the ablest or the most ambitious, or the most hard-working prosper most can be challenged on the grounds that it is questionable whether these qualities deserve differential rewards and on the grounds that it amounts to an equal right to become unequal. Hence, the original liberal notion of the equal moral worth of individuals degenerates into an equal opportunity to be unworthy, to be less deserving, to be treated with unequal respect.

Libertarians, such as Nozick (1974, pp. 239–47) and Lucas (1977) challenge the notion that inequality undermines self-respect or self-esteem. On the contrary, they argue that inegalitarian societies show more respect for individuals by acknowledging the distinctiveness of and the differences between individuals. In an egalitarian society, because there are no differences in income, power, authority, rank prestige or social status, there is no basis for self-esteem, precisely because self-esteem is based on criteria that differentiate people.

People generally judge themselves by how they fall along the most important dimensions in which they differ from others. People do not gain self-esteem from their common human capacities – self-esteem is based on differentiating characteristics: that's why its self-esteem. (Nozick, 1974, p. 243)

Nozick argues that an egalitarian society cannot be a society of greater self-esteem because of human factors like envy. According to

Nozick, the demand for equality is often rooted in envy. Seeing some people better off than others creates envy. So, even if there were greater equality in one dimension in which self-esteem is based, for instance if there were a greater equality of wealth, then this would be replaced by envy of other attributes which differentiate people. If they had the same amounts of money, then they would envy people along another dimension; they would envy those who were more beautiful, or more athletic, more intelligent or sympathetic or those who had a better quality of orgasm. Even if envy were more tractable, it would be objectionable to reduce one person's situation to lessen the envy of others. Those who are envious of other people with more money and authority should face facts and consider whether or not these inequalities are deserved, because some people have superior talents and have a right to give orders. The reason for some people suffering from low-esteem may be because these people are inferior and they know it.

One obvious difficulty with these arguments is that they confirm what they were meant to deny, that is, that inequality undermines self-esteem. If, as Nozick and Lucas argue, self-esteem is based on differentiation, on comparative success or achievement, then only those who achieve along the valued dimensions will have self-esteem. Those who fail, will not. The more opportunities there are for achieving differential and scarce rewards, the more opportunities there are for demoralization when these are not achieved. Other difficulties with these arguments rest on the plausibility of maintaining that an egalitarian society is one in which differences between people are not acknowledged or respected, and on whether arguments for equality are reducible to envy. I will deal with the latter argument first. Nozick suggests that people argue for equality because they are envious of people who have more. However, the suggestion that the resentment of the poor for the rich is really just envy by the deservedly poor for the deservedly rich is untenable. As we have already seen, in practice, it is implausible to suggest that the reason the rich are rich is that they possess some attributes that the poor lack; and, in theory, it is questionable whether such attributes merit different rewards. In addition to this, the resentment of inequality is not just an irrational feeling, or an unjustified response to other people's success, their resentment is informed by an independent belief that inequality is wrong, unjustifiable and unfair. Richard Norman argues:

If the resentment arises from a sense that the inequalities are unjustified, it is misrepresented by the 'argument from envy' ... What should be said, however, is that people feel resentment at inequalities because they believe that inequality is wrong. Their resentment is not just a feeling of envy, it is not just a perverse resentment of other people's success. They themselves would regard it as an ethically justified response, because of their antecedent ethical belief that inequality is wrong. They would claim, perhaps, that they have a right to equal treatment, and that the existence of inequality is an injustice committed against them. It is for such reasons that they feel resentment. The argument from envy, then, cannot account for this *antecedent* ethical belief. (Norman, 1987, p. 64)

The radical egalitarian condemnation of substantial inequalities of income, wealth, power and status depends on recognizing that these inequalities do undermine the idea of the fundamental moral equality of individuals. Equality of respect demands more than guaranteeing equal opportunities to compete, but must involve promoting greater equality in the conditions of life. Socialists will argue for this in terms of everyone having the resources and social conditions necessary to satisfy basic human needs. On similar lines writers like Nielsen (1985) and Norman (1982) suggest that the idea of equality of respect implies equal well-being or the opportunity to lead a worthwhile and satisfying life. Social inequalities are condemned because they violate the right to equal respect, the right to lead a worthwhile and satisfying life which all individuals are entitled to by virtue of being human. However, even if we take a strictly liberal line and stress the importance of individuals pursuing their own good in their own way, and the value of freedom of the individual to pursue their own ends and purposes, or to satisfy their given desires, it is clear that equal opportunities and/or a social system that generates inequalities cannot guarantee this. Inequalities in power, privilege, wealth and resources prevent people from satisfying their basic needs, from enjoying an equally worthwhile and satisfying life and from pursuing their own good in their own way. Given this, the connection between substantial equality and liberty should be clear.

According to radical proponents of the idea that liberty and equality are not only compatible but interdependent, substantial equality only conflicts with freedom, if freedom is defined narrowly as negative liberty. If freedom is defined as the absence of external impediments, then of course any attempt to implement equality will conflict with it. But if freedom is defined more broadly to include the power, ability, resources and capacities to do something (whether this is to satisfy given desires or needs, to pursue our own interests or to live a life shaped by our own ends and purposes), then clearly people are not equally free if they do not have equal access to the resources and conditions which would enable them to do so. Substantial equality is not a threat to freedom in this sense, but is supportive of it.

Egalitarians are concerned to create the social conditions which will enable all people to be equally free. They are aiming at an equality of freedom. Richard Norman, for example, argues that in practice this means that egalitarians have aimed at an equality of social power, wealth and education and that these in various ways constitute an equality of liberty. They have been concerned with unequal power relations between classes, races and sexes because these inequalities make people less free to control their own lives. Similarly, inequalities in wealth and resources which flow from and create inequalities of power, restrict people's freedom to live equally worthwhile and satisfying lives. Education, too, is an important source of liberty, because it is a precondition for people to be self-determining and for them to have, not the opportunity to compete, but to lead an equally worthwhile and satisfying life. Eliminating inequalities of power, wealth and education would not diminish liberty, but rather, would aim to make freedom more equal.

To the objection that equalizing liberty would restrict the liberty of those who formerly possessed advantages of power or wealth in order to increase the freedom of others, radical egalitarians acknowledge that this is true. Redistribution to those who were formerly worst off increases their liberty, but simultaneously diminishes the liberties of those who were formerly better off. However, the better off are not being deprived of anything they deserved or were entitled to in the first place. This objection assumes the fairness or justice of the existing distribution of resources. Redistribution is justified because it increases the total amount of freedom. Carritt illustrates this by an example of an island where one man has a monopoly over the water supply. If water ownership is equalized, then only the monopolist loses his freedom, and the others gain dramatically. From this he concludes that, 'to be forcibly deprived of superabundance or even of conveniences impair liberty less than to be forcibly prevented from appropriating necessities' (Carritt, 1967, p. 138-9). Greater equality is therefore conducive to a greater total sum of liberty.

Other advocates of radical egalitarianism admit that substantive equalities would restrict the freedom of non-interference, particularly those freedoms celebrated as free enterprise. Nielsen (1985) argues that it would not protect the unrestricted freedom to invest, retain or bequeath in the economic realms or the freedom to buy and sell, because this unrestrained power is in the hands of the few who thereby control the lives of the many. This freedom would be restricted in order to gain more liberty and more equally distributed patterns of liberty, so that more people would be able to do what they want and could have greater control over their lives. Nielsen adds that there is no good reason to think that this would be destructive of basic liberties. The restriction of these so-called freedoms involves no violations of civil rights nor does it harm the basic well-being of those restricted but it does enhance the basic liberties and well-being of others. Baker (1987, pp. 77–85) concurs, arguing that egalitarianism would restrict the property rights of owners and controllers of capital. This would leave some people unable to do what they do now. However, the restriction of the freedom of the minority to buy and control other people's labour, and to control the means of production which generates other inequalities of wealth and power is not more important than the freedom of the majority to exert control over their own lives and to have sufficient resources to lead a satisfying and worthwhile life. He maintains that this is not a question of the conflict between freedom and equality, but a question of freedom for the few at the expense of the many.

Macpherson also argues that there is an increase in aggregate liberty, 'If the gain in liberty by those who had had doors closed to them more than offsets the loss of liberty by those (relatively few) who had been in a position to take full advantage of market freedoms' (Macpherson, 1973, p. 103). It is this idea of the extension and equalizing of freedom that precludes the liberal fear that equality can only be brought about by centralized states with total control over the economy. For if freedom is to be equalized, then limiting political freedom or civil liberties in order to achieve it will be both contradictory and counterproductive. Political equality means extending democratic control over the way resources are used in order to extend everyone's freedom. Moreover, those who value political liberties should acknowledge how social and economic inequalities systematically undermine the exercise of these.

The final liberal objection to an egalitarian society is that this would require a levelling down. It would eliminate the differences between individuals and stifle the development of their talents and abilities. This argument makes the basic mistake of confusing equality with sameness and uniformity, and these are values that no egalitarian could possibly hold. One of the main reasons for advocating an equality of power and resources is so that all individuals, in their different ways, have an opportunity to develop their talents to the full, rather than these being restricted to a privileged few as they are in a competitive, hierarchical society. Beneath this claim that an egalitarian society will not respect the differences between people, is the persistent liberal idea that people should be rewarded for their talent and ability. An egalitarian society would undermine the liberty of the talented to retain the benefits accruing from them. It would penalize the talented by requiring ongoing redistribution to the less talented. However, as the arguments in this chapter have attempted to show, the talented are not being deprived of anything they are entitled to. The real issue here is not whether an egalitarian society would prevent talents from developing, or penalize people who had them, but whether it is justifiable that people should be rewarded for them by vast differences in wealth, power and control. An egalitarian society would not stop people from using their talents, nor would it entail that they were not respected or admired. It would entail that people were not able to sell them as a commodity on the market, and that they were prevented from accumulating wealth which would enable them to dominate and control the lives of others.

Conclusion

This chapter has tried to demonstrate the problems that arise from various liberal attempts to justify inequality. It has been argued that inequalities in social power, wealth, income and resources cannot be justified because they are deserved or because they are necessary as incentives.

Rawls and Dworkin recognized that the liberal commitment to the equal moral worth of each individual is undermined by the principle of desert which differentiates between people according to their merit, ability or skill. Their brand of liberal egalitarianism sought to avoid the injustice of unequal outcomes that results from undeserved inequalities. They tried to establish that a liberal commitment to equality involved redistribution and welfare to compensate for morally arbitrary and undeserved differences. However, neither Rawls's difference principle which allows the more fortunate to have extra resources if this benefits the least fortunate, nor Dworkin's redistributive scheme which compensates for unequal circumstances while holding people responsible for their choices, solve the problem of undeserved inequalities that result from unfair natural advantages or unfortunate circumstances. Commitment to the idea that human beings are of equal worth is undermined by rewarding people as they deserve as Rawls and Dworkin have shown. But commitment to the equal moral worth of each individual also implies that we should adopt a more substantive idea of equality than the liberal egalitarianism endorsed by Rawls and Dworkin.

Respect for moral equality demands more than equal opportunities to compete and more than redistribution to compensate for undeserved differences in income that are the effects of the operations of the market. It demands that we redress the injustice of the initial undeserved inequalities in income, wealth, power and status. These are undeserved and undermine the fundamental moral equality of individuals, their right to equal consideration and respect and their ability to lead equally worthwhile lives.

In one sense, advocating substantive equality is extending what it means to advocate the liberal idea of equal moral worth. But pursuing this liberal ideal to its seemingly logical conclusion is, in another sense, incompatible with liberalism. Most dramatically, because implementing substantive equality involves abandoning the concept of negative liberty and endorsing a richer notion of positive liberty. It involves rejecting the idea that respect for liberty takes precedence over and puts limits on the achievement of other social goals. It would also involve more radical reforms of liberal institutions than liberals have ever acknowledged. It would require the eradication of power relations and the entrenched inequalities of race, class and gender. It would require the redistribution of wealth and property ownership that flow from inequalities of power and an equalization of educational opportunities. It would require state intervention to ensure that everyone has an equal chance to develop their skills, to exercise choice and responsibility so that they can make a contribution to a common product according to their ability and so that they can be provided for when they cannot meet their own needs. In short, so that each person has the chance to lead an equally worthwhile life.

4

Justice

Within the liberal tradition there are several conflicting theories of justice. All take the idea of the equal moral worth of individuals as their starting-point and give different reasons for justifying departures from equality. In the last chapter, in the context of discussing these justifications, the traditional liberal idea of justice as desert was critically examined. Rawls's and Dworkin's theories were discussed in so far as their ideas of just distribution did not manage to overcome the problem of justifying undeserved inequalities.

This chapter will begin by examining utilitarian theories which take maximizing want satisfaction as the criterion by which to assess society from the point of view of justice. Utilitarians claim to respect the equal worth of each individual by giving each person's preferences equal weight in calculations of the overall good. It will then examine alternatives to utilitarianism by looking in detail at the procedural theory of justice offered by Rawls, Dworkin's defence of rights as trumps and Nozick's entitlement theory. All of these, in different ways, defend a conception of individual rights which cannot be set aside whatever the good consequences of doing so.

Utilitarianism

The theories of justice discussed in this chapter are not premised on the idea of justice as desert. As we have seen, Rawls rejected desert-based theories because they rely on morally arbitrary factors about people. Rawls's own procedural theory of justice, however, is primarily a response not to meritocratic theories, but to utilitarianism. Rawls believes that, in our society, a utilitarian approach to morality and politics predominates. Any alternative approach must therefore address itself to and defend itself against utilitarianism, which at first sight seems to provide the most rational conception of justice.

Utilitarianism is a general moral theory which assesses the rightness or wrongness of actions, policies, decisions and institutions in terms of their consequences. The right action etc. is the one which maximizes 'utility'. For the classical utilitarians, Bentham and J.S. Mill, 'utility' was defined as pleasure or happiness. Bentham explains the concept of utility in the following way: 'By utility is meant that property in any object whereby it tends to produce benefit, advantage, pleasure, good or happiness (all this in the present case, comes to the same thing) ... to the party whose interest is considered' (Bentham, 1967, p. 126). Mill explains the principle of utility thus:

The creed which accepts as the foundation of morals, utility, or the greatest Happiness Principle, holds that actions are right in proportion as they tend to promote happiness, wrong as they tend to produce the reverse of happiness. By happiness is intended pleasure, and the absence of pain; by unhappiness, pain and the privation of pleasure. (Mill, 1962b, p. 257)

It is assumed that happiness is the goal of human action. For Bentham, it is an empirical fact of human psychology that human beings are motivated to seek pleasure and avoid pain.

Nature has placed mankind under the governance of two sovereign masters, pain and pleasure. It is for them alone to point out what we ought to do, as well as to determine what we shall do. On the one hand, the standard of right and wrong, or the other, the chain of causes and effects is fastened to their throne. (Bentham, 1967, p. 125)

The principle of utility is both a psychological principle of human motivation and a moral principle based on it. It is a moral criterion by which to judge action. If the fundamental motivation of the individual is the pursuit of his or her own pleasure, each individual will be the best judge of what their own pleasure consists in. The individual knows their own experience better than anyone else. Bentham does not prescribe any content to what the human good consists in, except in so far as it is happiness or pleasure as defined by the individual in question. Given that experiences or sensations of pleasure or pain are the ultimate evaluative criteria, and that for the individual the right action is that which maximizes their own utility, it follows that collective principles like the interests of society or the common good can only be understood as an aggregate of these individual interests.

For Bentham, as we have seen in Chapter 1, the concept of society is a fiction. Society is a collection of individuals each seeking to satisfy their own interests. There is no collective good over and above the sum of individual interests and these are defined in terms of their sensations of pleasure. The principle of utility as a decision-making tool for moral activity and for social and political policy aimed to calculate the right course of action by summing up the individual desires for pleasure. In this calculation all individuals are to be considered equally. In Bentham's formulation, everyone is to 'count for one and no more than one'. He developed a 'felicific calculus' to assess and weigh various pleasures and pains according to their intensity, duration, certainty, propensity and remoteness. The amount or quantity of pleasure produced overall was the criterion by which to judge alternative courses of action. The formula 'the greatest happiness for the greatest number' expressed this general societal aim. The idea that decision-making should be based on maximizing happiness or utility and this could be calculated, inspired many nineteenth-century social, political and legal reformers who sought to apply this principle with the hope of bringing about radical change in society.

Mill accepted Bentham's general formulation of the principle of utility, that happiness was the criterion of moral action, but he challenged Bentham's view that pleasures were merely quantitative, that 'pushpin was as good as poetry' if the quantity of pleasure gained from each was equal. He introduced a qualitative distinction between 'higher' and 'lower' pleasures. The higher pleasures, the intellectual and the aesthetic, the cultivation of the mind and feeling were superior. Mill thought this distinction was consistent with utilitarianism.

It is quite compatible with the principle of utility to recognise the fact that some *kinds* of pleasures are more desirable and valuable than others. It would be absurd that while, in estimating all other things quality is considered as well as quantity, the estimation of pleasures should be supposed to depend on quantity alone. (Mill, 1962b, p. 258)

Mill tries to justify this distinction on supposedly empirical grounds by arguing that if people experienced both quantitative and qualitative pleasures they would prefer the latter. This distinction, however, poses problems for calculating utility in any straightforward objective or neutral way. It suggests a move away from merely identifying and summing what it is that individuals desire, to discriminating between and evaluating their desires. It seems to call for moral judgements about what is desirable and valuable rather than taking as given and incorrigible what individuals actually desire.

If what individuals desire is not simply taken at face value or accepted by virtue of the fact that they desire it, then inevitably, in order to discriminate between desires, some standard of judgement about what is good for human beings is implied. Ideals and values other than feelings of pleasure must be acknowledged. But Mill, like Bentham, was concerned to bring all human desires, ideas and values under the single concept of utility or happiness or pleasure. Now, if all that human beings aim at, want or value is defined in terms of pleasure and is reducible to the pursuit of happiness, then there is no room for evaluating, criticizing, grading or choosing between desires and for determining what is desirable whether or not it is what people do in fact desire. This point is clearly illustrated in Mill's so-called proof of the Principle of Utility as the standard by which to judge moral action.

Questions about ends are, in other words, questions about what things are desirable. The utilitarian doctrine is, that happiness is desirable, and the only thing desirable, as an end: all other things are desirable as a means to that end. What ought to be required of this doctrine — what conditions is it requisite that the doctrine should fulfil — to make good its claim to be believed.

The only proof capable of being given that an object is visible is that people actually see it. The only proof that a sound is audible is that people hear it: and so of the other sources of our experience. In the manner, I apprehend, the sole evidence it is possible to produce that anything is desirable, is that people do actually desire it. If the end which the utilitarian doctrine proposes to itself were not in theory and in practice acknowledged to be an end, nothing could ever convince any person that this was so. No reason can be given why the general happiness is desirable, except that each person, so far as he believes it to be attainable desires his own happiness. (Mill, 1962b, p. 288)

Mill's notion that the only way to show that something is desirable is the fact that people desire it has been criticized, most notably by G.E. Moore (1959, p. 67) as a fallacious inference. According to Moore, Mill illegitimately deduces the conclusion that something is desirable from the fact that people desire it. This is because 'desirable ' does not mean 'is desired' but 'ought to be desired'. The fact that something is desired cannot entail the value that it ought to be desired. Therefore Mill's argument is invalid.

MacIntyre (1967, p. 239) has argued that this is a mistaken reading of Mill. Mill does not claim that the premise 'all men desire pleasure' logically entails the conclusion 'they ought to desire it'. Rather, his argument is a factual assertion 'that all men desire pleasure' and it is this that can be challenged. First, because it is patently untrue that all men desire pleasure (martyrs and Puritans do not); second, because there are other desires and goals people have: pleasure is only one of the things people desire; and finally, because if all desires are explained in terms of pleasure, this reductionism which identifies whatever is desired with pleasure is vacuous and uninformative. It cannot explain different desires.

These arguments show the difficulty of trying to fit all human desires, ideas, goals and values into a unitary concept like happiness or pleasure. But there is also a problem of taking 'what is desired' to be equivalent to 'what is desirable'. Even if we disagree with Moore, that Mill did not intend to deduce that pleasure ought to be desired from the fact that people desire it, Mill still does insist that 'the sole evidence that something is desirable is the fact that it is desired'. And this means there can be no criticism or judgement or evaluation of desires over and above what people happen to want. If this is so, then there is no basis for the qualitative distinction Mill makes between 'higher' and 'lower pleasures'. Furthermore, the distinction itself is incompatible with a utilitarianism which has happiness or pleasure as its single evaluative criterion because it implies that there are some pleasures which are more desirable and valuable than others.

Modern utilitarians abandon the maximization of happiness or pleasure as the end to be achieved, and substitute instead want satisfaction or the satisfaction of preferences. It is considered to be a virtue of the theory that these wants and preferences are not judged or criticized but taken as given. They are observable in behaviour and their aggregate satisfaction is to be maximized. In political and economic terms, this doctrine is translated into the view that the function of government and the market system is to maximize the satisfaction of expressed wants which are revealed in demands made in the market or are 'read off' from what people actually consume or use. No normative judgements are made about the true ends or purposes of human beings, if political and economic policies correspond to individual wants. People simply have the desires and preferences they can demonstrably be seen to have and these are sovereign. Hence, there is no danger of coercion or justification for paternalistic policies.

Political and economic policies claim to satisfy the wants people have and do not seek to interpret their wants or to judge or impose what is in their best interests. Here utilitarianism is underpinned by the assumptions of modern liberal thought: that society is a collection of individuals who are the best judges of their own interests and that these interests can be aggregated together to form the general interest.

The disadvantages of assuming that individuals are the best judges of their own interests and of taking their given desires as expressive of their interests, is that, as for Bentham and Mill, there can be no distinction between what an individual desires and what is desirable. The stress on the sovereignty of individual desire obscures the fact that wants and preferences are not just raw data but are produced in specific social and political circumstances. Wants are determined by what is produced, consumed and by the perceptions of what is available to individuals in a particular society. Individuals may not express wants through ignorance of what will satisfy them, they may have mistaken perceptions of what will satisfy. What they want may be limited to what is available and possible. What is desirable may be different from the actual desires individuals currently have or would have if they had adequate information or a wider range of opportunities. The fact of wanting something does not make it desirable or valuable. We can come to want almost anything at all, including things that are bad, trivial or harmful for ourselves or for others.

Utilitarianism, because it gives equal weight to each person's wants, cannot distinguish between preferences. It cannot rule out the satisfaction of those preferences we have which may be detrimental to our interests, nor can it condemn as illegitimate the anti-social preferences we may have which discriminate against other people.

Balancing preferences in the same scale with no differentiation between them creates a framework in which there are no theoretical tools to criticize, evaluate, grade or discount what any individual happens to want. And so, liberal and utilitarian theories, while attempting to remain neutral between different conceptions of the good, foreclose the possibility of discovering this and may even sanction policies and institutions which are detrimental to that good. This is nowhere more apparent than in the clash between utility and justice. This problem is not immediately obvious. As Rawls (1993, p. 73) says, 'surely the simplest and most direct conception of the right, and so of justice, is that of maximising the good'. However, utilitarianism is an aggregate theory: it focuses on the overall net happiness or satisfaction of the greatest number, and justice is a distributive notion. Theories of justice offer criteria for the proper distributive shares which justify who gets what and why.

In utilitarian calculation, there is no principle of distribution. No ethical significance is attached to how the sum of satisfactions is distributed amongst individuals. This means that although each person's preferences are given equal weight, if the aim is to maximize overall satisfaction, then individuals or groups can be sacrificed for the greater good. This violates our normal moral convictions and our common-sense notions of justice, because the aim of maximizing utility excludes no class of actions as absolutely wrong in themselves, independent of their good consequences for the majority. All other moral considerations are subordinate to the single standard of utility. The various claims of justice – distribution according to desert, merit or needs, equal shares, equal rights, etc. – can be disregarded if respecting these claims is contrary to the general happiness.

The theories of Rawls, Dworkin and Nozick discussed in this chapter are particularly concerned to defend different conceptions of individual rights which cannot be set aside whatever the good consequences of doing so. Utilitarians' hostility to the notion of natural or human rights is notorious. Bentham described them as 'nonsense on stilts' and Mill thought that appeal to abstract rights could not be independent of their appeal to utility.

It is proper to state that I forego any advantage which could be desired to my argument from the idea of abstract right, as a thing independent of utility. I regard utility as the ultimate appeal on all ethical questions. (Mill, 1962b, p. 134)

Many utilitarians, however, including Mill, try to reformulate utilitarianism to avoid the obvious disadvantage that it offers no protection to individuals when their moral claims are overridden by the principle of utility. Mill argued that though utility is the ultimate appeal in ethical questions, utilitarianism does not license actions which we would normally class as immoral or unjust. For example, though the notion of abstract rights has no justification independent of utility, rights can be defended precisely because their protection will bring about the greatest happiness for the greatest number.

> To have a right, then, is I conceive, to have something which society ought to defend one in the possession of. If the objector goes on to ask, why it ought? I can give him no other answer than general utility. (Mill, 1962b, p. 309)

Similarly, justice as a system of moral rules is not disregarded, but is justified by the principle of utility, because of the contribution these rules make to humans well-being.

> While I dispute the pretensions of any theory which sets up an imaginary standard of justice not grounded on utility, I account the justice which is grounded on utility to be the chief part, and incomparably the most binding part, of all morality. Justice is the name of certain classes of moral rules, which concern the essentials of human well being more nearly, and are therefore of more absolute obligation, than any other rules for the guidance of life, and the notion which we have found to be of the essence of the idea of justice, that of a right residing in an individual, implies and testifies to this more binding obligation. (Mill, 1962b, p. 315)

The emphasis on the good consequences of moral rules rather than of actions is marked by the modern distinction between rule and act utilitarianism. The classical utilitarianism of Bentham is a form of act-utilitarianism whereby each particular action is subject to utilitarian calculation. An action is right if its consequences are better than any alternative. Because in any particular case an action may promote the general happiness at the expense of justice for individuals, act-utilitarianism cannot be considered to be a theory of justice. In rule-utilitarianism, the standard of utility is applied to moral principles, rules and practices and not to individual acts. Thus, it is right to act according to principles of justice, to respect individual rights, even if on a particular occasion disregarding them would have better consequences for the general welfare. This is because the general following of rules produces the greatest good. Rules, then, are assessed according to the utility of abiding by them.

Now it may be the case that, generally speaking, acting in accordance with the rules of justice has good overall consequences, but there is no necessary connection between following rules and general utility. Breaking a promise or violating an individual's rights can sometimes have better overall consequences than strictly adhering to or respecting them. If, in this case the rule-utilitarian abides by the rules, then this will produce a non-utilitarian result. If the rules are absolutely binding in all circumstances then the rule-utilitarian is not a utilitarian at all. Moreover, as Smart argues:

The rule-utilitarian presumably advocates his principle because he is ultimately concerned with human happiness: why then should he advocate abiding by a rule when he knows that it will not in the present case be most beneficial to abide by it? The reply that in most cases it is most beneficial to abide by the rule seems irrelevant. (Smart and Williams, 1973, p. 10)

The rule-utilitarian is faced with the problem that, from a utilitarian point of view, it would be irrational to always adhere to rules, the breaking of which would lead to better consequences. Strict adherence to the rules of justice is on occasion incompatible with maximizing utility. This problem arises because if the rightness of actions depends on the sum of happiness produced, then there can be no reason why we should consider or value the claims of justice when they conflict with utility. Utilitarianism is incompatible with justice in so far as there are no criteria for the distribution of benefits and burdens and for the way people ought to be treated which are not reducible to their useful effects. Utility could only approximate or be equivalent to a theory of justice if the claims of justice always coincided with what was generally useful, and if individual interests and general interests always coincided in such a way that the individual could not be sacrificed for the greater good.

Rawls: A Theory of Justice

Aims and method

Rawls's theory is an attempt to provide an alternative to utilitarianism and to remedy its defects by making justice its central concern. He writes:

If, then, we believe that as a matter of principle each member of society has an inviolability founded on justice which even the welfare of everyone else cannot override, and that a loss of freedom for some is not made right by a greater sum of satisfactions enjoyed by many, we shall have to look for another account of the principles of justice. The principle of utility is incapable of explaining the fact that in a just society, the liberties of equal citizenship are taken for granted, and the rights secured by justice are not subject to political bargaining nor to the calculus of social interests. (Rawls, 1993, p. 74)

Rawls aims to identify principles of justice which correspond to our intuitive convictions about the primacy of justice and to show that true principles are the result of a selection procedure that everyone can agree to as fair. Rawls believes that an acceptable theory of justice should be in tune with our intuitions about justice. He wants to demonstrate that the principles of justice he proposes coincide with our intuitions about justice once we have reflected on them, so that the principles match our 'considered judgements' about justice. He calls the method of matching our moral convictions and principles 'reflective equilibrium'. This involves taking our strongest moral convictions and then working back to the principles which justify them. For example, we are sure religious intolerance and racial discrimination are unjust. This conviction is a 'provisional fixed point' with which principles of justice must be compatible. If there are discrepancies between intuitions and principles, we can modify and revise either, going back and forth between them so that, eventually there is an equilibrium between the principles and our considered judgements.

Rawls claims that his two principles of justice meet our considered judgement about justice and this is an explanation and a justification for them, as is his attempt to show that these principles are a result of a fair selection process. The selection procedure that Rawls adopts is a version and revival of the social contract theory found in Hobbes, Locke and Rousseau. In these theories individuals in the pre-social state of nature enter into a contract to form civil society. In Rawls's theory of justice the guiding idea is that principles of justice for the basic institutions of society are selected and agreed to by hypothetical individuals in a hypothetical original position. This original position corresponds to the state of nature in traditional contract theories. Rawls asks what free and rational individuals concerned to further their interests would accept in an initial position of equality. That is, what principles would they choose, if they were to choose impartially, if they were ignorant of their own interests. The principles they choose are called 'justice as fairness' and these match our considered judgements about justice in reflective equilibrium.

The situation of ignorance is called the 'original position' of the contract. The parties to the contract are individuals (heads of families). They are to choose principles of justice which are to 'provide a way of assigning rights and duties in the basic institutions of society and they define the appropriate distribution of the benefits and burdens of social cooperation' (1971, p. 4). The conditions under which they choose are what Rawls refers to as the typical circumstances of justice. These are when 'mutually disinterested persons put forward conflicting claims to the division of social advantages under conditions of moderate scarcity' (1971, p. 128). There are formal constraints on the principles they choose. They must be general and universalizable. They must be feasible as a public conception and they must be capable of ordering priorities between conflicting claims and settling disputes about the design of basic institutions. The principles the contractors select must meet their considered judgements about justice in reflective equilibrium better than any others they could have chosen.

The contractors operate behind a 'thick' veil of ignorance. They have general information. They understood that their society is one in which the circumstances of justice obtain. They understand political affairs, the principles of economic theory, the general laws of human psychology and the basis of social organization. They are ignorant of their class position and social status and the generations to which they belong. They do not know what natural abilities or assets they possess, nor do they know their own conception of the good, the special features of their own psychology or the particular circumstances of their own society (1971, p. 137). This veil of ignorance is to ensure that the contractors choose impartially, that they evaluate different conceptions of justice on the basis of general considerations rather than bias in favour of principles that would advance their own particular interests.

It is assumed that the parties in the original position are disinterested (not interested in one another's interests) and are rational in the sense that 'in choosing between principles each chooses as best he can to advance his interests' (1971, p. 142). Since they do not know the details of their own particular life plans or interests or conceptions of the good, as rational agents they must choose out of a concern for desires they are bound to have whatever their actual interests turn out to be. These are desires for 'primary social goods' – which are 'rights and liberties, opportunities and powers, income and wealth' (1971, pp. 92, 263). They are primary social goods because whatever individuals' rational plans are, these are the goods they would prefer to have more of rather than less; and whatever their ends or interests are, primary goods are the means to them. They are 'things which it is supposed a rational man wants whatever else he wants' (1971, p. 92). Rawls provides a short list of traditional conceptions of justice (e.g. utilitarian, intuitional, egoistic and mixed conceptions) plus his own two principles from which any contractors must choose. They must agree unanimously which option is the best in so far as it maximizes their well-being as measured by their index of social primary goods.

The role of the contract is both analytic and justificatory. It is a device both to identify what rational individuals would choose if they were impartial, and to justify the principles which result from that choice. Rawls writes, 'The idea of the Original Position is to set up a fair procedure so that any principles agreed to will be just. The aim is to use the notion of pure procedural justice as a basis of theory' (1971, p. 136). The original position meets the constraints of pure procedural justice which means that if there is a fair procedure which has been properly followed, then the outcome is fair. The original position represents choice under a fair procedure, therefore the principles selected under this procedure are fair or just.

Problems with methods and procedures

Rawls argues that an acceptable theory of justice must match our considered judgements about justice in reflective equilibrium and it is this which justifies them. However, as many critics have pointed out, reflective equilibrium as a procedure for matching intuitions and principles is ultimately a subjectivist one (see Hare, 1975). It cannot provide any stronger justification for the principles Rawls selects than straightforward intuitionism, that is, than claiming that our intuitions validate the principles. Reflective equilibrium can be seen as an attempt to systemize intuitions (Rawls's own), but a match between intuitions and principles does not prove that the principles are just, only that they are coherent.

The justice of the principles cannot be made to depend on their agreement with Rawls's convictions, even if he thinks these are 'widely held' and that they are 'commonly shared presumptions'.

For example, it can be doubted that there is 'a broad measure of agreement' particularly among traditional liberal theorists, for Rawls's claim that it is one of the fixed points of our considered judgements that no-one deserves his place in the distribution of natural endowments (1971, p. 104). Moreover, since the outcome of his theory has to match our considered judgements about justice, it is obvious from the wide-ranging criticism of them (too egalitarian, not egalitarian enough, no room for desert, etc.) that they do not. Even if Rawls's principles matched most people's considered judgements (rather than his own), this would not be enough to show that they are just. They may merely reflect commonly held prejudices or preconceived ideas about what justice is. Having an intuition about justice is not enough to show that that intuition is right.

Similar points can be made about Rawls's justification of the contract made in the original position because it conforms to pure procedural justice. According to Rawls, 'pure procedural justice obtains when there is no independent criterion for the right result: instead, there is a correct fair procedure such that the outcome is likewise correct or fair, whatever it is, provided that the procedure has been properly followed' (1971, p. 86). However, following a fair procedure is in itself not enough to show that the outcome will be just. Now, it may show that it is fair *according* to that procedure, but it does not follow that the outcome is just. When someone gambles, wins a lottery or a game, we might say that they won according to the rules, but we often think that the outcome is unjust precisely because we are applying independent criteria. We say things like: 'She didn't deserve to win'; 'That's not fair, you always win'; 'He shouldn't have won, he doesn't need the money.'

This is all the more obvious when we are considering criteria for the just distribution of resources. We do not assess the justice of the outcome according to the criterion of procedural justice, by agreeing the fairness or otherwise of the procedures involved in allocation. We assess the outcomes by how far they meet the independent criteria of distributive justice, such as desert, merit or need. If defence of these criteria can be given, then Rawls's notion of pure procedural justice alone cannot validate the outcome of the contract. As Lyons writes: 'If there are grounds external to the contract argument for judging the justice of social arrangements, then Rawls' "justice as fairness" notion would seem to be discredited' (Lyons, 1975, p. 158).

Bias in the original position

Other criticisms have been directed at whether or not Rawls's procedure is fair in the first place. It has been argued that bias in the original position undermines it as a fair device for selecting principles. The veil of ignorance is designed to ensure impartiality, to rule out the parties seeking to advance their own special interests. People in the original position only know that they have desires for those primary goods which are necessary to fulfil any rational plan. However, Nagel (1975) has argued that Rawls's list of primary goods is not neutral between all conceptions of the good or relevant to all plans of life.

The primary goods Rawls identifies are less relevant to plans of life which characterize human beings as producers, creators and social beings; which do not require wanting more income or wealth; which emphasize the achievement of qualitative rather than quantitative goals; which focus on the development of human capacities rather than the consumption of utilities or which embody interactive, empathetic and reciprocal relationships rather than disinterested ones. Rawls's conception of what 'men' desire whatever else they desire is not a neutral conception, but a liberal individualist conception of what is necessary for the asocial individual to pursue the gratification of their material self-interested desires.

A whole barrage of criticism has been concerned to expose the liberal assumptions embodied in the contractarian argument and the original position. Notions of the individual as prior to society, and a view of society or social arrangements as the result of agreement by individuals each acting to further their own interests, inform Rawls's contract argument and are standard liberal fare. So, too, are the characteristics of the parties in the original position. They are independent individuals, abstracted from society; they are free and equal; autonomous and self-sufficient; mutually disinterested and motivated by self-interest. They are rational in the sense that they have the capacity to calculate the most efficient means to their own ends. These are not characteristics of people in general, but of modern, western, liberal individualistic men (Fisk, 1975; Miller, 1976; Lukes, 1978b). The original position is infected with the premises, concepts and values of liberalism. So, then, it is not surprising that the choices and conclusions of these ideologically biased individuals will reflect them too.

Communitarian and feminist criticism

Communitarian criticism focuses on whether people in the original position would be able to choose anything at all (see MacIntyre, 1981; Sandel, 1982; Taylor, 1982; Waltzer, 1983). This is because the asocial, atomistic, solitary, self-seeking free and equal person represented in the original position is so abstracted it is difficult to conceive of such a 'stripped down' individual being capable of choosing or of their choice being motivationally relevant to actual existing people. Sandel (1982, p. 21), for example, argues that Rawls relies on a metaphysical concept of the self which makes no sense. The person in the original position is an abstraction, a 'radically disembodied subject'. Such a pre-social individual independent of their particular interests, desires, values, conceptions of the good and communal ties which constitute their identity would be incapable of deliberation and choice.

Waltzer (1981, p. 389) asks why we should take any notice of the conclusions of people in the original position which is just an imaginary construction by Rawls, who is the only actual participant in the perfect meeting. We make choices, not by asking what the abstract individual would choose under universalizing conditions, but by asking the question in the context of shared social practices and meanings. Thinking about principles to govern distribution in abstraction from these will result in principles of justice which are of little use in the context of particular social circumstances. Similarly, Woolf (1977, p. 179) argues that even if the people in the original position could choose – so what? The veil of ignorance 'abstracts from all that is human and social'. Therefore, it is hard to see how it could be relevant to people in actual societies or why they should take any notice of what the people in the original position decide.

In some respects much of feminist criticism of Rawls resembles communitarian criticism in that it challenges the abstractness of the original position and its application to actual social contexts, (for example, Benhabib, 1987). Some feminists, however, believe that this is the result of a typically male conception of human nature and the application of male values. The model of the self-interested, individualistic, rational and autonomous man in the original position does not allow there to be a role for the nurturing, co-operation, care and empathy which are characteristically female qualities. Moreover, it is clear that the parties to the contract *are* men. Rawls assumes that they are male heads of households (1972,

p. 171). Therefore, neither female qualities, nor women themselves are represented in the original position. The choices that are made there represent a false universality which excludes or ignores women's particular interests (see Pateman, 1988).

Some feminists argue that Rawls's emphasis on impartiality, impersonality, rationality and universality, his appeal to the fairness of procedures and principles is based on male norms of moral reasoning (Gilligan, 1982). This kind of moral orientation ignores what is distinctive of women's moral reasoning which arises from considering particular needs in the context of particular psychological and social relationships. Rawls' model of 'man', then, is abstract, unrelated and inapplicable to women as well as to specific situations and contexts.

The two principles

In the original position, the parties choose two principles of justice for institutions:

First Principle
> Each person is to have an equal right to the most extensive system of equal basic liberties compatible with a similar system of liberty for all

Second Principle
> Social and economic inequalities are to be arranged so that they are both:
> (a) to the greatest benefit of the least advantaged, consistent with the just savings principle, and
> (b) attached to offices and positions open to all under conditions of fair equality of opportunity. (1971, p. 302)

The principles are subject to two priority rules, or 'lexical ordering'. The first is that 'liberty can only be restricted for the sake of liberty', and the second is that the second principle takes priority over the principle of efficiency and over 'maximising the sum of advantages'; and that fair opportunity takes priority over the difference principle, i.e. 2(a). Given the requirements of intergenerational justice, a certain level of savings must be maintained 'savings must on balance mitigate against those bearing this hardship'. The General Conception of Justice embodied by these two principles, as they are governed by priority rules is that: 'All social primary goods — liberty and opportunity, income and wealth and the bases of self-respect — are to be distributed equally unless an unequal distribution of any or all of these goods is to the advantage of the least favoured' (1971, p. 303). According to Rawls, these principles are chosen because the parties to the contract would adopt a 'maximin strategy' when choosing from their prescribed list of options. They must be sceptical in a situation where they do not know their own interests or position in society. Therefore, they would rank alternatives by their worst possible outcomes and choose the principles whose worst outcome is better than the worst outcome of any other (1971, p. 152).

The 'maximin strategy' would lead to Rawls's two principles being ranked higher than any alternative. The priority of liberty ensures that no-one, even those in the worst position, can be deprived of important liberties. The difference principle ensures that the worst off fare well without endangering liberty. The advantage of these principles is that they are ones which we can rely on people adhering to, as they create stability. People would accept them because, unlike under utilitarian principles, there is no risk that anyone would have to accept lesser liberties for the sake of others. Individuals would not be sacrificed for the general good. Therefore, the principles include everyone's good in a scheme of mutual benefit. In Part 3 Rawls argues that the parties who select the principles do so to promote their share of primary goods, and these are what any good life requires and that a just society governed by these principles will be stable and well-ordered.

These principles embody a large element of pure procedural justice according to Rawls (1971, p. 304). In order to apply pure procedural justice to the distribution of goods and services it is necessary to set up and administer impartially a just system of institutions. With the proper 'background institutions' the 'resulting distribution is just however things turn out' (1971, p. 275). Here again, we see the idea that if the procedure is fair so is the outcome, and the absence of appeal to independent criteria to justify the resulting distribution.

According to Rawls, the institutions which embody the principles are those of a constitutional democracy. A just political constitution is one that upholds the first principle of liberty by securing basic political liberties. A just economic order is one that upholds the second principle, that is, equal opportunities and the difference principle. Fair equality of opportunity and the difference principle require the government to secure equal opportunities in education and culture, and in the economy by preventing monopolies and trade restrictions. There will be taxation to provide a social minimum income for the worst off. The just savings principle requires that one generation cannot take advantage of the next by consuming all its wealth. It requires that one generation saves for the welfare of future generations. Thus just institutions which ensure that whatever arises from them is just include a rather familiar liberal scenario: equal rights, equal opportunities, competitive markets, the prevention of monopolies and taxation to generate a social minimum.

Problems with the two principles

1. A rational choice?

The first problem to be addressed is whether or not Rawls's Principles of Justice are or would be the solution to the problem of rational self-interested choice. Rawls claimed that his two principles represented the most rational choice, given the fair procedure for their selection and the constraints of the contract situation. Utilitarians have complained that Rawls has rigged the original position in order to get his desired anti-utilitarian result. Much of this criticism is directed at the 'maximin strategy'.

Rawls argued that the parties would adopt this strategy because it would be rational for them to do so since they do not know their own interests or the probability of social arrangements outside of the veil of ignorance. This uncertainty produces rational preferences for minimizing risks. But Barber (1975) argues, this strategy embodies a particular controversial and conservative psychology (risk aversion) which the original position was designed to exclude. The veil of ignorance was meant to prevent the parties from knowing their particular psychological dispositions. Moreover, this strategy assumes not uncertainty outside the veil, but the prospect of utter calamity. It requires the parties to be thoroughly pessimistic about their chances of being in the worst position once the veil is lifted.

This preoccupation with securing the minimum and insuring against the worst possible outcome is not typical of choices under uncertainty nor is it irrational to have no aversion to risk or to be a rational gambler. If the parties were not obsessed by avoiding risks they could rationally choose utilitarian principles. The possibility of greater gains if they were the best off would outweigh the risk of being the worst off.

It is not only the maximin strategy which militates against utilitarian principles being chosen. It is also Rawls's insistence that knowledge of probability outside the veil of ignorance is impossible (1971, p. 154). This limitation on knowledge is an important condition for securing impartial choice. Critics like Hare (1975) have argued that although ignorance of the parties' own particular interests is necessary for impartiality, knowledge of the objective probabilities of ending up in any particular place in society is not, and it is arbitrary to exclude the possibility of such knowledge. If the parties had knowledge of probable outcomes, they would predict how they would be likely to fare in society and this would permit the selection of utilitarian principles. Given that the hypothetical deliberators do have knowledge of the general facts about society, psychology and economics, it is likely that they could make predictions anyway. They could calculate the likelihood of having certain abilities and of ending up in certain kinds of social situations and base their choice on this. Lyons (1975) argues that even if the deliberators adopted a maximin strategy, there is no reason to think that Rawls's principles would be chosen over utility. Utilitarianism in theory and in practice protects against the feared worst outcomes since the general welfare could not be maximized if they were allowed.

Although Rawls's principles were meant to be antithetical to utilitarianism, there are many utilitarian dimensions to Rawls's own thought, and the principles themselves can be seen as a modified form of utilitarianism. Rawls's theory shares with utilitarianism the view of the individual as prior to society, a view of society as being marked by the conflict of interests, a model of 'man' as a utility maximizer, a seeker after gratification, and an instrumental view of reason. The parties are invoked in calculating the most efficient means to further their own interests.

Some of Rawls's conclusions are utilitarian too. Rawls claims that in contrast to utilitarian principles, the difference principle does not require people to lower their prospects of life for the sake of others (1971, pp. 178, 180). However, there is a sense in which both the better off and the worst off are required to do this. The better off who have received more resources as incentives will receive less than they would in a free market society, where the paying of differential rewards is not limited by the beneficial effect they have on the worst off group. And the worst off have accepted inequalities (which may only marginally benefit them and which may benefit

others substantially) which they would not have to accept in a
system which did not justify inequalities by appeal to the dubious
claims of incentive arguments (see Chapter 3). The usefulness of
inequality in society when it benefits everyone is typically defended
on utilitarian grounds and Rawls' defence is no exception.

2. The difference principle

Criticisms of the difference principle focus on the legitimacy of its
claims regarding the better off and the worst off and its justification
in terms of equality.

It has been doubted whether the difference principle would have
much appeal or even be just with respect to the better off. Once the
veil of ignorance is removed and individuals know their place in
society, why should the better off accept sacrifices to benefit the
least advantaged? Nagel (1975) and Fisk (1975) argue that in a
class-divided society, the better off (the ruling class) would not be
able to tolerate the constraints imposed on them by the difference
principle. Nozick (1974) argues that it would be unjust to treat the
better off as a means to the welfare of others, to treat them as means
to ends as this conflicts with individual liberty, with the right to
keep what individuals have justly acquired by their own labour.

It is doubtful whether people in the original position would
choose the difference principle when it permits inequalities which
might only marginally benefit the worst off. It is also doubtful
whether it would profit those who are actually worst off in society,
since, as we have seen, Rawls identifies these with those in the worst
material position, rather than those in the worst condition or
situation.

The most fundamental problem with the difference principle,
however, is whether it is a principle of justice at all. It will be
remembered that Rawls rejected desert as a criterion for unequal
distribution because such judgements were morally arbitrary.
However, Rawls justifies unequal distribution by appeal to
incentives. This criterion is not morally arbitrary, it is simply not
moral. It results in arbitrary, non-moral characteristics – undeserved
natural assets being rewarded as they are in a meritocratic system
and this, according to Rawls, is unjust. It also means that
inequalities are justified by appeal to the non-moral criterion of
self-interest. That is, people are motivated, not by justice which
recognizes the fundamental moral equality of all human beings, but

by greed, by a desire to acquire as large a share of resources for themselves as possible.

Rational self-interest motivates people to work for differential rewards and justifies inequality when this benefits everyone. There is a contradiction here between Rawls's premise of moral equality and his non-moral justification for inequality. If everyone is of equal moral worth regardless of their abilities and it is unjust to discriminate on these grounds, for justice requires a presumption in favour of equality, then on moral grounds there can be no need for the difference principle to justify inequality. If the difference principle and inequality are required for non-moral reasons because people are motivated by self-interest, then implementing the difference principle will be contrary to their self-interest. This is because, if people are motivated by a desire to gain as much as they can by the use of their abilities, why would they accept the redistribution of wealth called for by the difference principle and the responsibility this implies to the worst off?

If distribution ought to be equal on moral grounds, this contradicts the justification for incentives which results in some people having more than others. If incentives are justified, this contradicts the premise of the *prima facie* justice of equality. These arguments call into question Rawls's Principles of Justice as principles of justice (see Grey, 1973; Lyons, 1975; Narveson, 1976, 1978). Rational self-interest may explain why people in the original position adopt the difference principle, but it is not a moral justification for it. If inequality is necessary because people are self-interested, then the difference principle is a principle of expediency, but not a principle of justice.

3. The concept of liberty

The concept of liberty which Rawls uses is another target for criticism. Daniels (1975a), for example, argues that Rawls uses a narrow definition of liberty that is to be secured by the first principle. Rawls defines freedom in a typically liberal way as negative liberty, as freedom from the constraints of law, public opinion and social pressure (1971, p. 206). The liberties defined by the first principle are the familiar civil and political liberties (the right to vote, hold public office, freedom of speech and assembly, liberty of conscience, freedom of thought and expression, the rights over property and freedom from arbitrary arrest (1971, p. 61)). The protection of these liberties to be enjoyed equally is to take priority over all other social goods.

As we have seen in Chapter 2, definitions of freedom which only include political and legal constraints as restrictions on liberty arbitrarily exclude economic and ideological factors which have the effect of limiting liberty. They fail to acknowledge that the inability to take advantage of political and legal rights as a result of ignorance or lack of resources is an impediment to freedom. Liberals circumvent this objection by distinguishing between liberty and its worth and here Rawls follows suit. Inequalities in the ability to exercise rights due to unequal economic means do not count as inequalities of liberty, but only in the worth or value of liberty (1971, p. 204). But, even if this distinction could be maintained, it is still a pertinent question whether there is any point to having formal freedoms if we are unable to exercise them. Failure to take this point seriously leads Rawls to underestimate the effects of the inequality of wealth, income, power and authority allowed by the second principle on the equal basic liberties guaranteed by the first principle.

Daniels argues that for this reason the two principles are incompatible. The liberty of equal citizenship is undermined by and is incompatible with the significant social and economic inequalities which are allowed by the difference principle. Being poor and ignorant affects the ability to make use of political freedom. Equal liberties are not of equal worth if the ability to pursue our own ends and purposes cannot be achieved due to inequalities of wealth and power. If equal political liberties are important, then under the veil of ignorance it would be rational to choose not only an extensive system of equal political liberty, but to choose principles which also secured the equal worth of these liberties. It would be rational to reject the difference principle which allows unequal distributions because this undermines the principle which secures equal liberty.

4. The priority of liberty

Other criticisms focus on the rationale for granting priority to liberty. Rawls does admit that under extreme conditions when bare survival is at stake, people cannot take advantage of political freedoms. In these cases it may be rational to sacrifice basic liberties and give priority to other goods. This denial of liberty is justified 'only if it is necessary to raise the level of civilisation so that in due course these freedoms can be enjoyed' (1971, p. 152). Rawls claims that once certain levels of well-being have been reached, people would prefer increases in liberty rather than social or economic goods. He thinks that it would be irrational for them to accept a lesser liberty for greater material means or amenities (1971, p. 542). This is not obvious. It may be rational for people to give pride of place to political and legal rights if they are rich liberals. But it may not be irrational for the poor, the sick, the uneducated, the unemployed or the homeless to attach more importance to improvements in their well-being than they do to their right to vote or hold public office, or their freedom to complain about their lot.

5. Self-critique

It is generally thought that in *A Theory of Justice*, Rawls has presented not an impartial, universal theory but a theory that rationalizes liberal beliefs and values. In his later writings Rawls admits as much. He claims that he is not engaged in identifying universal principles of justice, but rather the principles appropriate for modern democratic society. He is constructing a fair procedure for devising principles of justice for people conceived of as free and equal moral agents. This conception of a person is not abstract or pre-social, but is a social conception because it is implied in the American tradition. In this tradition people are conceived of as free and equal, but there is no shared agreement about what social institutions should be like to conform to the freedom of equality of citizens (Rawls, 1980, p. 517). He claims that 'justice as fairness' is a political conception of justice (Rawls, 1985, p. 224). It is political because it applies only to the political sphere, because it does not presuppose accepting any particular comprehensive moral, religious, or philosophical doctrine and because it is formulated in terms of certain fundamental ideas viewed as latent in the public culture of liberal democratic society (Rawls, 1988, p. 252).

According to Rawls, his theory is a systematic attempt to articulate and make coherent the values and ideas of liberal democracy, and to construct principles of justice that will be acceptable to all members of pluralistic society and so produce stability and social unity. 'Justice as Fairness presents itself not as a conception of justice which is true; but one that can serve as a basis of informed and willing agreement between citizens viewed as free and equal persons' (Rawls, 1985, p. 230). It is a practical solution to the political problem of how to build an 'overlapping consensus' given competing moral, religious, intellectual and philosophical ideas. The task of political philosophy is to devise a procedure for constructing workable principles that can be agreed by all, despite their varying conceptions of the good.

Thus, it is claimed, critics who accuse Rawls of deducing universal principles from abstract premises which embody a pre-social view of human nature are mistaken. He is taking existing social practices as his starting-point, the moral values and judgements of a particular community, the liberal democratic conception of human beings as free and equal. His theory is not universal in application but culture-specific, appropriate for liberal democratic society. Now this may render Rawls's theory immune to the charge of false universality but it also makes the 600 pages of *A Theory of Justice* look less like the powerful work of magisterial grandeur it was originally greeted as. For it is rather an odd defence of liberal principles of justice to say that they are liberal principles of justice; to say that people conceived the way liberals conceive them would choose liberal principles; to say that a liberal theory of justice informed by liberal beliefs and values is one that liberals could accept.

In order to defend his theory, Rawls cannot appeal to the fact that the political culture is liberal and his theory represents a systematic articulation of fundamental liberal ideas, because how would he defend the theory to non-liberals in a non-liberal culture? He would have to defend the truth of liberal premises and it is precisely this which opponents of liberalism question. They do not question the fact that people in liberal democratic societies hold these beliefs, they question whether or not they are true. Critics of Rawls attacked his premise of the abstract asocial individual as his starting-point for constructing principles of justice. Rawls answers that the free and equal person in the original position is a social conception because this is the concept of a person that people in liberal democracies share. However, this answer misses the point.

A social conception of a person does not mean that people in society use it, it means that the conception acknowledges the social nature of human beings. It means that people who hold a social conception argue for the truth of a conception of human beings which recognizes their interdependence, their involvement with each other, their co-operative and productive capacities, and their shared interests. They argue that conceiving human beings as free and equal, autonomous and self-sufficient, separate and independent, mutually disinterested and self-seeking is a false conception of the person because it does not acknowledge their social nature. Even if everyone in liberal democratic society shared the liberal conception of a person, it would not make it a social conception. The fact that people in society share a conception may make it a societal conception, but it does not make it a social conception. It is this conception that Rawls must defend, independent of people's actual conceptions if he is to defend his principles of justice, otherwise after all the grandiose talk of monumental theories, what we have is a rather uncontroversial meek claim that liberal premises about the nature of human beings and what they value produce liberal conclusions about justice.

Dworkin: Justice as Rights

Dworkin in *Taking Rights Seriously* (1977) argues that justice is a matter of determining what rights people have and treating them accordingly. This is because only a recognition of individual rights can prevent people being treated as means to ends as they would be under unqualified utilitarian doctrines. For Dworkin, 'if someone has a right to something then it is wrong for the government to deny it to him even though it would be in the general interest to do so' (Dworkin, 1977, p. 269). Rights are anti-utilitarian in the sense that they cannot be overridden by policies aimed at the overall good of society. They 'trump' utilitarian arguments by having precedence over and by acting as restraints on the pursuit of other moral and political goals.

The ultimate basic right to be protected is the right to equal concern and respect which Dworkin regards as 'a postulate of political morality' (1977, p. 272). This right is fundamental and axiomatic in that other specific rights are derived from it. Dworkin combines rights with his conception of individuals as worthy of equal concern and respect, and it is this liberal commitment to the equal worth of each individual which informs his analysis of justice and which provides arguments for the protection and just treatment of individuals. Justice involves the right to treatment as an equal which Dworkin distinguishes from the right to equal treatment. The right to treatment as an equal means that the government must treat people with equal concern and respect. It does not treat citizens as moral equals if unequal distribution is justified on the grounds that some people are more worthy of concern, or if liberty is constrained on the grounds that one citizen's 'conception of the good life is nobler or superior to another' (1977, p. 273). Dworkin's defence of liberal neutrality is derived from the basic moral principle of treating individuals with equal concern and respect. Liberal society must be independent of and neutral between different conceptions of the good because individuals are not treated as equals if one conception is preferred or imposed over others.

This notion of treating people as equals does not mean that one person's interests should not be sacrificed for another, and the idea of rights as trumps does not imply that the role of the state should be confined to the protection of basic rights and should not intervene to advance the general welfare. For Dworkin, there is no general right to liberty *per se*, only rights to specific liberties. Unsurprisingly, the specific liberties to be protected as rights are the old liberal favourites – freedom of speech, worship, association, personal and sexual relations.

The state may intervene to restrict the use of property or freedom of contract, impose taxation for education and culture and prohibit racial and sexual discrimination when doing so promotes overall social welfare. Dworkin believes that 'the vast bulk of the laws which diminish my liberty are justified on utilitarian grounds' (1977, p. 269). Consequently, Dworkin is not opposed to sacrificing some liberties to considerations of utility. He even suggests that, despite the trump role of his preferred liberties, his theory could be viewed as a modified form of utilitarianism. This is because utilitarianism, like Dworkin's own theory, is based on egalitarian premises. Utilitarianism provides a conception of how governments treat people as equals because each person's preferences are balanced on the same scale, with no distinction between them. No person's preferences are discounted or given more weight than others. However, Dworkin argues, if utilitarianism is not checked in practice by rights, it will disintegrate into a corrupt theory which contradicts its own egalitarian premises.

If utilitarians are neutral between preferences and count all preferences equally, then problems arise when some of the preferences that are counted are themselves not neutral. For example, Nazi preferences include the preference that Aryans have more and Jews have less of their preferences fulfilled. If the Nazi preferences are counted, then utilitarianism's most fundamental tenet that no-one is entitled to have their preferences fulfilled more than anyone else is contradicted because the preferences that are being counted are that some preferences count more than others. If utilitarianism is not qualified to restrict such preferences, then its egalitarian character in which 'everyone is to count as one' is destroyed. Dworkin, therefore, endorses a modified or purified utilitarianism in which this 'corrupting' element is not allowed to affect determining decisions.

Dworkin identifies the elements which corrupt utilitarian arguments by distinguishing between personal and external preferences, both of which utilitarians count in calculating the general welfare (1977, pp. 234–8, 215–18). Personal preferences refer to an individual's assignment of goods or opportunities to himself; external preferences are preferences for the assignment or denial of goods or opportunities to others. In determining collective goals majority preferences should count, but only when decisions are based on personal preferences. Utilitarianism refined in this way 'is the only defensible form of utilitarianism' because it treats people as equals (1977, p. 276).

External preferences are excluded for two reasons. First, for the formal procedural reason that to count external preferences is a form of double counting in that both my own personal and external preferences are counted. Second, because counting external preferences involves counting preferences for how others should live and for the goods and opportunities they should or should not have, and as such is a denial of equal concern and respect. Dworkin argues that a practical way to restrict external preferences is to secure a set of rights which act as trumps over utilitarian arguments. Then, we can

enjoy the institutions of political democracy, which enforce overall or unrefined utilitarianism, and yet protect the fundamental right of citizens to equal concern and respect by prohibiting decisions that seem, antecedently, likely to have been reached by virtue of the external components of the preferences democracy reveals. (1977, p. 277)

Dworkin defends and identifies the list of rights which are to trump utilitarian arguments not by appeal to their intrinsic value, nor because of their instrumental importance in achieving the ideas of the good life or the ends of human nature, but by considerations of a procedural nature. That is, he distinguishes the liberties which are to be enshrined in rights by anticipating the likely outcome of a decision-making procedure that counts personal preferences. He assumes that if unrestricted utilitarian calculation of the general interest is made, then these are the rights that are likely to be overridden. A procedure which counts external preferences will then fail to treat people as equals and a set of rights are needed to counteract this corrupting element in the decision-making process.

Problems with personal and external preferences

Dworkin is attempting to deal with the problems which arise when aggregating the given preferences people have without criticizing or judging those preferences by reference to some substantive theory of what good or appropriate preferences might be. On the one hand, in keeping with his liberal convictions, he wants to remain neutral between different conceptions of the good life, but, on the other, he wants to distinguish between kinds of preferences, only some of which have legitimate weight in decision-making. To do this, he cannot appeal to a theory of human nature or objective human interests since this is inconsistent with his liberalism. He, therefore, can only rule out certain kinds of preferences on procedural grounds or in terms of their form rather than their content.

External preferences are ruled out because a procedure which includes them is unfair as it is thought to be analogous to double counting. They are also ruled out by reference to the foundational value of equal concern and respect, which, according to Dworkin, is a value prior to any other conception of the good. Dworkin explains that if external preferences about how other people should live are counted and some people are denied liberty or discriminated against as a result, then this amounts to not treating them as equals. They are denied moral independence, their conceptions of the good or ways of life are, in effect, deemed to be inferior to others. However, it is not clear why external preferences are a denial of equal concern and respect because of the form they take. Particular types of external preferences are not objectionable *because* they are external, that is, simply because they express views about how others should lead their lives, but because of their moral content. Certain kinds of external preferences about the assignment of goods and opportunities to others are objectionable, not because of their externality, but because they express hostility to the welfare of others, and have a negative impact on their freedom, on their equality of opportunity and on their equal rights generally.

Moreover, discrimination and denials of liberty to minorities are not unjust only when they reflect external preferences of certain types, they are unjust whether or not they are the result of a procedure which aggregates external preferences. They are unjust whatever the reasons for their justification. The distinction between external and personal preferences as made by Dworkin cannot bear the weight of his argument for defending rights. Rights cannot be defended on the grounds that they are needed to counteract policies which may be made by aggregating external preferences. First, because not all policies based on external preferences would infringe rights, and second, because if it were possible to count only personal preferences in decision-making, such a procedure would not necessarily protect individual rights or stop individuals from being exploited or discriminated against.

Dworkin does not distinguish between the kinds of external preferences which violate rights and those which do not. He clearly wants to exclude only those external preferences which express hostility to the rights of others, but, by ruling out all external preferences, he rules out counting altruistic preferences which are also external and which may be necessary to protect rights. Political decisions and policies which promote social welfare, health, education, foreign aid, defence, policing and other public goods are as often motivated by a concern for the interests of others, for the concern for the community as a whole, as they are by personal preferences for the goods and services that should be assigned to ourselves.

To justify rights as a shield against external preferences, Dworkin would have to distinguish between external preferences that were motivated by hostility to the interests of others and those which were motivated by a concern for them. This would involve justifying the exclusion of the former and the relevance of the latter in political decision-making by reference to their moral content and not to the faulty procedure of double counting and the external form they take. Moreover, in making external preferences the culprit in the denial of rights, Dworkin seems to imply that if it were possible practically for a decision-making process to count only personal preferences, then there would be no danger of rights infringement. However, policies that were determined by weighing personal preferences equally would be no guarantor of rights. If rights are needed, they are needed as a shield against certain kinds of external preferences *and* certain kinds of personal preferences too.

Dworkin assumes, like classical utilitarians and modern welfare economists, that rational preferences are those which are based on self-interest. He implies that all that is wrong with utilitarianism is the weight it gives to external preferences, the fact that it cannot restrict itself to aggregating personal preferences. This is why rights as trumps are needed to counteract this defect. However, personal preferences may be as irrational and uninformed, as prejudiced and selfish as external ones. And any process which aggregates self-interested preferences, which weighs each person's preferences equally, would be just as likely to generate a utilitarian result which had as morally dubious results as any procedure that included external preferences. Overall satisfaction of personal preferences may depend on the unequal treatment of others and the infringement of their rights.

From this we can conclude that the distinction Dworkin makes between personal and external preferences is not adequate to distinguish between preferences which violate rights and those which do not. More generally, we can conclude that justice requires distinctions to be made between those preferences which are morally legitimate and those which are not. Justice must mean something other than the maximization of preferences *per se*. If liberals remain neutral between conceptions of the good and give equal weight to each individual's preferences, then they cannot make the distinction necessary for just distribution, because they cannot rule out any preferences as illegitimate. Dworkin's attempt to preserve neutrality and rule out preferences on procedural grounds to temper the inegalitarian aspects of utilitarianism fails.

In order to rule out some preferences, we have to criticize not the procedural fairness by which they are satisfied or the form they take, we have to make judgements about their content. What individuals value for others and for themselves must be judged, criticized and evaluated, and this inescapably involves a theory about what kinds of preferences are good or appropriate for human beings. This solution is not available to Dworkin or those of a liberal persuasion who require that governments and the state remain neutral in relation to different conceptions of the good life or the good society. But there must be some such solution, if the good life or the good society is to be realized.

Nozick: The Entitlement Theory of Justice

Nozick's theory of justice is in the tradition of classical seventeenth-century liberalism, eighteenth-century individualist philosophy, nineteenth-century *laissez-faire* capitalism and twentieth-century libertarianism associated with the ideas of the Austrian economists, von Mises and Hayek. *Anarchy, State and Utopia* (1974), like Rawls's *A Theory of Justice*, was hailed as a major contribution to contemporary political philosophy. Even those who were wary of its conclusions welcomed its analytic sharpness, intellectual rigour, originality and ingenious arguments. In some respects *Anarchy, State and Utopia* is diametrically opposed to Rawls's *A Theory of Justice*. Rawls attempted to provide a theoretical justification for the provision of welfare and redistribution to achieve this. Nozick's theory strikes at the heart of any conceptual justification for the welfare state. For Nozick, justice is not concerned with achieving particular distributive patterns, but with respecting rights. These rights are so fundamental that only a minimal state can be defended.

However, in other respects *Anarchy, State and Utopia* displays important continuities with Rawls's and Dworkin's brand of welfare liberalism. All these theorists are responding to a defect in utilitarianism, which, if unrestricted, sacrifices some individuals for the sake of others. Rawls, Dworkin and Nozick all see themselves in the Kantian tradition where justice requires that people be treated as ends in themselves and this places limits on the way people can be treated to benefit others or to benefit society generally. All agree that a just society, therefore, will secure some basic liberties and rights which are not subject to utilitarian calculation. They disagree on the nature and extent of the rights that are important for treating people as ends in themselves.

Nozick defends a limited set of near-absolute Lockean rights – the rights to life, liberty and property. Each individual as long as they do not violate the same rights of others has the right not to be killed or assaulted; the right to be free from all forms of coercion and limitations on freedom; the right to acquire and transfer property and the right not to have property legitimately acquired taken or the use of it limited. For Nozick, these rights are fundamental constraints on how people can be treated without their consent. They are constraints because there is no case for infringing them by appeal to the consequences of doing so. Rights cannot be violated because doing so would produce more good or would benefit society generally. 'Individuals have rights, there are things no person or group can do to them without violating their rights' (1974, p. ix). According to Nozick, it follows from this that the only legitimate state is the nightwatchman state defended by nineteenth-century liberals.

The minimal state 'limited to the narrow functions of protection against force, theft, fraud, enforcement of contracts, and so on, is justified' because 'any more extensive state will violate persons' rights not to be forced to do certain things, and is unjustified' (1974, p. ix). The state, then, may intervene to protect these basic rights, it may impose taxation or restrictions on liberty in order to secure internal order and external defence and the performance of its nightwatchman functions. It may not, however, impose taxation or restrictions on the liberty of some to increase the welfare of others since this would violate their rights not to be treated in certain ways without their consent.

If these rights are so absolute, then Nozick must provide a strong argument to show that human beings have these and only these limited rights. It is a common criticism of Nozick that he fails to do this. In *Anarchy, State and Utopia*, Nozick himself voices the same theoretical worry. 'This book does not present a precise theory of the moral basis of individual rights' (1974, p. xiv). However, there are inter-related strands of argument which aim to provide a rationale for the constraints that rights impose. Nozick argues that the non-violability of rights 'reflect the underlying Kantian principle that individuals are ends and not merely means; they may not be sacrificed or used for the achieving of other ends without their consent: Individuals are inviolable' (1974, p. 31). There can be no sacrifice of the individual for other persons or for the overall social good because there is no social entity 'with a good that undergoes some sacrifice for its own good. There are only individual people, different individual people with their own lives. Using one of these people for the benefit of others, uses him and benefits the others' (1974, pp. 32–3). What underlies the existence of rights as side-constraints, then, is 'the fact of our separate existence', the fact that each individual is a separate person. Theories which appeal to an overall social good ignore this and do not respect the fact that each individual is a separate person. Rights reflect the fact that no moral balancing act can take place between individuals, 'there can be no moral outweighing of one of our lives by others so as to lead to a greater overall *social* good' (1974, p. 33).

The moral foundation of rights in Kantian respect for individuals as ends in themselves and in the idea of the separateness of persons relates to the idea that there are some valuable characteristics of individuals, by virtue of which others are constrained in their treatment of them. Nozick considers traditional proposals for valuable human characteristics, such as self-consciousness, rationality, free will and moral agency and concludes that the significance of these is that they add up to being able to formulate and act upon one's own ends and overall conceptions of a life that one wishes to lead. Nozick suggests that the moral basis of rights as constraints is their connection to the individual's capacity to shape their own lives according to their own values and purposes, for it is this which gives meaning to life. He writes:

I conjecture that the answer is connected with that elusive and difficult notion: the meaning of life. A person's shaping his life in accordance with some overall plan is his way of giving meaning to his life; only a being with the capacity to so shape his life can have or strive for meaningful life. (1974, p. 50)

Rights reflect the Kantian notion of respect for persons, the separateness of each individual, and their protection is important for the capacity to pursue our own ends and purposes and for our ability to lead a meaningful life.

Justice, then, is only concerned with respecting individual rights. Nozick rejects all the familiar criteria of distributive justice. He rejects all rules for the allocation of resources which specify whether a distribution is just by looking at an end result produced, such as aggregate utility or greater equality. He also rejects what he calls 'patterned principles' which justify distribution according to some pattern: to each according to his ability, moral merit, need or social contribution. Instead, he advocates a procedural theory of justice called the 'entitlement theory'.

The entitlement theory is historical, but not patterned. It is historical because past circumstances or acts create entitlements to things, 'whether a distribution is just depends on how it came about' (1974, p. 153). Entitlement theory is not patterned, there is no pattern to which distributions must conform, what actually happened determines whether the distribution is just. That is, it is the procedures by which the holdings were acquired and transferred that make them just. They are just if they are legitimately acquired and transferred and, if so, people are entitled to the holdings they possess under the distribution. If a person has justly acquired private property or it has been justly transferred to them, then that person has an absolute right to it. No-one has the right to confiscate it on the grounds of greater equality, need or any other social good.

Justice in holdings consists of three major principles: justice in acquisition, justice in transfer and the rectification of injustice in holdings. The first of these, justice in acquisition, concerns how unheld things can come to be held legitimately, so that individuals can become entitled to ownership of previously unowned resources. Nozick considers Locke's attempt to specify a principle of just initial acquisition. Unconvincingly, Locke claimed that an individual has a right to whatever he mixed his labour with. Locke argued that each person owned his own body and his own labour. In mixing labour (which I own) with unowned resources, I establish a property right to those resources. So, if I mix my labour with something, I own it, I am entitled to it, with the proviso that I leave 'enough and as good' for others.

However, it is completely puzzling how or why mixing one's labour with something makes one the owner of it. Even Nozick is not sure and raises some salient and amusing objections to the notion that mixing labour establishes property rights (1974, pp. 174–5). For example, he asks what the boundaries are of what labour is mixed with. If an astronaut clears a space on Mars, does he own the whole planet, the whole uninhabited universe or just a particular plot? Why is mixing labour (which I own) with what I do not own, a way of losing what I own rather than a way of gaining what I don't? If I spill a can of tomato juice into the sea, do I thereby come to own the sea or have I foolishly wasted the tomato juice? Why should mixing labour entitle me to the whole product, rather than just the added value created?

Nozick does not try to enlarge on Locke to answer these questions. He merely proceeds to discuss the proviso that initial acquisition should leave 'enough and as good' for others. He re-interprets this to mean that initial appropriation is justified as long as 'the position of others no longer at liberty to use the thing is thereby not worsened' (1974, p. 178). Even if appropriation by some results in limited or no further opportunities for appropriation by others, it may still be justified, providing the appropriator compensates the others so that their overall situation is not worsened. In effect, instead of justifying how anyone can come to own anything and have exclusive rights over its use and disposal, Nozick defends property rights on the grounds that there can be no objection to them if no-one is worse off than they would have been without private appropriation. According to Nozick, the operation of the free market and private ownership are compatible with his Lockean proviso (1974, p. 182).

Absolute ownership rights gained from initial acquisition preclude any compulsory transfer of property associated with taxation policies to fund the welfare state. State provision of welfare requires coercion and transgresses the individual's right to keep what they have justly acquired. Individuals can transfer goods by voluntary exchange, trade or gift, but only when the individual has freely chosen to transfer goods is this compatible with individual rights. Therefore, welfare provision may result from generosity, charity or philanthropy, but not obligations. Neither individuals nor the state are obliged to help the poor. If a starving man drags himself to our table where we are entertaining friends to a sumptuous banquet, we are within our rights to leave him without a crust. Given the right to initial acquisition then, goods that are transferred in market exchanges are justly transferred and any attempt by the state to impose on these free exchanges is incompatible with the basic rights of the individual.

If property has not been justly acquired or transferred, if it has been acquired by coercion or in a way that worsens the situation of others, then rectification is possible and compensation may be paid. Nozick even goes so far as to argue that since we lack the historical information to make judgements, then something like Rawls's difference principle might be adopted as a rule of thumb to rectify the consequences of past injustices. 'Past injustices might be so great as to make necessary in the short run a more extensive state in order to rectify them' (1974, p. 231). But this is a once and for all adjustment.

Arguments for the entitlement theory

Redistribution and property rights

According to Nozick's entitlement theory, individuals have rights which put constraints on the way people can be treated. Only a minimal state is compatible with individual rights, any more extensive state violates them. Liberal egalitarians like Rawls and Dworkin favour taxing free exchange to compensate for natural disadvantages. This is unjust, because if people are entitled to their holdings, they have a right to dispose of them as they think fit. If initial acquisition is just, then Nozick's conception of justice fits the slogan: 'From each as they choose, to each as they are chosen' (1974, p. 160). Rawls argued distribution should not be influenced by factors such as natural assets which are arbitrary from a moral point of view. Nozick does not attempt to argue that people deserve their natural assets and, therefore, they are entitled to whatever they gain from them. He establishes property rights via the self-ownership argument. That is, he substitutes 'own' for deserve. People own their natural assets and, therefore, they are entitled to whatever they gain from them. 'Whether or not people's natural assets are arbitrary from a moral point of view, they are entitled to them, and to what flows from them' (1974, p. 226).

Redistribution policies violate the rights of people as self-owners. 'Taxation of earnings from labour is on a par with forced labour' (1974, p. 169) because it is like forcing someone to work for another's purpose. It involves 'appropriating the actions of other persons'. This process whereby others decide what purposes your work is to serve makes them a *part-owner* of you; it gives them a property right in you'. Nozick concludes:

End-state and most patterned principles of distributive justice institute (partial) ownership by others of people and their actions and labour. These principles involve a shift from the classical liberals' notion of self-ownership to a notion of (partial) property rights in *other* people. (1974, p. 172)

Since people have rights to self-ownership, no coercive intervention in free market exchanges can be legitimate or compatible with recognizing this.

Objection to patterns

Nozick also defends the entitlement theory by claiming that non-entitlement conceptions of justice require constant interference in the lives of individuals. Nozick argues any patterned principle D1 will be supplanted by another D2 by virtue of the voluntary economic transactions that people will subsequently engage in. Any return to D1 requires imposition, reversing the voluntary actions of individuals. He illustrates this by asking us to suppose that our favoured distribution D1 (equal shares, distribution according to need, etc.) is in operation. He then asks us to suppose that Wilt Chamberlain (a famous basketball player) signs a contract with a team stipulating that 25 cents from the price of each ticket goes to him. The fans are happy to pay and voluntarily donate a separate 25 cents. During the season one million people watch Wilt Chamberlain play and he ends up with 250,000 dollars, a sum larger than anyone else has. This new distribution D2 has upset the original pattern.

Nozick claims this new distribution is not unjust. Each person was entitled to the resources held under D1, each person voluntarily chose to transfer the resources that resulted in unequal distribution, no third party is worse off. They still have their legitimate shares. Redistribution to maintain D1 would be unjust because it would involve continually interfering to stop people from transferring resources as they choose, or because it takes from some people resources that have been transferred to them legitimately. The Wilt Chamberlain argument is designed to show that there is nothing unjust about the unequal outcome of a sequence of market exchanges, if each exchange is voluntary, and that interferences to restore patterns is incompatible with individual rights. 'A socialist society would have to forbid capitalist acts between consenting adults' (1974, p. 163).

Problems for Nozick

1. Mixing labour and self-ownership

Any justification for property rights must be supported by arguments which show how such rights can legitimately arise. If no principled basis for them can be found, there can be no case against redistribution in terms of infringing these rights. Nozick gives us no grounds for thinking that these rights exist, let alone that they have the absolute and unmodifiable character he attributes to them.

Nozick cannot explain how individuals come to have rights to private property by using Locke's mixing labour arguments. He acknowledges the difficulties involved in justifying the transition from self-ownership to entitlements in the original Lockean argument. Despite this, he claims that self-ownership of natural assets entitles people to whatever flows from them, therefore redistribution violates the rights of people as self-owners. I own my own body and natural assets and this entitles me to benefit from the products of my labour. In what sense, however, do I own my natural assets? To determine this, we must make the crucial distinction between saying something is mine in an identifying sense, and saying that I own it in a proprietorial sense. My natural assets are mine only in the sense that I happen to have a particular set of natural abilities. They are mine rather than yours. They identify me as the distinct person who has these abilities as a matter of natural fact. This is different from saying that I 'own' them in a proprietorial way, and that I have a natural right to them. They are mine but I do not have a right to them. Even if I did own my natural assets in a proprietorial way, a further argument would be needed to extend ownership to whatever I produced by exercising them. Owning my natural assets is not the same as owning the results of using them. Since Nozick fails to produce a supplementary argument to justify this crucial but elusive transition, no reason has been given for accepting that I have an absolute and inviolable right to profit from my natural assets.

2. The Lockean proviso

Nozick's further argument to justify exclusive property rights by invoking the Lockean proviso for legitimate acquisition also fails (1974, p. 178). He takes it that private acquisition of unowned resources is legitimate as long as no-one is worse off than they would have been without private appropriation. This argument provides a justification for unrestricted capitalism. 'I believe that the operation of a market system will not actually run afoul of the Lockean proviso' (1974, p. 182). He uses 'familiar social considerations' regarding capitalism's productivity and efficiency and the beneficial trickle-down effects of private ownership to support his notion that the market system is compatible with the Lockean proviso (1974, p. 177). But two points are immediately obvious: one is what Lukes (1978a, p. 197) calls 'extraordinary sociological and political naivety' of Nozick's faith in the advantages of capitalism.

The second is that the assertion that no-one is worse off than they would have been without private property will not do to legitimize it. This is because private appropriation and no appropriation at all are not the only conceivable states of affairs.

There are other social arrangements where, arguably, people would be better off than they would be either under capitalism or in the state of nature. For instance, Cohen (1986) argues they could be better off in systems which equalize chances of appropriation so that each person has equal veto over disposable land or in a system where the land is divided equally or collectively owned. In all these systems people would be better off in the sense that they would have more access to the resources necessary to shape their lives and to lead meaningful lives than they are under a system which licenses absolute property rights to unequal shares of the external world.

3. Kantian basis for rights

Considering the way in which people would be better off in different social and economic systems dovetails into criticism of Nozick's attempt to provide a moral basis for the existence of rights in the Kantian notion of respect for persons as ends-in-themselves. As many critics of Nozick have argued, the Kantian principle does not justify absolute property rights, but could justify rights to a more equitable share of resources and opportunities. As we have seen, for Nozick, the Kantian notion that individuals should be treated as ends-in-themselves respects the separateness of persons, the idea that individuals shape own lives according to their own conception of the good, and recognizes the intrinsic value of leading a meaningful life. This is, according to Nozick, the moral basis for the defence of a set of Lockean negative rights. However, the injunction to treat people as ends-in-themselves can be interpreted as requiring more than the right not to be interfered with in achieving those ends.

Plant (1991) argues that it could legitimate the right to the resources necessary to facilitate achieving those ends. Similarly, Nagel (1982) argues that the desirability of leading a life in accordance with one's own conception of the good cannot imply the absolute right of non-interference. Promoting self-determination requires access to resources as well as negative rights. Again, Scheffler (1982) claims that if the moral basis of rights lies in the value of leading a meaningful life, then this implies that there is also a right to a sufficient share of all the distributive goods and necessary material conditions whose enjoyment is necessary to have a reasonable chance of living a meaningful life. The promotion of these positive rights does not ignore the separateness of persons, but, rather, acknowledges it by ensuring that each individual has the resources they need. Moreover, the provision for these needs by taxation is not an infringement of the Kantian principle that people should be treated as ends-in-themselves for it does not violate anyone's right, nor does it restrict anyone's ability to shape their own lives or to lead meaningful lives. Lockean–Nozickean negative rights deny people rights to welfare and to the resources necessary to confirm their separate existence by achieving their ends, shaping their own lives and so give meaning to them.

4. Liberty and patterns

Nozick's entitlement theory, however, argued against patterned principles of distribution because they required restrictions on personal liberty and continual interference in people's lives. This argument presupposes that any state intervention to preserve or restore patterns is wrong because it is a violation of individual rights. But this argument only applies if there are overriding and absolute individual rights of private ownership and this has not been established. If there are no such rights, then restrictions to maintain patterns are not infringements of them. If justice is more than protecting property rights, then infringements may not only be justified, but be required by justice. Nozick believes that private property rights are required to protect personal liberty. But this is only so if freedom is specifically and simply the absence of interference to acquire and transfer property. If freedom is something more than this, and is concerned with one's ability to shape one's own life and achieve one's ends and purposes, then it is clear how rights to private property actually restrict rather than preserve freedom. Private property rights are, after all, an individual's right to exclude others from the use or benefit of the owned thing. They restrict non-owner's access to the resources owned by others. This denies them the opportunity to pursue their own projects and to lead meaningful lives. For this, they need access to resources which necessitates redistribution.

5. Impracticality

It is really difficult to see how *Anarchy, State and Utopia* could achieve such critical acclaim when Nozick provides no adequate foundation for the absolute and inviolable nature of the rights he defends and therefore no case against redistribution. This is even more puzzling when the hopeless impracticality of achieving justice as entitlement is considered. According to Nozick's theory of justice, presently existing capitalism is undoubtedly unjust, since it was surely built on past violations of the principle of justice in acquisition and present violations of the principle of justice in transfer in the form of taxation. Nozick glosses over the following practical problems:

- How we could have the historical information required to judge whether a particular distribution is just.
- How to apply the principle of just acquisition in a modern industrial society.
- How to separate out individual contributions to a total social product in order to match them with property rights.
- How to control the minimal state and monitor just institutions.
- How to apply the principle of rectification.
- How to make the transition to a society where justice as entitlement can operate.

The theory is little more than manipulative rhetoric. The chief function this serves is to provide justifications for those who would defend the privileges of the rich and cutbacks in public provision for the poor by using soundbites about rights and the entitlements of each individual. Nozick's theory aids attempts to make economic and social inequality not only acceptable but also morally defensible.

Conclusion

This chapter has examined liberal theories of justice which do not claim that desert is the criterion for just distribution. Utilitarianism was considered first in order to set the scene for the responses by Rawls, Dworkin and Nozick. The relevant criticism of utilitarianism for the purposes of understanding these alternative theories of justice is that utilitarianism is incompatible with respect for the individual rights that are to be secured by justice. Utilitarianism is an aggregate theory which provides no criteria for the just distribution of benefits and burdens that are not reducible to their useful effects. As a result, individual rights may be overriden if doing so produces beneficial effects.

Rawls, Dworkin and Nozick all defend different sets of individual rights which must be protected against utilitarian calculation and which take priority over other social goods. Rawls's theory is an attempt to defend the liberties of equal citizenship, which are not subject to political bargaining or the calculus of social interests. Dworkin argues that only a recognition of individual rights can prevent people from being treated as means to ends. He aims to provide a modified form of utilitarianism, where rights have priority over and act as restraints on policies aimed at the overall good. Nozick defends a set of near-absolute Lockean rights, which he regards as so fundamental that there is no case for infringing them whatever the good consequences of doing so.

The theories of justice defended by each of these theorists are radically different and encompass both ends of the liberal spectrum. Rawls and Dworkin advocate versions of welfare liberalism and Nozick defends a narrow set of property rights in the tradition of classical seventeenth-century liberalism and present-day libertarianism. However, they have in common a concern to prioritize individual rights over considerations of utility. The importance they attach to the different rights they defend is derived from the liberal principle of respect for persons, from Kant's injunction that justice requires that individuals be treated as ends-in-themselves and never as means to ends. The next chapter will take up the issue of respect for persons as ends-in-themselves in relation to arguments for both civil and political rights and social and economic rights.

5

Rights

Natural Rights

The continuing importance of rights in the liberal tradition received its first expression in Locke's writings towards the end of the seventeenth century. In the *Second Treatise*, Locke expounded a doctrine of natural rights grounded in natural law. Natural laws were thought to be an expression of God's will implanted in our reasoning which, in principle, were discoverable by all human beings. According to Locke, God willed the peace and preservation of all mankind. Consequently, God's natural law dictated that 'no-one ought to harm another in his life, liberty or possessions'. Under natural law each individual has a natural right to life, liberty and property and a natural duty to respect the same rights of others.

Locke's starting-point was the state of nature, a mythical state prior to the formation of civil society. In the state of nature individuals have equal freedom. No-one is by nature subordinate to the authority or will of another, and everyone has an equal right to do what is necessary to protect their own and other's rights and to punish transgressors of them. However, the state of nature is characterized by conflict arising from the exercise of natural rights. Individuals are biased in their own interests and are not prepared to accept the laws of nature as binding in their own particular cases or pay attention to the claims of others. In the state of nature, there is no impartial arbiter, and no authority to support and execute judgements when disputes arise. To avoid conflict and uncertainty, men agree to establish a political community and move from the state of nature to civil society. By means of a social contract, they agree unanimously to pool their natural powers so they can act together to uphold each other's rights. Trust is placed in political authority to enact the law of nature which involves protection of rights to life, liberty and property. The people hand over legislative and executive power to an authority in order to ensure the impartial protection and enforcement of natural rights lacking in the state of nature. Natural rights constrain all individuals, they are universal and inalienable claims that individuals have against each other and the state.

Several political and moral conclusions can be drawn from Locke's doctrine of natural rights, and these have remained stable features of liberal thought. First, is the linking of individual liberty and the right to private property which is still a persistent liberal claim. The others involve the legitimacy, role and limits of government. Government can only be established by consent. For Locke, since men enjoy equal rights under the laws of nature, no-one can transfer their rights to the arbitrary power of another or come under political authority without their consent. The role and responsibility of government are derived from and limited by natural rights. The function of government is the maintenance, protection and enforcement of rights. Any more extensive state is not morally justified. Natural rights set limits to the authority of government and, thus, if government violates individual's rights, then it loses claims to obedience and can be legitimately overthrown. Disobedience, resistance or revolution are justified when government violates natural rights or exceeds the limits of its authority.

The political impact and consequences of Locke's doctrine of natural rights are re-stated in the American Declaration of Independence (1776), which asserts each man's inalienable right to life, liberty and the pursuit of happiness, identifies the task of government as securing these rights and rests legitimate authority on consent of the governed and on its protection of rights. Paine in The Rights of Man draws on this and on the similar claims of the French Declaration of the Rights of Man and of Citizens (1789) in relation to the 'natural and unprescribable rights of man ... liberty, property, security and resistance of oppression', the preservation of which is the end of all political institutions (Paine, 1969, p. 166).

For Locke, the American and French revolutionaries and the doctrine of natural rights countered ideas of natural subordination and were used as a protest against established government, monarchical absolutism and paternalistic rule. In the modern liberal tradition, the notion of individual or specifically human rights has continuities with the natural rights tradition in so far as these are thought to be moral claims which an individual possesses by virtue of some human characteristic and which is independent of laws, customs or convention. Their primary function is to define the claim that the inviolability of persons gives rise to rights which government must protect and respect. Their advocacy has been used to counter utilitarian arguments and to delineate the ways in which people ought to be treated, regardless of utility.

However, the original notion of natural inalienable rights underpinned by a pre-social natural law was not without criticism in the eighteenth and nineteenth centuries. Thinkers as diverse as Burke, Bentham and Marx attacked the incoherence of the belief in the existence of pre-social rights and laws. For Burke, rights were not natural, but the product of convention and custom. Bentham challenged the notion of natural rights as a legal positivist and as a utilitarian. Natural rights were nothing more than 'nonsense on stilts', 'anarchical fallacies, metaphysical entities which could not be shown to exist'. There could be no pre-institutional or pre-social rights existing in the fictional state of nature. Rights were only institutional arrangements to guarantee the legal protection of rights. Such rights could be established only after the creation of society. No rights prior to or independent of their embodiment in positive law could be said to exist.

As a utilitarian, Bentham rejected the absolute claims of rights, as enforcing such claims could override the general happiness. Although Mill and subsequent rule-utilitarians have tried to reconcile individual rights with utilitarianism, these attempts cannot succeed unless protecting individual rights and promoting aggregate benefit are always compatible aims. Even if there are often utilitarian reasons for respecting rights, these reasons do not have the equivalent moral force that a theory of rights is designed to provide, since they cannot admit considerations independent of utility to back them, nor can they exclude utilitarian reasons for abridging them.

Marx also challenged the notion of natural rights in various ways. Doctrines of natural rights presuppose a bourgeois individualist model of human beings as isolated, self-sufficient, self-interested independent individuals abstracted from and outside of society. As such, they deny the social nature of human beings and the communal nature of human existence. They degrade 'the sphere in which man functions as a species-being' (Marx, 1978, p. 43). They license the pursuit of private gain, egoism and exploitation. Furthermore, the concept of natural rights is incoherent, since the existence and exercise of rights presuppose a social order and shared norms which are inconsistent with the state of nature as a theoretical starting-point. For Marx, the notion of natural rights possessed by all men was an ideological device to disguise ruling-class interests as universal interests. It created the illusion of equality between individuals by establishing formal equal rights and by obscuring the significance of social and economic inequalities outside the narrow political and legal sphere.

Human Rights

Twentieth-century declarations of human rights parallel earlier assertions of natural rights in that they seek to define the inviolability of persons against considerations of utility and the moral entitlement that each individual is owed by virtue of their natural capacities as human beings. The United Nations Declaration of Human Rights (1948) and the subsequent United Nations Convention of Economic, Social and Cultural Rights and the European Convention for the Protection of Human Rights and Fundamental Freedoms, identify human rights as the traditional negative rights which give rise to civil and political liberties – the right to life, liberty and property, equality before the law, the right to a fair trial, freedom of religion, speech and assembly, the right to participation in government and the absolute right not to be tortured. In addition to this, they endorse rights to social and economic goods, such as education, work, social security, rest, leisure, an adequate standard of living, health and well-being.

The traditional civil and political rights impose negative duties on individuals and the state to refrain from interfering with the rights of others. The social and economic rights directed towards providing minimum standards of living for each person assert claims on the fulfilment of basic human needs. They correlate with positive duties to provide for basic needs. It has often been disputed as to whether social and economic rights can be properly regarded as human rights or whether they are simply desirable ideals. Because of scarcity, it may be practically impossible for anyone to discharge the appropriate duties and these positive rights, and unlike negative rights, claims are not correlated with duties that can be assigned to any particular person.

However, before examining explicit criticisms of the status of social and economic rights, it is first necessary to defend the concept of these rights as human rights. It will be argued that both political and legal rights, on the one hand, and social and economic rights, on the other, can be defended as human rights since they both rest on the same moral foundation.

In the twentieth century, liberals have abandoned the natural law framework as a basis for natural rights and have instead adopted a Kantian justification for human rights claims. The Kantian conception of human beings as ends-in-themselves and therefore as bearers of rights provides the background for the argument for various justifications of different sets of rights as human rights. These rights are grounded in respect for human agency or autonomy and rest on conceptions of human beings as capable of choosing and pursuing their own projects, ends and values. Hart's classic statement of the equal right of all men to be free is defended as a natural right because it is one we all have if we are human beings capable of choice (Hart, 1955, pp. 189–91). Claims to particular rights are derived from this universal right to liberty held equally by all, to be constrained only if circumstances are consistent with the general principle of the equal right of all to be free.

Rawls's first principle of the equal right to liberty which has lexical priority over other rights similarly identifies a set of rights which allow individuals to pursue their own ends subject to a similar system of liberty for all. The liberal conception of individuals as rational autonomous choosers is a presupposition of these arguments. Rights to equal freedom are the means by which diverse individuals can pursue their own good in their own way. But whether civil and political and/or social and economic rights can be justified on these grounds reflects the differences between negative and positive conceptions of liberty. If freedom is simply the absence of deliberate interference, then, like Nozick, we could argue that freedom can be protected by a set of negative rights. We could defend the traditional civil and political liberties as human rights. If, however, we defend a positive conception of liberty, then we will argue that freedom involves not just absence of interference but the capacities, resources, and opportunities to enable individuals to act to achieve their ends and purposes, and this will be the basis for the justification of social and economic rights as human rights.

For example, Gewirth (1987) argues that freedom as the capacity for rational action in pursuit of ends, whatever they may be, requires positive rights to economic resources and aid. Gewirth's argument for negative and positive rights begins with liberal assumptions about individuals as moral agents with a capacity for choosing their own values and acting upon them. He claims that morality and rights are connected with human action, which itself is the general context of all morality and practice. Gewirth argues that rights are crucial to all actions because human rights have as their object the necessary conditions of action and of successful action in general.

Human rights are justified requirements that all persons have as their due, as what they are entitled to, as what they can justifiably demand that all persons respect either by non-interference or, in certain circumstances, by positive assistance. And the context of these goods are the necessary conditions of action and successful action in general. Thus, what human rights require is that the necessary goods not be received or interfered with by any persons, or groups, and also, in certain circumstances, that the necessary goods be provided for all persons who cannot obtain them by their own efforts. (Gewirth, 1987, pp. 59–60)

Gewirth argues that what is at issue here is the fulfilment of needs, the fulfilment of the needs of action which are the central concern of morality. He identifies freedom and well-being as the generic features and necessary conditions of action. Gewirth explains:

Freedom is the procedural feature of action; it consists in controlling one's behaviour by one's enforced choice while having relevant knowledge of the circumstances, and well-being ... is the substantive generic features of action; it consists in having the purpose-related general abilities and conditions that are required either for being able to act at all or for having general chances of success in achieving the purposes for which one acts. The components of such well-being thus fall into a hierarchy of goods, ranging from life and physical integrity to self-esteem and education. (Gewirth, 1987, p. 61)

Gewirth proposes that the concept of universal human rights is crucial to all action and therefore must be accepted in this context because it is the necessary condition of successful action in general. Without this, people either cannot act at all or cannot act with any general expectation of achieving their purposes.

Gewirth then claims that rights are based on needs which relate to capacities for moral agency. Freedom and well-being are generic rights in that they are rights to the necessary condition of acting at all. Each person has a positive and negative right to freedom and well-being which are justified claims to the carrying out of correlative, positive and negative duties. If freedom and well-being are necessary conditions of action, then we are committed to recognizing them as necessary conditions for every agent. According to Gewirth, the general moral principle, the 'Principle of Generic Consistency', requires that every agent act in accordance with the generic rights of their recipients as well as themselves. The recognition that their own agency requires freedom and well-being commits them to the view that others do too.

Gewirth establishes positive rights by a parallel argument. Each person has positive rights to freedom and well-being – the rights to assistance as well as the right of non-interference. Both negative and positive rights are entailed by the same considerations. They are needed as necessary conditions of action. Thus, it could be said that negative and positive rights, political, civil and socio-economic rights can be justified by appeal to what is necessary for human beings to act at all to achieve their own ends and purposes, whatever these may be.

The point of departure for those who defend each set of rights as human rights is the difference between what each believes is necessary to do this. Defenders of civil and political rights seem to believe that only negative rights of non-interference are required to act to achieve one's own goals. Defenders of social and economic rights give an account of the requirement for purposive and successful action in terms of fundamental human needs. The necessary conditions of action are what constitute the fundamental needs of every actual or prospective agent. These needs must be satisfied if any and each individual is to act to achieve their goals, and meeting these goals requires more than the absence of interference, but also requires the provision of resources and opportunities, that is, freedom involves positive conditions which are reflected in claims for positive rights and duties.

However, there are notorious difficulties in defining and defending a list of basic human needs which would reflect the components of Gewirth's notion of 'well-being' and these will be taken up in Chapter 8. However, for the moment, let us assume it is uncontentious to say that to act successfully to achieve any goal, human beings must at least survive since this is a necessary condition of any activity. Minimal survival needs, on this view, would generate at least positive rights to clean air and water, adequate food, clothing and shelter, basic health care and education and the provision of these where individuals or groups cannot provide for themselves. These are essential if human beings are to act to acquire any ends or values and they are universal in that they apply to all human agents at all times and places, even though the historically and culturally specific forms these needs take differ. Thus, it would seem that defending socio-economic rights as human rights depends on the validity of the claim that human beings have fundamental basic and universal needs as requirements for action and upon arguments which support what these requirements are. However, even if those who oppose socio-economic rights accepted these arguments, their criticisms about the status of positive rights would still need to be addressed.

Enforceability

Opponents of positive rights begin from the premise that the status of rights is closely linked to whether or not they can be enforced. Since rights logically imply reciprocal duties to observe them, every individual right creates a duty for other individuals and/or the state to respect them. But if an individual or the state has a duty to respect rights, then it must be the case that they are able to do so. 'Ought' implies 'can' and individuals or governments are not responsible for things they are unable to do in practical terms.

It is argued that we are always able to carry out our duty to respect negative rights. Cranston (1973) argues that negative rights, because they are injunctions not to interfere, only require restraint and because of this they can be universally applied and can generate perfect duties for everyone. Fried (1978) similarly argues it is always possible not to do something. We cannot run out of not harming one another, not lying to each other or leaving each other alone. In contrast to this, positive rights to resources require us to do something and this is not always possible because of scarcity. Implementing positive rights would be costly and impractical, therefore they cannot be universally upheld. Negative rights have costless duties which are always capable of being implemented and because of this they are categorical and universal and positive rights are not.

In answer to this it is often pointed out that duties to respect negative rights cannot be implemented by leaving people alone or without incurring costs. In order to enforce the duty of forbearance, a wide range of positive actions are needed. A whole array of institutions, personnel, practices and procedures are required to ensure such rights are respected. Government institutions, penal systems, courts, prisons, judges, police, lawyers, taxation policies, etc. are all involved in attempts to protect individual rights and to prevent and punish violations of them. Fried replies that this type of argument misses the point that negative rights can be satisfied simply by not interfering with their exercise:

My right to freedom of speech is not a right to be heard, much less a right to have my views broadcast and applauded. If my right implied these things, then certainly it would be equivalent to a positive right, and would run up against the limits of scarcity ... But what if others would deprive me of my freedom of speech – a hostile mob for instance? Surely it is the case that in asking for protection against the mob I make an affirmative claim upon the scarce resources of the community. But this objection misses the point too, for the fact that I have a right to freedom of speech against the government does not also mean that I have a right that the government protect any exercise of that right. (Fried, 1978, pp. 110–11)

However, if anything misses the point, surely it is this argument. There is no point having negative rights unless they can be exercised, protected and enforced. It is absurd to suggest that some rights can be satisfied by being left alone and that corresponding duties only involve doing nothing to violate them. Rights to freedom of speech are not simply claims to be left alone but claims to have what is necessary to protect and exercise that right. If having a right does not imply duties to provide the conditions which make it effective, then there is no value in having the right in the first place. Shue challenges the alleged distinction between negative and positive rights on these grounds.

The common notion that *rights* can be divided into rights to forbearance (so-called negative rights), as if some rights have correlative duties only to avoid depriving, and rights to aid (so-called positive rights), as if some rights have correlative duties only to aid, is thoroughly misguided. (Shue, 1980, p. 53)

This is because any kind of right requires the performance of multiple kinds of duties to make them effective. Shue argues that the useful distinctions are between duties, not between rights. The fulfilment of any right requires duties of forbearance, protection and aid, that is:

With every basic right, three types of duty correlate:
1. Duties to *avoid* depriving
2. Duties to *prevent* from deprivation
3. Duties to *aid* the deprived. (Shue, 1980, p. 52)

Consequently, the notion that political and civil rights only have correlate duties to avoid infringement is seriously misleading. Civil, political and economic rights require three kinds of duties which must be performed if the basic right is to be respected. This means that negative and positive rights cannot be distinguished on the grounds that only the former are universal and categorical because they involve costless duties. All sets of rights have corresponding negative and positive duties which involve costs and problems of implementation. If this is the case, then it can be seen that respecting economic rights is not necessarily more expensive, difficult, burdensome or impractical than implementing civil and political rights.

Duties to aid those in need would not be burdensome if duties to avoid and protect from deprivation were discharged. Strategies to make economic rights effective need not depend on massive transfers of resources or take the form of aid at all. They could depend on designing institutions and policies concerned with prevention, self-help and self-reliance. Where the provision of resources is necessary to make economic rights effective, there is no reason to think that this would be more expensive than guaranteeing the actual performance of so-called negative duties.

The costs of providing for defence and law and order far outweigh the costs of providing for basic subsistence needs. The money required to provide adequate food, water, education, health and housing for everyone in the world was estimated as $17 billion a year in 1973. This figure was approximately the amount the world spent on arms every two weeks at that time. Global military spending, despite its recent decline, still equals the combined income of half of humanity each year (*Human Development Report*, UN, 1994). Nor is providing for basic needs impractical. Cranston (1973, pp. 66–70) argues that the first test for the authenticity of a human right is practicability. But the UN report shows that, in practical terms, essential human needs could be met in all nations by the turn of the century. The most important global targets of universal access to basic education, primary health care for all, clean drinking water and sanitation, the elimination of serious malnutrition and the halving of moderate malnutrition, family planning for all who want it, and the extension of credit shares to ensure self-employment opportunities and sustainable livelihoods are easily manageable by restricting priorities in existing budgets.

Basic needs provision is only impractical, if impractical means incompatible with capital transfers of wealth, the existence of private property and the free market. That is, if present arrangements for material production, distribution and consumption are beyond challenge or change. The barriers to their satisfaction are chiefly political. Leontief's UN study makes this clear:

The principal limits to sustained economic growth and accelerated development are political, social and institutional in character rather than physical. No insurmountable physical barriers exist within the twentieth century to the accelerated development of the developing regions; the most pressing problem of feeding the increasing population of the developing regions can be solved by bringing under cultivation large areas of currently unexploited arable land and by doubling and trebling land productivity (in the developing countries). Both tasks are technically feasible but are contingent on drastic measures of public policy favourable to such development and on social and institutional changes in the developing countries. (Leontief *et al.*, 1977, pp. 10–11)

These considerations suggest that civil, political and economic rights involve both negative and positive duties, that neither are costless and that in principle there are sufficient resources to make their protection a practical possibility.

Correlative duties

Criticisms of socio-economic rights that try to uphold the distinction between negative and positive rights all trade on the assumption that negative rights only involve the duty of forbearance, abstaining from action or interference. Consequently, it is argued in the case of negative rights, the corresponding duty is clear and precise, whereas positive rights involve indefinite and open-ended duties. If there is a positive right to the resources necessary for autonomy and well-being, or simply for survival, then it is unclear how extensive the duty to provide should be. So, whereas the right to freedom of speech involves not only a costless but also a clear duty to refrain from interference, the duty to provide the means for survival or well-being is not only impractical, but there is no limit on what this would involve.

It is not possible to specify the level of provision necessary to satisfy basic survival or subsistence needs. So corresponding duties will be either indefinite and infinitely expandable or their specification and cut-off point will be arbitrary. However, if it is accepted that negative rights as well as positive rights imply both negative and positive duties if they are to be respected, then the objection to economic rights based on their imprecision or arbitrariness cannot hold. The same objection applies to the resources needed to protect and enforce civil and political rights. For example, the amount of criminal legislation, the extent of police powers, the kinds of positive actions, the range of social policies necessary to reduce theft, fraud, force, assault, rape and murder are unspecifiable and potentially limitless, relative to time and place and to the extent of the problem to be solved. However, this imprecision in the cases of both civil and economic rights does not mean that some appropriate and non-arbitrary standard of provision for the protection of both cannot be found or implemented.

Negative Responsibility

However, the argument that negative rights impose definite and clear duties of forbearance is also used by critics of subsistence or welfare rights to claim that, morally speaking, we only have negative duties. Our moral responsibilities only involve the negative duty to avoid harm and not the positive duty to provide aid. This is because we can only be held responsible for and thus be blamed for the harm we actually bring about. Therefore, we only have negative duties to refrain from action, to do nothing that violates rights and this gives us clear responsibilities. Positive rights require us to act, to do something and this extends our moral responsibilities too far. We cannot be held responsible for all the good that we could do, for all the things that we allow or fail to prevent. Therefore, there can only be negative rights with corresponding negative duties.

This argument for the moral distinction between negative and positive duties depends on the moral significance of the difference between an action and an omission of action. Those who claim we only have negative duties support the acts and omissions doctrine. This states that a failure to perform an action with certain foreseen consequences is morally less bad than to perform a different action which has identical foreseen consequences. That it is worse to kill someone than to allow them to die. We have a strict negative duty to avoid killing but we do not have a strict positive duty to provide them with resources which will prevent their death. Phillipa Foot's famous example summarizes the force of the acts and omissions doctrine.

Most of us will allow people to die of starvation in India and Africa and there is surely something wrong with us that we do; it would be nonsense, however, to pretend that it is only in law that we make a distinction between allowing people in the underdeveloped countries to die of starvation and sending them poisoned food. (Foot, 1967, p. 11)

Those who reject the acts and omissions doctrine want to show that we are morally responsible for omissions that cause harm, suffering and death, if there were actions which could have been taken which would have prevented the harm occurring. Of course, we cannot be responsible for omissions which are the result of ignorance or where there was no opportunity to intervene, but it is plausible to argue that we are morally responsible for the harmful consequences of our omissions when we could foresee their effects and when acting would have made a difference to the outcome.

To accept that the harmful consequences of omissions are equal to the equivalent harmful consequences of acts, it is necessary to show the causal efficacy of the omission in question. Harris (1980, Ch.3) argues that when we realize that harm could be prevented, we are entitled to see failure to prevent it as a cause. Honderich (1980, p. 68) also tries to show the causal connection between an omission and its consequences. An act, he says, in almost every instance would be a necessary condition in a given situation for the result to occur. Sending poisoned food would be a necessary condition in a certain situation for death to result, i.e., the death would not have occurred without the parcel. The act was part of the causal circumstances which was sufficient for the death.

Honderich says this also applies to the corresponding omission: buying a chaise longue for £500 means that he omitted to send money to Oxfam. The omission is seen by him as part of the causal circumstances sufficient for the deaths to result. Given this, he concludes, it is mistaken to think that sending poisoned food is more efficacious, more of a cause than not sending money to Oxfam. He notes, of course, that the causal circumstances are different. In the case of the act they are shorter and simpler and in the case of the omission many other people may be part of the causal circumstances, but this does not lessen the individual's responsibility for any particular omission.

Where a failure to act causes harm, suffering and death and this could have been foreseen and prevented, it is plausible to argue that we have a positive duty to act to avoid harm, just as we have a negative duty not to act to cause harm. The distinction between acts and omissions, negative and positive duties, cannot be based on the view that acts cause more harm, so we only have negative duties to refrain from them. If I fail to send starving people money, they will die just as surely as if I send them poisoned food and so, for this reason, it could be said that I have a positive duty to aid them.

In reply to this, it is often argued that acts are worse than omissions because they are intentional. Sending someone poisoned food is worse than not providing people with resources because omissions are not conscious or deliberate. For example, Fried (1978, p. 114) argues that the alleged right not to be deprived of a decent diet is only infringed, if I *intentionally* deprive you of a decent diet (either as my means or as my end). This is difficult to understand. If you are deprived of food, because I don't care about you or because I am indifferent to your plight, or because I am negligent or lazy, or because I prefer to protect my own interests, how can this mean that your starving to death as a result is not my fault, nothing to do with me? If you have a right to food and I have a duty to provide it if I can, then my motives for not discharging that duty are irrelevant to whether or not it is my duty and whether or not your right has been infringed.

The criterion of intention cannot provide support for the view that, morally speaking, harmful acts are worse than equally harmful omissions. We are equally morally responsible for acts and omissions if we have the power to prevent the effect in question. Our intentions are irrelevant to our responsibility to prevent the effect and irrelevant to the consequences of an action or inaction. Plant sums this up thus:

If killing and allowing to die are, in certain circumstances, morally equivalent then these acts and omissions cannot be correlated with rights in terms of forbearance and the provision of resources, because the failure to provide resources for life could then be regarded as morally equivalent to killing and thus an infringement of the right to life. A more general way of putting the point is this. If the fundamental duty implied by a negative right is the duty not to harm, then this may well imply positive duties because the failure to act (or forbear) can itself produce harm, and indeed a degree of harm which is morally equivalent to the intentional infliction of harm ... If this argument is accepted then it is difficult to maintain the idea that infringing a right is always an intentional action and that the right can always be respected by the appropriate form of forbearance. (Plant, 1991, pp. 279–80)

Limitless obligations and the problems of responsibility

One of the principal objections to the abandoning of the acts and omissions doctrine and accepting that we are morally responsible for the harmful consequences of failures to act, is that this would place an intolerable burden on people. They would have limitless obligations because the potential for not acting is endless. They would have moral responsibilities to unspecified others to remedy all the ills in the world.

Glover's, Harris's and Honderich's rejection of the acts and omissions doctrine certainly leaves them facing the problems of the boundaries of personal obligations. On their analysis, the £500 Honderich spent on his chaise longue 'would have made the difference', therefore, he was responsible for the plight of starving people. Both Glover and Harris have a problem with the individual 'cut-off' point. Harris answers this rather abstractly by saying that we can be 'rescued' from unlimited responsibility by the effect it would have on our own and our societies' moral consciousness. Glover says:

The moral approach advocated here does not commit us, absurdly, to remedying all the evil in the world. It does not even commit us to spending our whole time trying to save lives. What we should do is work out what things are most important and then try to see where we ourselves have a contribution to make ... As well as recognizing the variety of ways in which people can contribute to the world, it is also necessary to accept the desirabilities of people protecting things that are worthwhile in their own lives as well. This is partly because Yeats was right that too long a sacrifice makes a stone of the heart ... But it is also partly because someone's own worthwhile life is a good thing in itself, not merely an instrument for creating benefits for others. (Glover, 1977, p. 105)

What omissions are permissible then? Glover suggests as a 'rule of thumb' a compromise between what we value in our own lives and the death and starvation of others. After showing us how far our moral responsibility extends by providing us with reasons for rejecting the acts and omissions doctrine, Glover then abandons any notion of strict duties by substituting 'rules of thumb'. Harris, too, has a problem when he recognizes that human beings, though they can be made to feel guilty, are not saints. He says that a consequence of the boundlessness of our task is the gulf between our beliefs and our intentions to act upon them. We are like someone who sincerely wants to give up smoking but who knows he never will. We have sincere beliefs but we have acquired them too late in life to change our habits. If we cannot act to save our own lives, how much more impossible it will be to change our priorities to help others. However, meanwhile, we can sincerely hold that we ought to prevent literally all the harm we can and recognize that we are not going to find the saintliness to do anywhere near as much as we believe we should (Harris, 1980, pp. 152–3). We may then suffer guilt and remorse, but this is philosophically and morally preferable to the bad faith which comes from seeking ways to show that there is nothing wrong in failing to prevent them.

What ultimately Glover and Harris urge us to do is to change our attitudes, but they lament human fallibility, and consequently, the possibility of acting responsibly to eliminate misery is utopian. Our duty to aid others is a morality for saints and martyrs and we can limit its demands by reference to our private conscience which allows us to decide by 'rules of thumb' how far our responsibility extends.

An alternative approach which avoids the problem of boundless individual obligation and the politics of personal improvement is one which bases its ascription of moral responsibility on the nature of the causal process, not on judgements about the actions or inactions of contextless individual agents. A structural analysis of the socio-economic system (in which acts and omissions occur) is necessary to determine where moral responsibility lies. Otherwise, we end up in the impossible situation of trying to justify where to put the limits on individual self-sacrifice for the good of others.

Structural analysis is necessary to show the various kinds of mechanisms at work in the generation of an event, such as hunger or poverty. It is necessary to identify the source of deprivation, to discover from among all the possible causes, which together with other factors at work (such as individuals failing to contribute) produced the effect in question. For example, when we say that individuals failing to send money to Oxfam are responsible for the harm they could have prevented, the causal efficacy of their omission must be seen in the context of structural causation. That is, it must be seen in the context of socio-economic systems which require charities to meet basic needs but not to send men into space; in the context of governments who use food 'as a weapon', who withhold aid for political and ideological reasons; in the context of nations which control the world's food supply and the huge corporations that dominate the food trade. A statement from the World Food Conference 1975 confirms that:

The goal of agribusiness is not to increase food resources nor to contribute to their equitable distribution, nor yet to adapt existing technologies to the conditions of particular countries. Their goal is first and foremost to increase their markets and commercial outlets, to realise maximum production and cost reduction and to increase their profits. (George, 1976, p. 54)

The effects of agribusiness are less intensive labour farming and therefore loss of jobs, increased prices for basic commodities, the use of soil for cash crops rather than subsistence or self-reliance and ecological imbalance, pollution and depletion of resources. Here, it could be said that the structure of agribusiness causes hunger (see George, 1976; Lappe and Collins, 1977). Attributing causation and thus moral responsibility is a process of asking why, but asking why within a structural analysis of the logic of a system in which an act or an omission occurs. If this analysis is omitted, then the causal theory will have impoverished explanatory power. It will also have the effect of prescribing inadequate measures for deciding what to do to remove this harm, for protecting rights and for assigning duties. The point is, the causes of hunger and poverty and its alleviation are rarely dependent on the actions or inactions of individual agents but are produced by structures and their prevention is dependent on structural change.

Although this approach establishes causal responsibility within a socio-economic structure, the analysis of which reveals the underlying causes of harmful events, it is still relevant to say, as Glover and Harris do, that the individual's effort 'might have made a difference' in any particular case and so they had a moral responsibility to intervene. However, the status of the individual, the nature of their involvement, the degree of their responsibility depends on the sort of impact they might have made on the state of affairs and on their nature and importance. Hence, we can approach the question of moral responsibility in terms of the powers of various social agents – individuals, collectives and governments with various class complexions. For instance, an individual has the power to donate money to pay for food to be delivered to a drought-stricken area, but does not have the power to initiate irrigation schemes which would free that area from the threat of drought; a government may have the power to irrigate, but may lack the power to transform social relations such that its benefits would be shared by the poorest social strata, and so on. The difference between what various social agents have the power to do is not merely quantitative (i.e. governments can afford more money for famine relief than individuals) but qualitative, in that a government may be able to remove not only famine, but the structures that periodically generate famine.

Moral responsibility for an event or structure lies with those agents who have the power to produce or transform that event or structure, and responsibility for the existence of the structure is also responsibility for the events that are generated by that structure. Because structures have explanatory power over individual wills, we are directed to looking for causal factors in social and world structures, rather than in individual intentions, acts and omissions and to looking for solutions in the altering of structures rather than in the altering of individual wills, and to assigning responsibilities in terms of the powers of institutions and people to effect change.

If this structural account is correct, then the effects of a given structure cannot be alleviated by the cumulation of individual efforts, but only by organizing collectively to change that structure. This analysis avoids the problem of the individual's 'cut-off' point as regards responsibilities, since all those things which cannot be changed by individual effort cannot be said to be the individual's responsibility. An individual, *qua* individual is neither the determining cause of poverty, hunger, disease, unemployment or home-lessness, nor has the power to change their effects by individual donations. Therefore, they cannot be held personally responsible for them. However, an individual as a member of a society shares in the collective responsibility to change a structure that generates deprivation and to support policies and institutions that attempt to alleviate it.

The argument that every person has a right to resources to meet their needs does not create a burdensome or saintly duty on the part of any particular individual to meet any particular or every other individual's needs. The argument for rights to resources creates a requirement to institutionalize and allocate the corresponding duties to agents and agencies with the power to meet those needs. It implies that duties to avoid, protect and aid fall on those international and government agencies who have the power to use societal resources and to establish policies and priorities to meet their needs. In so far as the state and inter-state organizations have the power to do so, they are responsible for discharging the multiple duties to implement and institutionalize rights.

If states fail to act and the effects of their omissions are foreseeable and avoidable, then they are morally responsible for the deprivation which results. But since individuals, not as individuals acting alone, but individuals as part of a community have the power to collectively effect outcomes, then individuals will also have negative and positive duties which correlate to rights and they will be morally responsible for the consequences of failure to discharge them. Each individual has a strict negative duty to avoid violating every other individual's right, but, because positive duties to protect and duties to meet needs require the co-operative and coordinated efforts of many individuals, the fulfilment of an individual's positive duties will be mediated through social procedures, policies and collective processes. Therefore, each individual has a strict duty to support collective action to protect rights, to support institutions and policies designed to meet needs and to contribute to the collective endeavour to satisfy needs by working to produce wealth and resources, according to their opportunities, abilities and capacities.

Accepting that we are morally responsible for the harmful consequences of failures to act extends awareness to the range of events which are in principle within human control, and calls attention to the range of events for which human beings must accept responsibility. However, duties to protect and aid do not give rise to limitless and unassignable obligations. Duties fall on those who have the power to discharge them, on governments, intergovernmental agencies and on individuals mediated through collective procedures.

The Relationship between Civil and Political and Economic and Social Rights

In the liberal tradition the function of natural or human rights has been to define and limit the role of government to the protection of a set of civil and political rights. However, it has been argued here that social and economic rights, which require a more extensive state, can also be derived from those morally relevant features of human beings which make them the bearers of rights. Both sets of rights are grounded in the liberal value of respect for human agency or autonomy, in the Kantian conception of human beings as ends-in-themselves capable of choosing and pursuing their own ends and values and acting to achieve them.

Respect for human beings as rational moral agents requires not only freedom from interference which gives rise to negative rights, but also positive freedoms and positive rights. In order to act to achieve any ends, purposes or values, individuals must have the necessary conditions of action – the capacities, opportunities and resources to enable them to fulfil their own ends and realize their own values. Both sets of rights are derived from the same moral foundation, from the necessary conditions for human agency, from the claim that human agency requires more than the absence of interference, because the ability to act is restricted by lack of resources as well as by intentional coercion. Therefore, civil and political, social and economic rights are necessary for autonomy.

If this argument is correct, then the liberal prioritizing of civil and political rights is untenable. The kind of objection to the provision of economic resources offered by Nozick who argues that state-enforced redistribution interferes with individual's negative rights and thus restricts their autonomy, can be turned on its head. First, because the moral foundation on which the defence of negative rights rests, the Kantian respect for persons as ends-in-themselves requires access to social and economic resources. They are essential for autonomy. Second, because the absolute rights to acquire and transfer property which Nozick defends are precisely those that should be interfered with and restricted if autonomy is to be preserved.

The kind of priority Rawls gives to political and civil rights and the social and economic inequality his difference principle allows, undermine the value of freedom from interference civil and political rights were designed to protect. Liberty as equal citizenship is undermined and becomes incompatible with social and economic inequalities. Social and economic deprivation not only affects the individual's ability to make use of these basic liberties, but also prevents the individual effectively pursuing their goals and this diminishes their capacity for agency. Exercise of rights, to formal liberties depends on the fulfilment of social and economic rights, as does the ability to effectively pursue our own goals and values.

Given the crucial importance of social and economic rights for human agency, it is not at all obvious why political and civil rights should have priority over these other rights. The poor, the sick, the illiterate, the unemployed and the homeless are much more likely to give priority to welfare provision, health care, education and jobs than they are to their formal rights to complain, assemble and dissent, and it would be absurd for them not to. Nor would it be absurd for those with an adequate standard of living to prefer increases in social and economic resources and opportunities rather than increases in civil and political liberties. However, the exercise of some political and civil rights is necessary to guarantee rights to resources.

They are necessary to prevent violations of rights, to participate in arrangements for deciding how resources should be used and provided and for organizing resistance to failures to protect and aid. This implies that civil and political rights and social and economic rights are inseparable, interdependent and both necessary for autonomy. It also implies that civil and political rights as they currently stand should be extended so that the purely formal and nominal freedoms they enshrine truly reflect the capacity for autonomy and self-determination.

Conclusion

The primacy of civil and political rights is a distinctive feature of liberal political thought. Even the egalitarian theories of Rawls and Dworkin give priority to these traditional liberal rights. Although it has been argued here that social and economic rights can be derived from the same moral foundation as civil and political rights, it would be misleading to think that liberals, once they realized this, would commit themselves to endorsing all that advocating social and economic rights entail.

The moral foundation for both sets of rights was said to be Kantian respect for individuals as ends-in-themselves. But the individuals who require positive rights to resources if they are to be treated as ends-in-themselves are not the individuals of liberal theory. The individual in liberal theory is asocial, isolated, self-sufficient and self-interested, concerned to protect themselves against the conflicting interests of others. It is not difficult to see, then, why rights in this tradition are viewed as boundaries surrounding the individual to protect them from invasion by predators and why we are thought to have only a general moral duty to avoid harm and no obligation to aid. Your duty is to do nothing to invade my territory, you are not morally required to cross the boundary to aid me if I am in need.

The individual that is the subject of positive rights claims is a social interdependent being with needs that can only be intersubjectively realized; this individual requires for their survival and reproduction the co-operation, help, support and productive efforts of other people. According to this view, rights are not individual claims against isolated, antagonistic, self-interested and competitive individuals. Rights and their corresponding duties to avoid harm, protect and aid are organizational, co-ordinating devices which reflect our inter-relatedness; which express our respect for individuals as ends-in-themselves; which govern institutional arrangements for each individual's positive duty to contribute to and positive right to benefit from the collective and co-operative endeavour to satisfy human needs. To fully endorse social and economic rights, liberals would have to abandon the concept of the individual that is at the heart of their theory.

They would also have to embrace a conception of positive freedom which underpins arguments for social and economic rights and make substantive judgements about what capacities, resources and opportunities are necessary to secure the fulfilment of human ends and purposes. This would go against the grain of the liberal preoccupation with neutrality and the sovereignty of individual desires. Since the argument for social and economic rights is based on identifying objective and universal human needs that must be fulfilled if human beings are to act to achieve their ends, rights are regarded as legitimate claims on governments to satisfy human needs.

This conception of needs-based rights justifies enlarging the role of the state in a way that is obviously incompatible with traditional liberal and libertarian defences of the minimal state. The moral force of social and economic rights requires a more extensive state with powers to enforce these rights and their correlative duties. The functions of such a state are likely to extend beyond the more active role for government in society and the economy justified by welfare liberals. It would not simply provide for minimum subsistence needs to mitigate against the effects of market freedoms. This is because provision for needs and the protection of social and economic rights are incompatible with the maintenance of a capitalist market society.

Although it has been argued that capitalism has the material resources to meet fundamental human needs, they will not be met while capitalism remains the dominant system. With the best will in the world, the capacity of international organizations and national governments to control the use of resources and to implement policies to meet needs are restrained by institutions which regulate international finance and trade. The means necessary to meet needs threatens capital accumulation, property rights and the operation of market forces. These means require a redistribution of property, wealth and resources between countries and within them. They demand a reorganization of the productive process and the set of unequal relations it determines. The survival of capitalism depends on the continuing existence of capital accumulation, differential power relations and economic inequalities. The satisfaction of needs requires equal distribution patterns, the absence of exploitative and oppressive social relations and the reorganization of the processes of production, distribution and consumption so that these are geared to meeting needs rather than profit. It requires an equalization of power, wealth and resources. That is, it requires an improvement in the conditions for meeting needs, rather than simply state provision of either the public goods the market cannot provide or the welfare policies to counteract the effects of these remedial inequalities. For these reasons, though social and economic rights rest on the same moral basis as liberal arguments for civil and political rights, liberals could not defend or implement them without ceasing to be liberals.

6

Women's and Children's Rights

The last chapter discussed the liberal prioritization of civil and political rights and argued that social and economic rights could be derived from the liberal value of autonomy and Kantian respect for individuals as ends-in-themselves. This chapter will examine two specific problems in relation to the liberal concern for autonomy and rights. The first problem centres around the issue of whether or not women should have equal or special rights if they are to be autonomous agents. The second concerns the justification for the denial of rights to children on the grounds of their limited capacity for autonomy.

Equal Rights for Women?

In the history of political thought, the denial of civil and political rights for women and their exclusion from the political realm were justified by arguments and assumptions about the natural differences between the sexes. For example, thinkers as diverse as Aristotle, Aquinas, Rousseau and Hegel believed that these natural differences were reflected in men and women's social role and function. Women, by nature, were unsuited to political and economic activities, their natural place was in the home, their natural role was reproductive and domestic. The achievement of equal civil and political rights for women was in part a consequence of denying these natural differences and applying liberal principles to women. Mill in the *Subjection of Women* (first published in 1869) argued that since women, like men, were equally capable of reason, they should have equal opportunities with men to be free to pursue their own interests. For this they required equal civil and political rights. This kind of reasoning was reflected in nineteenth-century campaigns to end discrimination in marriage, property and civil laws, to achieve equal access to education and employment, and to obtain the rights to vote and hold public office. Early twentieth-century liberal feminists in the 1960s and 1970s pursued the same kind of argument, stressing the similarities between men and women as a basis for demanding equal rights. Distinctions between men and women had too often been used to exclude women from public life and to limit their rights to equal pay and job opportunities.

Emphasizing sameness was a way of combating exclusion and of demonstrating that there were no relevant differences between men and women which justify denying women equal rights. The same anti-discrimination argument has underpinned claims for black, gay and disabled rights. The ground for equal rights being the common humanity which transcends irrelevant and arbitrary differences. Discriminatory laws and policies which result in different treatment for similar individuals unjustly differentiates between people because they justify unequal treatment by reference to irrelevant distinctions.

The liberal emphasis on sameness and formal equality to guarantee equal rights for women has been criticized in much contemporary feminist debate because this position ignores the biological and social differences between men and women which are significant if equal rights are to be of equal worth. Some feminists claim that legal rights and social policies which are blind to gender differences tend to reinforce and perpetuate rather than undermine gender inequalities. Feminists who believe that it is the differences between the sexes rather than their similarities which are important, focus on women's reproductive function and their associated nurturing, co-operating, caring qualities and responsibilities. For some feminists gender differences are innate. They are the result of fundamental differences in male and female nature (Rich, 1977; Griffin, 1984). Others attribute them to the maternal practice of child care (Ruddick, 1980, 1990; Noddings, 1984), and others to the different experience of boys and girls which lead to differences in their moral reasoning (Gilligan, 1982). Because of these differences, the equal treatment with men that is safeguarded by non-discriminatory policies can actually disadvantage women. The right to equal treatment and equal access to the goods society distributes competitively does not take into account the fact that women are handicapped by their role in reproduction, by their domestic and childcare responsibilities and by their special vulnerability to sexual violence and harassment. To support equal rights is to take male values and qualities as the norm and to overlook the fact that these do not fit the different experiences and situations of women. This means that a system of equal treatment is gender-biased in that it is advantageous to men. In effect, it results in positive discrimination in favour of men because

Virtually every quality that distinguishes men from women is already affirmatively compensated in this society. Men's physiology defines most sports. Their needs define auto and health insurance coverage, their socially-designated biographies define workplace expectations and success-ful career patterns. Their perspectives and concerns define quality in scholarship, their experiences and obsessions define merit, their objectifica-tion of life defines art, their military service defines citizenship, their presence defines family, their inability to get along with each other – their wars and rulerships – defines history, their image defines God, and their genitals define sex. For each of their differences from women, what amounts to an affirmative action plan is in effect, otherwise known as the structures and values of American society. (MacKinnon, 1987, p. 36)

The claim that women have equal rights to jobs ignores the fact that paid employment itself is structured in such a way that it favours male norms, behaviour, lifestyles and career patterns. Women have to become like men in order to succeed. They have to take on male qualities and have typically male work patterns and lifestyles free from domestic and childcare responsibilities. Even if this were desirable, for the majority of women, it is simply not possible. The point is that women are not the same as men, nor are they in relevantly similar situations and circumstances. Therefore, many feminists claim that equal rights are not enough to ensure that women play an equal role in society. They argue that women should have special rights because of their special needs and disadvantages. For only by attending to differences 'can enable the inclusion and participation of all groups in political and economic institutions. This implies that instead of formulating rights and rules in universal terms that are blind to difference, some groups sometimes deserve special rights' (Young, 1990, p. 136). For example, women's childbearing capacities give them special needs and special rights – rights to pregnancy and maternity leave, special treatment for nursing mothers and childcare assistance.

Special Rights for Women?

The same/difference debate continues. Many feminists are opposed to emphasizing differences and claiming special rights because of them. First, because by acknowledging women's differences from men, feminists run the risk of these differences being used against them. Instead of providing a foundation for special rights, women's differences can inadvertently justify exclusion and discrimination. Rights to maternity leave can justify financial incentives not to hire women. Consequently, special rights programmes can serve to perpetuate the problems they seek to resolve. Second, because difference approaches reinforce assumptions about the appropriateness and naturalness of traditional gender roles and responsibilities. Special rights for women in relation to childcare provision draws attention away from men's joint responsibility for their children's welfare. Third, because focusing on women's differences from men implies women are the same as each other and this obscures the different needs women have as members of different races or classes. Some feminist writers, therefore, have suggested that the same/difference debate is misguided in the sense that neither the question of equal rights nor special rights addresses the wider issues of female oppression and the social conditions which create and perpetuate it. The problem facing women is classed as one of disadvantage (Rhode, 1992) or dominance (Flax, 1992), not one of difference.

If this is so, then feminists should challenge the social conditions and social relations which disadvantage and oppress women rather than concentrate on claiming either equal or special rights within them. To this end, the demand for some sex-specific rights will sometimes be necessary. When special rights are seen in the context of a strategy for ending disadvantage, domination and oppression, then the problems identified with emphasizing difference outlined above dissolve, in theory at least. First, because arguments for special rights are not based on differences *per se*, but on whether the different treatment which results from them will reduce or reinforce sex-based inequalities (Baachi, 1991, p. 82). If different treatment reinforces inequalities, then it is wrong (Rhode, 1989, Ch. 10). In this vein Young argues:

Most historical discriminations have been wrong not because they distinguished people according to group attributes, but because they aimed at or resulted in formally and explicitly restricting the actions and opportunities of group members. They have been wrong, that is, because they have contributed to and helped enforce oppression. If discrimination serves the purpose of undermining the oppression of a group, it may be not only permitted, but morally required. (Young, 1990, p. 197)

Second, because drawing attention to sexual difference in the context of gender oppression can be used to challenge rather than entrench traditional views of the appropriateness and naturalness of gender roles by questioning the male roles and standards that women are meant to conform to if they are to compete on an equal footing with men. Rhode argues:

So, for example, in employment settings, the issue becomes not whether gender is relevant to the job as currently structured, but how the work place can be restructured to make gender less relevant. What sort of public and private sector initiatives are necessary to avoid penalizing parenthood? What changes in work, changes in working schedules, hiring and promotion criteria, leave policies and childcare options are necessary to reconcile home and family responsibilities? (Rhode, 1992, p. 155)

While special rights because of women's different needs and circumstances may be necessary if women are to have the same opportunities as men within the present set-up, these alone will not alter the social structure and conditions which give rise to these different needs and circumstances. However, the aim of pointing to these differences is to make reproduction, parenthood, home and family responsibilities, issues of public and social responsibility, not issues of women's differences to men. These then become not the basis for demanding special individual rights for women, but reason for altering the social conditions which penalize reproductive activity, which perpetuate the division of labour in private life and which channel women into domestic labour and segregate them in the job market.

Third, awareness of women's differences does not necessarily imply that women are a homogeneous group with identical needs. By acknowledging the diversity of women's circumstances across time, classes, culture and social circumstances, focus on difference in the context of women's oppression can recognize its multiple sources and the varying needs these give rise to. Though as Baachi (1990, p. xi) writes, 'if society catered appropriately for all human needs, men and women included, discussions about women's sameness to, or difference from men would be of little significance'.

The issue of equal or special rights must be seen in the context of women's oppression and strategies to end it. With this in mind, we need to refocus attention from sameness or difference. On the one hand, arguments for sameness and equal treatment have been used to ignore women's special needs and disadvantages and to obscure the inequalities in power and responsibilities between men and women, leaving these unchallenged. On the other hand, demands for equal rights have been used to ensure that arbitrary differences have not justified disadvantaging women in education, employment or before the law. Similarly, emphasizing difference has been used to exclude women and can be used to justify special rights which work to their advantage. However, the point is that the special needs and disadvantages women have, which justify their special rights, though they arise from the realities of women's lives, arise in the first place because of inequalities in women's living and working conditions. They do not arise because of women's intrinsic difference from men.

Different treatment may sometimes be necessary and justified because of these realities, but the point is to change these realities and not to insulate debate about sameness or difference from the need for political, economic and social change. If difference is exaggerated without reference to this wider social context, then attention is diverted from the pre-existing social and economic inequalities and power differences which cause the actual differences between men and women and from the need to change the material conditions which gives rise to them.

Reverse Discrimination

Allied to the argument for special rights for women is the argument for preferential treatment, affirmative action or reverse discrimination in favour of them. Liberal feminists, like those who argue for special rights, have recognized that equal rights or non-discriminatory treatment does not always equalize opportunities for women because of past socially caused inequalities in their capacity to use opportunities and to compete on equal terms with men. Therefore, they advocate forms of preferential treatment as a temporary measure to offset the effects of past discrimination. This same argument is applied to other groups such as ethnic minorities and the disabled who remain disadvantaged even when formal discriminatory barriers are lifted. Reverse discrimination or affirmative action, as it is known in America, covers a wide range of educational and employment policies which aim to increase under-represented groups' access to fields previously dominated by white males. For example, head start and special training programmes for excluded or disadvantaged groups; preferential hiring policies where group members are selected and hired over white males with similar or comparable qualifications; quota systems which earmark a proportion of places or jobs for minority groups and the formerly controversial Labour party policy of imposing women-only shortlists on a constituency.

These policies have stimulated much academic debate on the justice of any form of discrimination, negative or positive (see Cohen, Nagel and Scanlon, 1976), and have met with fierce opposition from liberals. Liberal feminists advocate these policies and in doing so they seem to violate liberal principles of equal treatment, or equality as non-discrimination and the liberal notion of justice as reward according to merit or desert. Traditional liberal arguments against racial and sexual discrimination are derived from the principle of equal treatment. People ought to be treated equally if there are no relevant differences between them. Racism, sexism and denying people rights on the grounds of race or gender are inherently unjust because they involve distinguishing between people and treating them differently on the basis of morally irrelevant characteristics. Therefore, it is argued, if it is unjust to discriminate against someone on the grounds of race or sex, how can it be just to discriminate in favour of them on these same grounds? Furthermore, discrimination in favour of some individuals involves discrimination against others. Reverse discrimination policies violate the rights of other individuals to have equal opportunities to be rewarded according to their ability.

Liberal feminists attempt to respond to these objections by appealing to backward-looking arguments concerned with com-pensating for or rectifying past injustices or by forward-looking arguments that appeal to the supposed good consequences of reverse discrimination policies. Some backward-looking arguments propose that reverse discrimination is a way of compensating for competitive disadvantages caused by past discrimination. Women and minorities who have been treated unfairly in the past should be compensated to make up for past disadvantages and for other sorts of discrimination that they have suffered (Jarvis Thompson, 1973, pp. 364–84). Other backward-looking arguments claim that past discrimination should be reversed, not as a way of compensating for past injustices 'but rather as a way of neutralizing the present competitive disadvantage caused by those past privations and thus as a way of restoring equal access to those goods which society distributes competitively' (Sher, 1979, p. 52).

Boxhill (1993, pp. 333-4) argues that the most plausible version of these backward-looking arguments rely on the principle of equal opportunity. That is, the equal opportunity to compete and to be rewarded according to ability. Although reverse discrimination may seem to violate the right to be rewarded according to ability, it actually increases fair competition by compensating people who have been systematically denied equal opportunities. 'So preferential treatment need not make the competition for desirable places unfair. On the contrary, by compensating women and blacks for being denied equal chances to acquire qualifications, it may make that competition more fair' (Boxhill, 1993, p. 336). In this sense then reverse discrimination is in keeping with the liberal principle of equal opportunities and not a denial of it.

A whole host of other objections, however, have been levelled against reverse discrimination as compensation. Some of these objections revolve around whether reverse discrimination is appropriate compensation for past disadvantages. Sher (1979, p. 48), for example, raises the objection that if the point of reverse discrimination is to compensate a wronged group, it is not clear that proper compensation for that group can be achieved by the preferential hiring of its individual members. This objection is linked to doubts about whether increasing access to educational places or jobs is in fact the appropriate mechanism of redress for disadvantages caused by poverty, poor diet, health and housing, or the effects of traditional gender roles and racial and sexual stereotyping on expectations, confidence and motivation.

The liberal feminist defence against this, and the one that Sher himself gives, is that reverse discrimination is a way of compensating not for the privations themselves, but for the effects of past privations. It is appropriate compensation because it is a substitute for the lost ability to compete on equal terms. However, if the justification for reverse discrimination is compensation for or rectification of past injustice, then surely this could justify compensatory preferential access to the goods and services like food, housing and health care, which would be more effective in restoring the lost ability to compete on equal terms than policies which merely benefit a few in higher education and employment? Moreover, if the basic concern is to equalize opportunities, then we need not only be concerned to compensate for the effects of their previous denial. We should be more concerned with tackling the foundational causes of racial and gender injustice. Reverse discrimination policies, although they may compensate some individuals for past competitive disadvantage, have little effect in tackling the structural causes of group domination and oppression.

Other objections to reverse discrimination concentrate on the fact that these policies only benefit some individuals and not necessarily the right ones. It is argued that if compensation is justified at all, then only those individuals who have actually been directly discriminated against deserve compensation. Reverse discrimination policies tend to benefit the least disadvantaged member of groups, typically favouring middle-class women and members of minority groups who have escaped competitive disadvantages and who therefore do not deserve to be compensated. Witness Labour activists' fear that women-only shortlists will allow a collection of pushy London professional women to seize power in the party (the *Guardian* 14 May 1995). To this, liberal feminists will reply that all women regardless of their class have been adversely affected in the past and the present by discriminatory practices and attitudes and this justifies their reversal.

Arguably it is the case that all women are disadvantaged, and we can agree with the liberal feminist position to the extent that there is no case to be made for abandoning reverse discrimination on the grounds that only some relatively advantaged members of the group benefit. However, surely the fact that the most advantaged benefit and that the majority of the group do not, and could not, are grounds for questioning the adequacy and appropriateness of a policy that is meant to compensate for past injustice?

A related aspect of the problem of who deserves compensation is the position of working-class white men who also have suffered competitive disadvantage. Reverse discrimination policies tend to ignore the disadvantages of class and can lead to discrimination against working-class males in favour of middle-class members of under-represented groups. In principle, however, if the criterion for compensation is past discrimination, then working-class white males could claim that they deserve compensation or reversal of their disadvantage. In practice, however, their theoretical exclusion highlights both the class blindness of liberal theory and the shortcomings of such policies to combat disadvantage on anything but a minor scale.

Forward-looking arguments for reverse discrimination rely on its supposed good consequences in helping to equalize opportunities or by reference to the goal of improving the position of disadvantaged groups in order to create a more fair and just society (Wasserstrom, 1980). It is thought that reverse discrimination will ensure that women and blacks take up important positions and that these new 'role models' will encourage other members of disadvantaged groups to set their sights higher, thereby eliminating a self-perpetuating model of under-achievement. Liberal feminists also defend reverse discrimination on the grounds that it is necessary to counteract both deliberate and unconscious bias against women and black people in education and employment. Reverse discrimination can create equal opportunities by forcing employers and institutions to rethink what counts as qualifications for positions and places. Given that disadvantaged groups may not have had the opportunity to gain traditional formal education, criteria for the job in question need to be translated into abilities, skills, competences and experiences necessary to do the job effectively. Merit need not be measured by formal paper qualifications, but by transferable skills and relevant experience gained from other social activities, responsibilities and life events. Qualifications for certain jobs or places may even include race and gender if the aim is to create a better racial and sexual balance or to promote racial harmony.

Opponents of forward-looking arguments dispute their beneficial effects. They claim that reverse discrimination policies undermine the self-respect of women and ethnic minorities as they patronizingly assume that they cannot compete without special advantages. This populist argument relies on the notion that creating or restoring equal opportunities amounts to providing extra opportunities which are unnecessary. Opponents also argue that reverse discrimination will lead to a lack of excellence, low standards and will undermine efficiency. This argument is underpinned by the questionable assumption that, given equal opportunities, only white males will achieve effectively and efficiently. A more compelling argument and one that is certainly true is that reverse discrimination policies do not have good consequences because they cause resentment, and rather than promote racial and sexual harmony they fuel prejudice and discontent. Consider the furore over

Labour's women-only shortlist policy and the white male backlash in America where the Supreme Court has recently (May 1995) ruled that scholarships offered by Maryland University to black students are unconstitutional, and where hundreds of thousands of people have signed the 'California Civil Rights Initiative' demanding a ban on reverse discrimination. Fears are now rife that this has negative implications for the demise of affirmative action policies in over half of America's universities. Underpinning the resentment caused by such policies is the belief that they violate the right to equal treatment. The Supreme Court ban on reserved places was made on the grounds that the policy violated the Constitution's guarantee of 'equal protection' because the scholarships were limited to African-Americans. And certainly liberal feminists' advocacy of affirmative action seems to challenge the primacy of the liberal principle of equality as non-discrimination.

Liberal feminists, however, argue that reverse discrimination is not discrimination. Discrimination, it is argued, means taking race or gender to be relevant criteria for differentiating between people in contexts where they are not relevant. In the context of achieving equal opportunities, race and gender are relevant criteria, relevant to the aim of creating a fairer society (Radcliffe Richards, 1980, p. 142). What appears to be discrimination is not discrimination at all. Whatever the success of this argument, it still remains the case that the liberal feminist defence of reverse discrimination raises questions about the validity of the liberal idea of equal treatment and the idea of equality as sameness, precisely by showing that justice, even as equal opportunities to compete, sometimes requires different or special treatment.

Resentment is also felt on behalf of the unfairness to the angry white males who feel that they lose out through the practice of reverse discrimination, for without it they would have been selected for places and positions. It is argued that these individuals are not responsible for past injustices and therefore do not deserve to pay for them. The standard and obviously unsuccessful liberal feminist response to this is that individual responsibility or lack of it for past injustices is irrelevant. What is relevant is that unless reverse discrimination is practised, men will benefit more than women or ethnic minorities, and the point of reverse discrimination is to generate equal opportunities with those white men. What appears to be injustice to individuals by violating their right to equal opportunities to achieve according to merit, is not injustice at all, because they are not being deprived of anything they have a right to. They do not have a right to benefit from white male advantages gained from the original unfair discrimination. Nor do they have a right to be judged or rewarded according to traditional criteria or qualifications. The right to be rewarded according to merit or desert may include abilities and qualities necessary to perform the job or to do the course and sex and colour may be relevant qualifications. The liberal defence of reverse discrimination, then, is that it is necessary to guarantee equal opportunities and since disadvantaged groups suffer from past and present discrimination, it is not unjust to white men.

Liberal feminists justify reverse discrimination both as compensation for past injustice and for the good consequences in achieving equal opportunities and creating a more equal society. But even if reverse discrimination policies were widespread and factual claims about its beneficial effects true, reverse discrimination would have the following disadvantages from the point of view of justice. The most disadvantaged members of minority groups are not compensated or substantially affected by these policies. They ignore class disadvantages as grounds for compensation or as symptoms of injustice. And, if we are concerned to equalize opportunities and to rectify racial and gender injustice we should tackle their causes, not just their manifestations. It is not even clear that these policies have effectively rectified the effects of injustice. It is estimated that 12 per cent of Maryland undergraduates are blacks even though they make up only 25 per cent of the population. Only one in seven black Americans have college degrees compared to one in four whites. Despite thirty years of affirmative action in America, the number of blacks enrolled in universities has failed to rise in twenty years (the *Guardian* 14 May 1995). There is even less reason to believe that reverse discrimination could have anything more than a minor effect in altering the basic structure of group inequalities and the issue of white male supremacy. This would require fundamental changes in the structure of the economy, the distribution of benefits and burdens, the social and domestic division of labour, access to goods, services and resources and the reduction of inequalities in property, wealth, salary structures, power, education and employment.

Furthermore, the whole debate about equal opportunities and reverse discrimination is bounded by the liberal framework which accepts the justice of a social system with vastly differential rewards and the justice of the criterion of merit (however merit is defined) for treating people differently. Those opposed to reverse discrimination argue that it offends against equal opportunities to compete according to ability and to achieve scarce rewards. Advocates argue reverse discrimination is justified when these opportunities are unequal in order to award jobs and positions to those who would have been best qualified or the most deserving had they not been discriminated against. In so doing, they justify the inequalities which are the outcome of differential rewards according to merit or desert. Chapter 3 challenged the idea of justice as desert and the differential economic and social rewards that result from it as being fraught with theoretical, practical and moral problems. If these arguments are correct, then as Nagel argues, there is little gained from merely transferring the same system of differential rewards adjusted to include ethnic minorities or women.

If it is unjust to reward people differentially for what certain qualities enable them to do, it is equally unjust whether the distinction is made between a white man and a black man or between two black men, or two white women, or two black women. There is no way of attacking the unjust reward schedules of a meritocratic society (if indeed they are unjust) by attacking their racial or sexual manifestations directly. (Nagel, 1979 p. 99)

Children's Rights

It is generally accepted that women and members of ethnic minorities were discriminated against in the past and denied equal rights because of irrelevant characteristics. Some philosophers see the denial of children's political rights as a form of arbitrary discrimination and unjust exclusion from citizenship, and that in time this exclusion will be seen as absurd as the denial of women's suffrage seems today. In all societies children are denied many of the political rights that adults possess. Harris writes:

In addition to the long list of political and legal disabilities imposed on children – inability to vote, to initiate or defend legal proceedings on their own account, consent to sexual relations and so on – they are also positively controlled and their lives almost completely regulated by adults. (Harris, 1982, p. 35)

This regulation is usually justified by reference to the paternalistic protection of children which is pursued by governments, legislators, social welfare agencies, teachers and parents. Children are seen as legitimate exceptions to the anti-paternalism expressed in the liberal belief in individual autonomy. Writers in the liberal tradition from Locke, Kant, Bentham and Mill to Hart, Rawls and Nozick insist on the importance of individual autonomy – the freedom of the individual from interference to pursue their own good in their own way. In Mill's classic formulation, interference with a person's right to pursue their own good in their own way is only justified when this causes harm to others. A person cannot be interfered with or coerced for their own good or because it would make them happier or because in someone's opinion it is right to interfere. But even the fiercest opponents of paternalism do not hesitate to accept it for children. Mill wrote of the Liberty Principle,

It is perhaps hardly necessary to say that this doctrine is meant to apply to human beings in the maturity of their faculties. We are not speaking of children, or of young persons below the age which the law may fix as manhood or womanhood. Those who are still in a state to require being taken care of by others must be protected against their own actions as well as against external injury. (Mill, 1962a, p. 135)

Mill believed that society had a special duty to intervene when individuals lacked the capacity for rational thought and therefore were not responsible for their actions. Among those in the non-rational category, according to Mill, are the mentally ill and children. Children, then, are an exception to the anti-paternalism principle because they lack rationality – the abilities, capacities and experience that make it wrong to impose on adults. Therefore control and intervention in children's lives is justified in order to protect the interests of children.

Is lack of rationality sufficient ground for denying rights to children?

Many writers are critical of the weight given to rationality as a criteria to distinguish adults and children and the subsequent argument that because children lack rationality they should be denied the rights adults possess. This is because, however anyone attempts to define rationality and the capacities and abilities a rational person should have, this does not provide a criterion for distinguishing between adults and children, but merely the rational and the irrational. And, in that case, some rational children should be given full political status and some irrational adults should be disenfranchised. For example, Schrag (1977) argues that if rationality means the ability to be independent and self-sufficient, then rationality does not distinguish between children and adults, since many children are independent and some adults are not. The old, the handicapped, the sick and the unemployed are not self-sufficient, but this does not justify coercion for them. If rationality means 'capable of being improved by free and equal discussion', then clearly some children are capable of being improved in this way and therefore they should not be coerced for

as soon as mankind have attained the capacity of being guided to their own improvement by conviction or persuasion ... compulsion either in the direct form or in that of pains and penalties for non-compliance, is no longer admissible as a means to their own good. (Mill, 1962a, p. 136)

If rationality is explained on utilitarian lines, then this too fails to distinguish adults and children. Scarre (1980, p. 123) writes that 'rational actions are those which are directed towards maximising the expected utility of the agent'. Rationality means 'the ability to plan systematic policies of action ... essential to solving the practical problems of living'. Scarre believes that paternalism is justified when 'decisions are not based on rational calculations and that they are likely to result in a diminution of his stock of existing good or under-achievement of his possible stock of good'.

According to Scarre, children lack the ability and experience to act rationally in these ways and therefore they should be subject to paternalistic intervention. However, as Franklin (1986) and Harris (1982) have pointed out, many adults do not display these abilities and many children do. On the one hand, it is clear that many children do have the ability to plan systematic policies of action, whether or not we approve of these is irrelevant to the fact that they have this ability. On the other hand, most if not all adults (even utilitarians) do not obsessively calculate the consequences of their actions for their utility-maximizing potential before embarking on them and many non-utility-maximizing actions are not irrational. Many decisions adults make result in under-achievement of their possible stock of future good, but this does not mean that decisions made earlier in life were irrational at the time. Even if such decisions are later acknowledged to be mistakes, this would not justify paternalist intervention by others who could foresee their bad effects.

Moreover, the decisions that adults make which diminish their existing good are often based on rational considerations. As Harris argues, Scarre's narrow account of rationality 'seems to make self-sacrifice, lack of competitiveness and modesty, etc; irrational' (Harris, 1982, p. 40). These considerations lead to the conclusion that the capacity for rationality, however it is defined, does not distinguish adults and children and because of this it could justify paternalism for many 'irrational' adults as well as justifying political rights for many 'rational' children. If this is to be avoided, other criteria for the distinction must be found.

Can paternalism be justified on utilitarian grounds?

Schrag (1977) rejects arguments about the relevant capacities which underpin the traditional distinction and advocates paternalism on utilitarian grounds. Paternalist interference maximizes the happiness of children. If left to their own devices, even though they may have the capacity to make decisions, they will make disastrous mistakes detrimental to their happiness. Because of their lack of understanding and experience, children will make unwise choices. By denying them rights, adults seek to protect them and promote their happiness. Against this, Harris argues (1982, p. 39) that the emphasis on understanding and experience and the likelihood of making unwise choices do not distinguish adults and children either, so this cannot provide an argument for denying children rights. The ability to make wise choices and avoid mistakes is not necessarily connected with age. Adults have not displayed any distinguishing tendency to make wise choices, avoid disaster or harm to themselves. It is adults who smoke cigarettes, who eat fatty food, waste scarce resources and irreparably pollute the environment. It is adults who fight pointless wars, persecute people because of their race or religion, produce nuclear weapons while people starve and who allow people to die from preventable diseases. If the ability to make wise choices is a criterion for political rights, this suggests that paternalism should be advocated for adults and that society should be ruled by an experienced and far-sighted élite who have the ability to recognize and the will to prevent the harmful consequences of unwise choices.

Lindley (1986, pp. 129-31), too, argues that the various criteria which have been used to distinguish adults and children, apply equally to both. If it is argued that children should be denied the vote because they are too irrational, too ignorant to use it wisely, or because they do not understand the issues, or because they will make choices harmful to their future happiness, then a large number of the adult electorate ought to be denied the vote too. They are ignorant of political issues, unaware of the consequences of casting their votes, and, anyway, governments typically pursue policies aimed at the short-term interests of ill-informed adults.

Criteria for extending political rights to children

The point these critics are making is that criteria used to distinguish adults and children do not do so. They merely distinguish the competent from the incompetent, the rational from the irrational and this excludes not just some children but also some adults, and is consistent with paternalist rule by an élite who possesses the relevant qualities. Because of this, Harris argues, we should abandon the traditional distinction between adults and children and replace it with a distinction between persons and non-persons. This is a less stringent criteria which does not exclude so many people and thus avoids paternalism. According to Harris:

If we value people, and if we are committed to a conception of equality which protects a person's dignity and independence by requiring that each person is shown the same concern and respect as that shown to any, then we need some account of who is valuable and who is protected by the principle. It would be parochial in the extreme to suppose that adult human beings were the only qualifiers. (Harris, 1982, p. 47)

For Harris, a person is a being who values their own life. To do this they must have a conception of their life as their own; they must be self-conscious; they must have decisions to take, plans to make and things to do. This requires some self-awareness, intelligence and language. If these characteristics constitute a person who is thereby deserving of equal concern and respect, it is difficult to exclude from political rights all but the youngest children. Age 10 would be a more likely candidate than age 18 for political status.

Granting political status to all those who are persons, means that they have the right to vote, to work, to initiate and defend legal proceedings, to own property, make wills, enter into contracts, be criminally responsible and have the right to due process of law (Harris, 1982, p. 51). Lindley (1986, pp. 122–3) also argues that by the age of 10 years old, non-mentally handicapped children are people and as such they are fit subjects for the Kantian principle of respect for the autonomy of persons as ends-in-themselves.

Lindley's criteria for personhood are consciousness, the possession of the concept of the self as the subject of experiences, the possession of beliefs and desires, and the capacity to evaluate and structure beliefs and desires and to act on the basis of these. Franklin also concurs with age 10 as the probable age for granting political status. Rather than distinguishing between persons and non-persons, he endorses a proposal made by Holt (1975, p. 118) for the right to vote for people at any age. Franklin writes:

Eligibility, on his account, is determined by awareness and interest in political affairs. Everyone should have the right to vote when their interests, knowledge and involvement in politics are sufficiently developed to motivate them so to do; as interest develops so participation will increase. (Franklin, 1986, pp. 39–40)

Franklin argues that few very young children would exercise their right to vote, but that, by the age of 10, children could have developed the understanding and motivation to do so. All the objections to young people voting – their ignorance of political affairs, that they would be irresponsible voters, that they would vote on the basis of personality rather than on policies, that they would be influenced by their parents – even if true, cannot be reasons for excluding children since these same factors do not ban adults from voting. Franklin believes that the denial of political rights to children offends fundamental democratic principles:

First, they offer a clear example of the violation of the democratic principle that no individual or group should be subject to laws which they have not participated in making ... Second, they are the only grouping in a democracy whose political rights are entrusted to another group to be exercised on their behalf without the restraint of a mechanism of accountability or democratic control. (Franklin, 1986, p. 24)

All these writers have tried to show that the division between citizens and non-citizens, adults and children based on criteria such as rationality, understanding, competence, responsibility and experience cannot be sustained and in this respect their arguments are convincing. These ideas have had some effect in practice (though not necessarily because philosophers have advocated them).

The recognition that children can be rational, competent, responsible and capable of making decisions appears to have informed the thinking behind both the recent Children's Act (1989) and the UN Convention on the Rights of the Child (1989), both implemented in 1991. The Children's Act is the most far-reaching change to child law this century. For children involved in court proceedings, children's welfare is given paramount consideration above the needs and wishes of parents or anyone else. Children can apply for a range of orders on issues affecting their lives if they can convince the judge that they understand the consequences of their actions. The much publicized cases of children vetoing adoption orders and 'divorcing their parents' to live with grandparents or foster parents, result from the recognition that children can make rational decisions and they ought to be allowed to take legal action on their own behalf when they can demonstrate this.

The UN convention similarly recognizes the right for children to be consulted and taken account of in all matters which affect them, and the right to challenge decisions taken on their behalf in the courts and by other official bodies. The convention extends and endorses some other legal and political rights to children such as protection in law and in the administration of justice, to participation, freedom of expression, thought, religion and association. Arguably, underpinning these initiatives are notions of children both as rational agents capable of making informed choices and as persons who value their own lives with the capacity to evaluate and structure their beliefs and desires. It is implicitly acknowledged that children are persons who are deserving of equal concern and respect and to whom the Kantian respect for autonomy applies. The extension of democratic rights of participation to children could be said to imply that they have or could have the interest, knowledge and motivation to exercise them.

The development and exercise of autonomy

The arguments given by Harris, Lindley and Franklin to support children's political and legal rights can be seen as arguments for an extension of the liberal principles of egalitarian, democratic participation, equal concern and respect, and respect for the sovereignty and autonomy of individual desires to children. This may well be justified and acceptable in theory to liberals, but unless the problems of the development of autonomy and the ability to exercise it for both children and adults are addressed, then these rights are merely formal and empty. All these writers object to paternalism on the grounds that adults make short-sighted, reckless, ill-informed and unwise decisions which harm them and since this does not justify coercing them, why should children's similar decisions be curtailed and controlled by adults, supposedly acting in their best interests? Children, in their view, are not an exception to the liberal non-discrimination principle: there are no relevant differences between children and adults which justify their different treatment. However, the similarities between children and adults in respect of their deficiencies is a poor argument for giving children similar rights to adults. This seems to me not to be an argument for giving children equal rights to harm themselves and to make stupid decisions, but to be a reason for calling into question two things.

First, the notion embodied in Mill's Liberty Principle, that it is all right for *adults* to harm themselves, and second, the lack of attention paid to the development of autonomy and the ability to make decisions. It calls into question a notion of freedom that is meant to be based on respect for the individual, but which blithely and proudly accepts that individuals should be allowed to ruin their own lives, as long as they do it in their own way. That this freedom to do what is stupid, irrational or wrong and this right to ruin your own life is defended on *moral* grounds is to me simply unintelligible. However, if we think that people should be protected from the harmful consequences of their actions, this does not license paternalism or mean that 'egalitarian democracy is absurd and we should have the courage to be full-blooded elitists' as Harris (1982, p. 54) suggests it does. The alternatives are not between allowing everyone to make unwise choices, adults and children alike, and allowing no-one to. The fact that adults make ill-informed and unwise choices instead suggests that we should pay more attention to the development and exercise of autonomy, rather than accept unwise choices as an expression of freedom, with the small comfort that children's choices are not likely to be worse than adults.

Now, it is clear that the education system does little to foster the development of autonomy. There is no tradition in the UK of acknowledging the rights of children and young people to participate in the process of education. Children have no rights to be consulted with regard to educational provision, school choice, school suspensions or exclusions or on any issue relating to their education or problems in school. Children have no formal rights to participation in matters of school policy or administration, or to be involved in decisions on, for example, school uniform, arrangements for school meals, supervision in the playground, discipline or the curriculum. The basic civil liberties of freedom of expression, association, thought, conscience and religion are severely curtailed for children and young people. Section 28 of the Local Government Act 1988 prohibits intentional promotion of homosexuality through publishing material or teaching by local authorities. The Education (No. 2) Act 1986 gives head teachers in England and Wales a duty to forbid the pursuit of political activities by junior pupils. Rules on school uniform often restrict a pupil's right to freedom of expression. Though parents have a right to withdraw children from religious worship and education, children themselves do not have this right.

The content of education, too, fails to promote autonomy in that it does not provide children with the necessary knowledge, understanding and skills to participate fully in a democratic and multi-cultural society or to question and challenge received ideas. The recent introduction by the National Curriculum Council of cross-curricular themes – Education for Citizenship, Health, Economic and Industrial Understanding, Environmental and Careers Education – and their emphasis on personal and social development, communication, problem-solving and decision-making skills suggest that it has been recognized that the acquisition of these skills and learning about rights, duties, responsibilities, the economy, the environment and the world of work are necessary for the development and exercise of autonomy.

However, the introduction of these initiatives is the product of social, political and economic forces which require major changes in education generally and is significant in that they help to meet both the ideological and practical needs of an advanced and complex market economy. Ideological requirements are transmitted by selecting a narrow content which legitimizes existing social relations and endorses a business, individualistic and consumerist ethic. Practical requirements are secured through emphasis on process – the development of skills and attitudes necessitated by the organization of the productive process in a changing technological society (Ramsay, 1993, p. 28). These, together with increasing emphasis on traditional values, a return to basics, meeting the needs of industry and vocational training reflect the ideological changes which are taking place in the context of the need to prepare pupils for their future roles in a particular kind of society. Those who advocate equal rights for children because they are concerned with extending autonomy to all persons should also advocate examining the content and process of education and the effect the current system has in undermining the capacity for autonomy.

Furthermore, there is no point in arguing for political rights for children, so that they, like adults can be free to pursue their own interests, if no account is taken of the inequalities that will prevent their effective exercise. Even if we take the right to education as it presently exists, we can see that children's access to education is severely hindered by poverty, under-resourcing and administrative structures and policies. There is growing evidence that a disproportionate number of children being excluded from schools in England and Wales are boys of Afro-Caribbean origin. Children living in temporary homeless accommodation and children in care have their education disrupted because of the insecure and poor nature of their housing and lack of adequate provision. Children from poor homes face hidden costs of education for uniforms, school dinners, books and equipment. Many disabled children and those with learning disadvantages are unable to be educated in ordinary schools. Children with special educational needs are not having them met because local authorities are unable to provide sufficient resources. There are marked disparities of education provision between affluent and poor areas, state, voluntary aided and public schools. Lack of resources adversely affect the fabric of schools, buildings, facilities, equipment, textbooks and quality of teachers.

The equal right to education, like any equal right that adults possess, is rendered less meaningful by these inequalities. Generally, the ability to exercise any formal, legal or political right that children have, or should have, will be affected by inequalities that result from differences in gender, race, class, wealth and levels of educational attainment. And it is to these social, economic, educational and cultural inequalities that attention must be given if we are interested in the exercise of autonomy. Arguments for equal formal rights often obscure this, though the presuppositions of such arguments – the promotion of autonomy and equal respect –

should suggest that the conditions necessary to develop autonomy and to exercise rights are at least as important as the rights themselves. As Lindley writes:

The problem for liberals is that some values which lie at the heart of liberalism are, in their implications, radical. It may well be that the values cannot be instantiated in a class-divided society, with widespread economic and political inequality, and deep conflicts of interests. And yet liberal theory has in practice been precisely a theory for such societies. At least as far as children are concerned, it seems to be true that liberal democratic society is unable to deliver what its own principles declare to be essential. (Lindley, 1986, p. 139)

The different needs of children

A further problem with arguments for extending equal rights to children is that they downplay the different needs of children which legitimize their different treatment. In this sense there are parallels to the feminist debate about sameness or difference, equal and/or special rights for women. Children's difference is acknowledged in the United Nations Convention of the Rights of the Child which states that children, because of their vulnerability, need special care and protection and therefore special rights to meet these needs. The convention provides a minimum standard for children and young people's civil and political, economic, social and cultural rights. These standards are defined within three main categories – participation, provision and protection.

The articles concerning participation include civil and political rights, the right to be consulted, to have information and to challenge decisions taken on their behalf. These are based on the concept of the child as an active and contributing participant in society, and are underpinned by the idea that children, like adults, possess capacities relevant to the exercise of autonomy. They aim to extend to children, the same rights adults possess. The articles concerning provision cover the basic rights of the child to survive and develop. These range from an adequate standard of living, education, health care, food and clean water to the cultural, artistic, recreational and leisure facilities which allow the child to develop. The articles concerned with protection deal with the exploitation of children at work; physical, sexual and psychological abuse; discrimination and other mistreatments.

The convention makes it a duty for state parties to protect

children and, where necessary, to provide rehabilitation for them. These rights do not aim to give children any greater independence from adults or to give them equal status, but advocate special rights to protection and provision to meet the special needs of children. Such 'paternalism' does not undermine autonomy, but seeks to enhance it. The convention, however, also recognizes that children's autonomy, like that of adults, is not secured simply by providing them with negative rights to non-interference. Equal respect for human agency also requires positive rights to the provision of resources and opportunities and the carrying out of correlative negative duties of forbearance and positive duties to protect and aid.

It seems to be the case that, in principle, liberal theory is inconsistent when it advocates paternalism for children, because the characteristics it uses to distinguish adults and children do not in fact justify their exclusion from political and civil rights, any more than these characteristics justified the former exclusion of women. However, arguments for the political equality of children are no more then an academic indulgence unless they are also accompanied by arguments to support the economic, educational and social measures designed to promote the development and exercise of autonomy. The prioritizing of political rights typical of liberal thought is even more acutely problematic when applied to children, given the crucial importance of economic and social resources and opportunities for human agency and given the special vulnerability of children. Arguing for political status for children is simply barking up the wrong tree here and is irrelevant to the alleviation of the poverty, hunger, disease, exploitation and oppression that children, in particular, suffer world-wide. The opening statement of the 1995 WHO report *Bridging the Gaps* reads:

Every year in the developing world 10–12 million children under five die, most of them from causes which could be prevented for just a few US cents per child. They die largely because of world indifference but most of all they die because they are poor. (WHO, 1995)

It is estimated that in the 1990s, 100 million children will die of preventable diseases or hunger. In 1990, more than a third of the world's children under 5 were undernourished. In 1993 across the world 51 million people of all ages died, a quarter of these were children. Some 12 million children live in poverty in the USA, some 3 million in Britain. In Brazil death squads murder street children, in South Africa thousands of children are tortured. In the Far East child prostitution is rife. Some 60 million children in the world work today. In Colombian mines they work for twelve hours a day. In India they work as bonded labourers weaving carpets. In Brazil, Portugal and Italy, they work in dangerous glass factories. In Britain, there are 2 million children in part-time work. Britain has the worst record in Europe (apart from Portugal) for protecting children in employment. It is hard to see how giving children political status could do anything to further the interests of these children.

Conclusion

In this chapter I have discussed the issues of equal or special rights for women and children. It was argued that equal political and legal rights for women are not enough if their opportunities are to be of equal worth. However, demands for special rights and positive discrimination in favour of women could be justified on liberal grounds if these are necessary to increase equal opportunities for women to pursue their own good in their own way. It was argued that liberal theory is inconsistent in advocating paternalism towards children. The liberal commitment to autonomy which is the moral foundation for rights justifies the extension of political and legal rights to children.

However, even if special rights for women and equal rights for children could be derived from liberal premises, these alone would not be sufficient to guarantee autonomy to either. In relation to children, attention must be paid to the conditions for the development of autonomy, to the inequalities that undermine this, and to their special needs which give rise to positive rights to protection and aid. Neither equal nor special rights for women are sufficient to end oppression as these do not fundamentally alter inequalities in power, social and economic inequalities or the unequal division of domestic labour that undermine women's ability to compete in the world of public life. The next chapter will take these issues further by examining the liberal division between the public and private sphere. Although gender inequality is incompatible with the liberal principles of individual autonomy and equal opportunities, liberal principles cannot be applied to women without regard to the paternalistic structure of private life.

7

The Public and the Private

This chapter will address two issues that arise from the liberal distinction between the public and the private spheres. The first concerns feminist criticism of the distinction itself and their claim that it obscures and serves to reinforce gender injustice. The second focuses on the feminist view that prevailing ideas of justice reflect the male norms and values that are typical of liberal thought and that have traditionally been associated with the public sphere. Emphasis on female values and experiences, traditionally associated with the private sphere, can reveal the inadequacy of the male model and provide a corrective or an alternative to liberal conceptions of justice in both the public and the private sphere.

In trying to set limits to the role of the state, liberal theory distinguishes conceptually between the public and the private sphere. The public sphere is thought of as those areas of life where the state may legitimately intervene; the private sphere, those areas of life where the individual is to be left alone, free from state interference. The aim is to protect an area of social or personal life that is free from the exercise of political power.

There has always been controversy amongst liberals over just which aspects of life are public and which are private. Early liberals thought that the personal life of individuals, the family and the economy were private matters in which there could be no legitimate intervention. State intervention was only legitimate in so far as it preserved individual freedom by protecting civil liberties. Liberals in the twentieth century still give priority to the role of the state in preserving civil liberties and individual rights but narrow the scope of the private sphere. They advocate some state intervention in the economic realm to provide welfare, education and a minimum standard of living as a means to promoting individual liberty. The state, however, still cannot legitimately intervene in private lives. It is generally accepted that sexuality, child-bearing, child-rearing and the family fall within the scope of the private sphere and therefore should be exempt from state interference.

Feminist Criticisms

The liberal separation of the public and private has been the target of feminist criticism. According to Pateman (1987, p. 103) 'it is ultimately, what the feminist movement is about'. Pateman argues that liberalism makes two distinctions between the public and the private. The first distinguishes the family and the domestic from the public world. Here, the public encompasses all aspects of life apart from the domestic and is conceptualized as separate from the private domestic sphere. The second intersects the distinction between the public power of the state and the private relations of civil society by a division within civil society. The private here refers to the market, the economy, and to the social as opposed to public political life. Civil society is conceptualized in abstraction from the domestic sphere, that is, the domestic is not seen as part of civil society. To this, Kymlicka adds a third distinction, that between the personal and social. He writes, 'modern liberalism is concerned not only to protect the private sphere of social life, but also to carve out a realm *within the private sphere* where individuals can have *privacy*' (Kymlicka, 1990, p. 258). This form of liberalism's public/private distinction is often characterized as the legal 'right to privacy'.

These three divisions − between the domestic and the public; between civil society and the state; and between the personal and the social have been challenged by feminists.

1. The domestic and the public

Feminists argue that the dichotomy between the domestic and the public gives the impression that two separate spheres exist side by side. This is misleading because it obscures the unequal relations between men and women.

Phillips writes:

The private is very often taken to mean the family, and in the family men and women are unequal. In the name of freedom, liberalism can exempt from political interference the arena in which women are most subordinate and controlled. In its desire to keep separate the worlds of public and private, it offers us 'equality' in the former while hypocritically ignoring real differences in the latter. The split between public and private may present itself as a neutral, 'sex-free' distinction, but its effects are unequal between women and men. (Phillips, 1987, p. 13)

Feminists have also drawn attention to the ways in which the domestic and public worlds are inter-related and structured by liberal patriarchy, so that far from being separate spheres, the private and the public, the personal and the political are intimately connected and reverberate upon each other. They have explored the ways in which women's reproductive roles and domestic responsibilities affect their access to jobs and to participation in public life generally. They have shown how women's paid employment and how inequalities at work reflect and reinforce their subordinate position in the private domestic sphere in that typical 'women's work' is an extension of their domestic roles, and the low pay and low status attached to this work mirror the devaluing of their domestic tasks. The exploitation of their labour in the paid work force and in the home are continuous with each other, two sides of their oppression. They have analysed how women's low pay and marginalization in the public world help to maintain women's economic dependence on men and how this enables men to dominate women sexually and to exploit their domestic labour. They have shown how the reproductive and domestic labour performed by women is connected to other aspects of patriarchal power in the public world and other dimensions of economic and social life. Women in the home attend to men's domestic, sexual, emotional and material needs, and serve the interests of the capitalist economy by limiting competition for jobs and by socializing, reproducing and maintaining the workforce.

Feminist critiques of the domestic/public dichotomy also show how these categories are inter-related in the sense that the private domestic sphere is structured by public and political factors, decisions and policies. The domestic is not the realm of freedom, but has constantly been subject to political regulation and interference. The state intervenes in the family by enforcing laws on and defining the rights, responsibilities and status of family members in relation to marriage, divorce, child support and child custody. It implements laws and policies on abortion, rape, child-care and the allocation of welfare. It propagates an ideology of the family. It is concerned with the decline and disintegration of the nuclear family and it recommends a return to family values.

Feminists have shown not only how the private is constructed by the public through legislation on marriage, sexuality and the policies of the welfare state, but also that this construction both presupposes and reinforces the subordinate status of women and stereotypical views of their roles and responsibilities (Wilson, 1977; Barker, 1978; Olsen, 1985; Nicholson, 1986). For example, Wilson argues that the welfare state and welfare services and state policies from education to housing are based on the view of women as passive dependents, nurturers and carers. The policies and institutions of the welfare state are nothing more than the 'state organisation of domestic life' (Wilson, 1977, p. 9).

Radical feminism of the 1960s and 1970s extended the challenge to the liberal separation of the domestic and public spheres, not just by showing how the private and public are inter-related or how the former structures the latter, but by proclaiming and taking literally the slogan 'the personal is the political'. If the political is defined in terms of power, then power is not only manifest in the state, the traditional domain of the political, but it pervades every aspect of personal life. This critique further highlights aspects of the family and sexual life which had hitherto been thought of as paradigmatically non-political. Radical feminists claimed that the family is a central part of society's power structure and the chief institution of patriarchy (Millett, 1985, p. 33). Within the family women are exploited domestically, manipulated emotionally, and coerced and abused sexually. It is here that women are exposed to the physical violence which is the most overt form of male power. It is here, where early socialization takes place, where gender identities are formed and reproduced, where sex-role stereotyping is learnt and internalized. Within the family, the unequal distribution of domestic work and child care, prestige and self-esteem, leisure time and consumption, physical, economic and emotional security reflect the coercive power of men over women. The notion that the 'personal is political' also highlights power relations in aspects of sexuality and sexual relations. These are not private or individual matters, but are bound up with male definitions, male desires and images, so that heterosexuality itself, sexual relationships between men and women, the sexual objectification and portrayal of women, rape, pornography and prostitution – these are all manifestations of male authority and power and replicate these relations of dominance and submission. In these analyses the domestic, the personal and the sexual cannot be separated from the political.

2. The state and civil society

Different feminist criticism, then, challenges the separation of the domestic and public spheres, either by showing that these spheres are inter-related or by denying theoretically that such a distinction exists. However, as Pateman points out, there is another sense in which liberals conceptualize the distinction between the public and the private which has consequences for the oppression and exclusion of women. In separating the public power of the state from the private relations of civil society, liberalism conceptualizes the private in abstraction from the domestic. She writes:

Precisely because liberalism conceptualises civil society in abstraction from ascriptive domestic life, the latter remains 'forgotten' in theoretical discussion. The separation between the private and the public is thus re-established as a division *within* civil society itself, within the world of men. The separation is then expressed in a number of different ways, not only private and public but also, for example, 'society' and 'state'; or 'economy' and 'politics'; or 'freedom' and 'coercion'; or 'social' and 'political'. (Pateman, 1987, p. 107)

Here, the political is contrasted to the private, conceptualized as the social and economic, and the domestic is not conceptualized at all. Socialists have typically complained about this liberal separation of the state and civil society because it ignores how inequalities in the so-called private sphere, in income, wealth, social power and education affect equality in the political sphere.

Similarly, feminists have argued that the demand for equal political and legal rights for women ignores biological differences and inequalities in men and women's respective social roles and responsibilities which prevent them from exercising equal freedom. However, feminist critiques of the state/society distinction extend these arguments, because this distinction does not include domestic life. The family is excluded from civil society. This omission makes it seem as though society is composed only of male individuals who have no family ties or social bonds, no family background or history. Not only does this give a false picture of the independent and self-sufficient man as the universal human being, it also totally ignores the value and significance of the domestic, procreative, nurturing and supportive labour done by women to produce and sustain such robust individuals. As Phillips notes:

because the family is now completely out of the picture, liberalism can more plausibly pretend that we are indeed the private and isolated individuals on which its theories rest. In seemingly universal concern over the limits of the state and the freedoms of the individual, liberalism talks in effect of a world occupied by men. (Phillips, 1987, p. 15)

These men are the abstract, rational, autonomous individuals of liberal political theory, who are motivated by their own interests and whose interests conflict with others. The individual therefore is a man who 'needs a sphere in which he can exercise his rights, pursue his (private) interests and protect and increase his (private) property' (Pateman, 1987, p. 107). Consequently, women and women's nature seem to have no place in society, and the domestic and the familial have no place in political theory or in theories of justice.

3. Divisions within the private: the right to privacy

The third distinction between the public and the private is in fact a division within the private sphere which delineates an area where individuals can have privacy and retreat from both public and private life. This is defined in legal terms as the right to privacy and is interpreted to mean that any societal or state interference in the home, the family, marriage, motherhood, procreation or child-rearing is an invasion of the right to privacy. Feminists have challenged the value of this so-called right for women. Protecting the institutions of the family and marriage from interference leaves women vulnerable to economic dependency and exploitation, sexual abuse and physical violence within the home, and simultaneously ignores the value of their domestic services and the contribution they make to society in general. Women's subordination is de-politicized as it becomes a private matter beyond public scrutiny, social reform or legal redress. MacKinnon sums up this criticism in the following way:

It is probably not coincidence that the very things feminism regards as central to the subjection of women – the very place, the body; the very relations, heterosexual; the very activities, intercourse and reproduction; and the very feelings, intimate – form the core of what is covered by the privacy doctrine. From this perspective, the legal concept of privacy can and has shielded the place of battery, marital rape and women's exploited labour; has preserved the central institutions whereby women are *deprived*

of identity, autonomy, control and self-definition ... This right to privacy is a
right of men 'to be let alone' to oppress women one at a time. (MacKinnon,
1987, pp. 101–2)

However, Kymlicka (1990, pp. 260–2) argues that the tendency to
remove the family from the scope of public justice arises not
because the liberal value of privacy entails this exclusion, but
because individual privacy is equated with the collective privacy of
the family. That is, because the family as a collective unit is assumed
to be a single individual. The right to privacy is attributed to
families, not to their individual members. Consequently, individuals
have no claim to privacy within the family and family members have
no right to protection from each other. However, Kymlicka argues
the right to privacy which protects the family as a collective is
inconsistent with the liberal values of individual autonomy and
equal rights for individuals. If the right to privacy is applied to
individuals rather than families, this would be consistent with
liberal principles, and would legitimize state interference in the
domestic sphere to protect individual privacy within the family and
to prevent abuse. Kymlicka claims

Once it is detached from patriarchal ideas of family autonomy, I believe that
most feminists share the basic liberal motivations for respecting privacy –
i.e. the value of having some freedom from distraction and from the
incessant demands of others, and the value of having room to experiment
with unpopular ideas and to nourish intimate relationships (Allen, 1988).
(Kymlicka, 1990, p. 261)

If this is the case, then the scope of the private sphere is
considerably narrowed and liberals must abandon their belief in
the family as the centre of private life and the concept of privacy in
relation to it. The liberal right to privacy is uncontroversially
reduced to the right to get away from people now and again. This
would make privacy rather a peripheral value in liberal thought and
hardly the target of so much criticism.

Kymlicka's argument overlooks the fact that critics have objected
to the liberal concept of privacy, not because they do not
acknowledge that people sometimes want time and space for
themselves, but because the notion that a realm of privacy needs to
be protected against interference is connected with an inadequate
conception of liberty and of human nature. In liberal thought it is
assumed that individuals are free to pursue their own interests and

self-fulfilment if they are left alone – this is why liberals value privacy. However, critics point out there is little value in protecting a private area of non-interference because leaving people alone is only marginally important to their freedom. Assiter sums this up in the following way:

> the ends the liberal believes he or she is preserving by defending negative liberty and privacy depend on rejecting these very notions. 'Negative' freedom is not sufficient for genuine liberty. Freedom or the ability to fulfil one's purposes has little to do with privacy, and much more to do with the provision of means, material and mental, for the fulfilment of one's ends. (Assiter, 1989, p. 29)

Liberals value privacy as negative liberty because they do not conceptualize human beings as social beings who intersubjectively relate to each other to meet their needs and to fulfil their ends and purposes. They see human beings as isolated and independent individuals who are 'self-contained and self-sustaining needing a private area of withdrawal from society not merely for rest and refreshment, but as a condition of self-realisation. They assume that the private (home) offers scope for self-realisation where liberal values can be preserved' (Arblaster, 1984, p. 43).

Again, what is being challenged is the liberal conceptions of the abstract individual and negative liberty which support the value and importance liberals place on freedom from interference in the private sphere.

The Public/Private Distinction: An Essentially Liberal Characteristic?

The public/private distinction is generally thought to be a defining feature of liberal thought and many feminists have taken this distinction to be liberalism's fatal and most fundamental flaw. However, Elshtain (1981, p. 6) argues that the distinction between the public and the private and the relegation of men and women to each respectively, pre-dates liberalism and has been part of political thought from Plato to the present day. Eisenstein too, notes that 'the assignment of public space to men and (domestic) space to women is continuous with western history' (1981, p. 22). Political theorists as diverse as Nietzsche, Hegel, Kant and Rousseau have accepted the relegation of women to the private domestic sphere.

Traditional justifications for assigning these separate spheres to men and women were made by appeal to the different biological and psychological natures of each. The exclusion of women from the public realm and their domestic and subordinate role were seen as a reflection of their biological role. Their psychological character traits made them unsuitable for social and political life (Okin, 1981). Their particularist, emotional, irrational, non-universal nature was thought to be incompatible with and dangerous in political life governed by universal, impersonal, rational and conventional criteria (Kennedy and Mendus, 1987, pp. 3–4, 10). Thus the public/private distinction not only reflects the natural subordination of women, but also expresses oppositions between the nature and culture, the particular and the universal, emotion and reason, and women are associated with the negative sides of these dichotomies. Liberalism, then, inherited the distinction. However, the prevailing idea of the domestic and private as women's territory and of the public as men's was further entrenched by the development of industrial capitalism and the rise of commodity production. When production moved away from the home, life within the home seemed more obviously private. The demands of capitalist production and its accompanying sexual and class division of labour meant that women were excluded from public economic activity and confined to their 'natural' place in the home. So, as Pateman argues, 'The old patriarchal argument from nature and women's nature was thus transformed as it was modernised and incorporated into liberal capitalism' (Pateman, 1987, p. 108). The public/private distinction did not originate with liberalism, but was inherited and endorsed by it. In what follows I will argue that although liberals inherited rather than invented the distinction, they should not have endorsed it if they were to consistently apply liberal principles to women. And that it is not just because liberals accept the public/private distinction that they are unable to deal adequately with the injustice of gender inequality. All the concepts, values and principles of liberalism mitigate against doing so. To challenge women's oppression is to challenge liberal principles themselves.

Liberalism should not have endorsed the public/private distinction which reinforces the subjection of women. Gender inequality is incompatible with liberal values of individual autonomy and equal opportunities. Pateman argues, 'In theory, liberalism and patriarchalism stand irrevocably opposed to each other. Liberalism is an individualist, egalitarian, conventionalist doctrine; patriarchalism claims that hierarchical relations of subordination necessarily follow from the natural characteristics of men and women' (Pateman, 1987, p. 105). Liberals who believe in the equal worth of each individual, and who are opposed to all forms of supposedly 'natural' authority, should have rejected any justification of natural hierarchical relations between men and women. However, early liberals who opposed the idea that hierarchical relations were ascribed by nature, did not extend their opposition to relations in the domestic sphere. The theoretical basis for this apparently contradictory position was provided by Locke.

Locke introduced the separation between the public and the private into liberal political theory by differentiating between political and paternal power. He aimed to counter patriarchal argument for absolute power in the government realm, but continued to justify patriarchal power in the family. In the *Second Treatise*, Locke argued against Filmer's case for patriarchal government by claiming that political power is conventional and that legitimate authority can only rest on the consent of free and equal individuals. In contrast to this, paternal power in the private sphere is based on natural bonds. Fathers have natural authority over children during their pre-rational stage. When children reach maturity and become free and equal individuals, then their consent is required for any continuing authority to be exercised over them.

Locke takes paternal power to include the rule of husbands over wives. The subjection of wives to husbands has a 'foundation in nature' and, given women's natural inferiority, domestic authority 'naturally falls to the man's share, as the abler and stronger' (Locke, 1967: Treatise I, p. 47: 210; Treatise II, p. 82: 364). Locke then challenges hierarchical relations in the public sphere and reinstates them in the private domestic sphere. He legitimizes the subordination of women and their exclusion from public participation by appealing to traditional assumptions about women's natural inferiority. However, adopting these old assumptions creates problems for liberal theory. Ideas of natural authority and natural subordination conflict with ideas of the free and equal individuals who must consent to authority. Liberalism's individualistic, egalitarian and universal character is not easily reconcilable with assumptions of natural inequality between the sexes.

Mill tried to tackle this contradiction in liberal thought. In *The Subjection of Women*, Mill attacked the prevailing arguments from nature which justified inequality between the sexes and women's relegation to the private sphere. He argued that the subordination of women only appears natural because ideas about their innate inferiority are so entrenched by custom. There is no evidence to suggest that the apparent differences between men and women are rooted in nature. Women's supposedly inferior qualities and capacities – their submissiveness, narrow-mindedness, irrationality and emotionality – are rather the result of legal and social pressures, different attitudes towards the sexes and their different upbringing, experiences and education. Not until women were given equal opportunities to develop their capacities could anything be known about their alleged natural differences.

Mill, then, attempted to undercut the ground for the unequal treatment of women against the force of contemporary ideas that had used nature to legitimate women's exclusion from the public sphere. He could then proceed to apply liberal principles to both men and women without the previous contradiction in liberal thought between natural freedom and equality, on the one hand, and natural inferiority, on the other. Women, like men, were free and equal individuals, equally capable of reason and motivated by self-interest. Therefore, they should be free from interference to pursue their own interests and have equal opportunities to achieve them. This requires that women should have the same opportunities as men to participate in public and political life. There should be an end to legal discrimination in marriage, free access to education and employment and equal, legal and political rights for women, in particular, the right to vote and hold public office.

Despite Mill's emphasis on women's equality, he nevertheless saw the sexes as playing different roles in society. These conformed to those delineated by the traditional public/private distinction which justified the appropriateness of the domestic for women and the public and political for men. Although he advocated equal freedom for women to enter the public realm and to pursue a career, he assumed that the majority of women, even after gaining equal opportunities, would choose marriage and domesticity. He compared this 'choice' to a man's choice of a career.

Like a man when he chooses a profession, so, when a woman marries, it may in general be understood that she makes choice of the management of a household, and the bringing up of a family, as the first call upon her exertions, during as many years of her life as may be required for the purpose; and that she renounces, not all other objects and occupations, but all which are not consistent with the requirements of this. (Mill, 1989, pp. 164–5)

Mill assumed that the traditional division of labour in the family, with men earning the income and women managing the household and caring for children, was 'the most suitable division of labour between the two persons' and that 'it is not ... a desirable custom, that the wife should contribute by her labour to the income of the family' (Mill, 1989, p. 164).

Mill tried to make liberal theory consistent by extending and universalizing liberal principles to women. He challenged out-moded ideas of women's natural inferiority which legitimized their relegation to the private sphere. But, Mill lapsed back into the equivalence of these arguments by substituting 'suitable' and 'desirable' for 'natural'. This was a tantamount to endorsing the naturalness of the traditional sexual division of labour which he had previously denied. Feminist critics of Mill have been quick to point out that his failure to confront gender roles in the family undermines his own arguments for sexual equality.

Mill's acceptance of a sexually ascribed division of labour, or the separation of domestic from public life, cuts the ground from under his argument for enfranchisement ... How can wives who have 'chosen' private life develop a public spirit? Women will thus exemplify the selfish, private beings, lacking a sense of justice, who result, according to Mill, when individuals have no experience of public life. (Pateman, 1987, p. 116)

Okin (1980, p. 228) argues that Mill's acceptance of the naturalness of the traditional family sets limits on his application of the liberal principles of freedom and equality to married women. He assumes that women as rational and autonomous individuals, will 'choose' to be housewives, without examining how their freedom of choice is conditioned and constrained. He assumes that after legal reforms men and women will have equal opportunities to pursue their own interests and self-development, but circumscribes these for the majority of women. He does not see the inequalities involved in women having to choose either marriage or a career and men having both. He does not question the effects of women's economic dependence and domestic responsibilities on their equal participation in public and political life.

Mill's arguments are inconsistent in the sense that he did not fully extend liberal principles of autonomy and equal opportunities to the domestic sphere. Although his arguments against natural inferiority suggest that he thought that the family was a conventional rather than a natural institution, he accepted the natural sexual division of labour and so ultimately upheld patriarchal ideas of the separation between the public and private.

Contemporary liberal theorists still endorse this ideological separation and ignore power relationships within the family, the unequal distribution of domestic labour and the connection between this, women's economic dependence and their ability to participate in the public world. Liberal theorists of justice concentrate on freedom and equality in the public realm and, by so doing, imply that the family is a non-political, private institution. Okin, in her examination of justice, gender and the family, argues that contemporary theories of justice neglect gender inequalities because they assume the traditional, gender-structured family.

In one way or another, ... almost all current theories continue to assume that the 'individual' who is the basic subject of their theories is the male head of a fairly traditional household. Thus the application of principles of justice to relations between the sexes, or within the household, is frequently, though tacitly, ruled out from the start. (Okin, 1990b, p. 9)

Rawls is a typical example of this position, who simply assumes that the traditional family is just (Rawls, 1971, pp. 128, 146). Consequently, questions of justice within the family are not raised or discussed (see Okin, 1990a, Ch. 5).

Liberal feminists also, accept the division between the public and the private and until recently have neglected the family. This is because liberal feminists, like their male counterparts, concentrate on equal rights and opportunities in the competitive world of public life. But liberal feminists must also examine injustice in the private sphere of the family as well as public discrimination if they are to successfully challenge gender inequality and if they are to consistently apply liberal principles to women. As the analysis of Mill made clear, liberal principles cannot simply be applied to women in the public sphere without regard to the paternalistic structure of private domestic life. However, the principles of liberty and equality cannot just be applied to the domestic sphere or to private matters such as contraception, abortion, pornography, prostitution and sexuality, in abstraction from the rest of society.

As feminist critiques have shown, tackling the problems of the paternalist structure of private life necessarily involves seeing how the separate spheres are inter-related. And this, in turn, implies that the dichotomies and oppositions in the liberal conception of the public and the private have to be abandoned.

Liberalism's failure to tackle women's oppression in the private sphere is not just a consequence of their inheriting and endorsing a traditional gendered public/private distinction. Nor is this failure explained by the sad fact that liberal philosophers have ignored the domestic and the private for the same chauvinist reasons as non-liberal philosophers do. As Kymlicka would have it, 'because male philosophers had no interest in questioning a sexual division of labour from which they benefited' (Kymlicka, 1990, p. 253). For, even if and when this is rectified by extending and consistently applying liberal principles to the family, domestic and sexual matters, liberalism cannot deal adequately with the oppression of women, because liberalism does not recognize how the public and the private spheres are inter-related. So that, for example, when contemporary liberal feminists apply liberal ideas of freedom of speech, individual rights, autonomy and equality before the law to private matters such as pornography and prostitution, they cannot adequately account for or give adequate solutions to these problems.

In opposing restrictions on pornography in the name of the freedom of the individual and by defending prostitution as a market exchange between free and equal consenting adults, they assume the existence of private individuals abstracted from their social and economic circumstances. They ignore power relationships in the production and consumption of pornography; the economic and social factors that cause men to demand commercial sex and women to sell it; the coerciveness of a social system that distorts women's sexuality and sexual relationships; the eroticization of male power in the context of their social, economic and political domination. They do this because, more generally, they ignore how the public world influences the private and how private choices are restricted.

Moreover, the public/private distinction is not just an inherited one, or one perpetuated because it serves male interests. It is logically connected to liberal ideas and values, and their inability to tackle women's oppression is also a consequence of the inadequacy of these. So in order to explain gender inequality and develop

strategies for overcoming it, not only do we need to reject the notion
of separate public and private spheres, but we need to reject liberal
principles, concepts and values.

The Inadequacy of Liberal Ideas

The categories of public and private are a consequence of the
distinctly liberal premise of private, isolated, autonomous individuals each pursuing their own interests, in conflict with others.
From this premise it follows that such an individual needs a private
space free from the intrusion of others, in which to pursue their
own interests, and, that public power is necessary and justified to
protect private interests and to prevent and arbitrate between
conflicts of interests. The state founded upon the consent of
individuals is thus seen as a legitimate authority for enforcing justice
and protecting rights, and as a neutral arbiter of conflicting
interests.

This conception of the state and its role has led liberal feminists
concerned to extend to women liberal values of liberty and equality,
autonomy and individual rights to demand legal reforms to solve
the problem of women's oppression. The inadequacy of this tactic is
tied up with the inadequacy of the liberal conception of the state as
neutral and impartial arbiter of conflicting interests. Both Marxists
and radical feminists reject liberal conceptions of the state because
they believe that the state is not neutral, but is an instrument of
economic and patriarchal power which reinforces and legitimizes
both capitalist and male domination. Therefore, reliance on the state
to achieve reforms, protect interests, enforce rights and guarantee
equality through legislation is a blind and limited strategy. Blind to
the resistance and opposition from those with vested interests in
maintaining women's subordination. Limited, because legal reforms
alone are insufficient to remove the structural inequalities which
hinder women's liberation. Part of the failure of liberalism to
account for women's continuing oppression is connected with the
inadequacy of the liberal conception of the state. Therefore,
feminists must reject this conception; feminist demands cannot be
met by the liberal state.

Feminists must also reject as inadequate, liberal conceptions of
equality. Formal equality is not enough to end women's oppression.
First, because this ignores the differences in other aspects of life
which undermine formal equality. Just as liberalism is blind to how

differences in power, wealth and educational opportunities affect political equality, so it is blind to how the sexual division of labour, economic dependency and family responsibilities restrict opportunities for women. Second, because formal equality denies the different interests and needs of men and women which require different, not equal, treatment to achieve equality. The demands for full legal equality and 'sex-blind' legislation overestimates the effects of achieving equal rights and leaves both the stated goals of liberal feminism unfulfilled and the structures of oppression intact.

Liberal feminists, however, have not just opposed restrictions that deny women equal rights, they have campaigned for legislation that prohibits discrimination against women. They have demanded not only equal pay but equal pay for work of equal value, not just equal access to education, but state intervention to promote gender equality in education. In order to extend equal opportunities, they have argued for the state provision of child care facilities and welfare benefits as well as legislation for maternity leave and flexible working arrangements. These changes, however, would require extending state intervention in a way that is potentially incompatible with a protected private sphere and with individual liberty. This means that liberal feminist demands are at odds with traditional liberal ideas of state intervention as a threat to individual autonomy. And in so far as they believe that the state can be instrumental in achieving equal opportunities, liberal feminists themselves bring into question the liberal value of freedom as freedom from interference.

The value of freedom as freedom from interference is connected with the public/private distinction since government intervention is seen as a restraint on freedom. Therefore, individuals need a private arena where they can be left alone. Individuals are free when no-one, the state or another person, interferes with them. The inadequacy of this conception of freedom has been examined in Chapter 2. There, it was argued that the ability of individuals to make choices and to pursue their own ends can be restricted by both internal and external barriers, by lack of opportunities, resources and capacities, material and mental, as well as by deliberate interference, and that the provision of these increases rather than restricts freedom. This suggests that if an adequate account of women's liberation is to be given, liberalism's narrow conception of negative liberty must be replaced by a positive conception which sees the overcoming of internal barriers as essential to women's ability to make genuine choices, and which sees state intervention to promote opportunities and to provide resources as a means to women achieving their own ends and purposes, rather than as a restriction of individual liberty.

So far, it has been argued that liberals fail to tackle women's oppression because of their separation of the public and private and as a result of inadequate conceptions of the state, freedom and equality. However, the most fundamental reason for this failure is their limited and partial view of human nature which itself is the basis of the public/private divide. The liberal conception of human nature underpins the public/private distinction, in that the qualities needed for public life and justice are those associated with the rational, independent, competitive, autonomous, individual and this same individual requires a private realm to retreat to. Feminists have levelled a barrage of criticism against this conception of human nature as a starting-point for political theory (see Chapter 1). First, because implausibly, it ignores the importance of co-operation, support, interdependence and the nurturing qualities traditionally associated with women, which are values intrinsic to and qualities necessary for social organization. Second, related to this, the liberal stress on reason as the defining mark of the individual and the criterion for citizenship, is male-biased. It focuses on male norms of rationality, logic and technical calculation, and subsequently underestimates the value of typically female ways of thinking and acting that are based on intuition, empathy, caring and responsibility. Third, the emphasis on the value of mind over body implies the superiority of the mental over physical activities and so devalues domestic work and child care as well as other forms of manual labour. Fourth, liberals, by assuming that male individual is the human individual, impose partial goals and values in the guise of a false objectivity and universality.

Liberal perspectives on human nature, then, pose problems for feminist theory in that the experiences, qualities, and characteristics arising from the social roles and responsibilities of women are not conceptualized as part of that nature, and so liberalism cannot provide an adequate understanding of human motivation and behaviour, nor make adequate provision for society's current reproductive and domestic needs, let alone provide the basis for a strategy for ending women's subordination. However, the most fundamental problem with the liberal theory of human nature is the idea of abstract, rational, autonomous individuals who are the sole generators of their own wants and the best judge of their own interests; and it is this which makes it impossible for liberals to see the connection between the public and the private spheres. The idea of the autonomous, rational individual, independent of social determinations obscures the economic, social, political and patriarchal forces which determine individuals, their opportunities, choices, needs, wants, interests and beliefs. This accounts for the liberal failure to acknowledge the socially determined nature of private life and therefore their failure to see how inequalities here affect equality in public life.

Abstract individualism cannot analyse the structural and causal factors which continue to reinforce the subordination of women. Furthermore, the idea that individuals are the best judges of their own interests, on which defence of the private sphere free from interference depends, is considerably shaken if it is acknowledged that individuals are socially determined. If it is accepted that economic and patriarchal forces mould women's interests, ambitions and expectations and that they, like men, are subject to sex-role conditioning, then the sovereignty of expressed desires and the validity of the concept of the abstract individual can be challenged. These criticisms show that an adequate conception of human nature must take account of so-called female qualities and characteristics and do this in relation to their social determinations. This implies an alternative theory of human nature and the abandoning of liberal conceptions.

In this section it has been argued that the division between the public and the private was inherited by liberalism, but that the public and the private are distinctly liberal categories following from liberal premises. To be consistent, liberals should have rejected traditional conceptions of the public and the private which entrenched the suppression of women. They should have extended and applied liberal principles to both public and private spheres. But, even if and when they do, they cannot provide an understanding of the nature and causes of women's oppression nor strategies for ending it, because they cannot see the interconnectedness of the different spheres, and this is a result of their own concepts and values. It is not just the separation of the public and the private that makes liberalism unable to tackle women's oppression, but the inadequacy of their conceptions of the state and human nature and the limitations of their values of freedom and equality.

Public and Private Virtues: An Ethic of Justice and an Ethic of Care

The division between the public and the private also gives rise to the idea that there are different standards of morality appropriate for each. It has been a common theme in western political thought that the qualities associated with gender form the basis for different moralities and modes of reasoning, and that these are related to the different spheres men and women occupy. The qualities associated with women were the qualities opposed to those of the real citizen who participated in politics. Women, because of their lack of reason, their emotional and particularist nature, were more suited to the private, domestic sphere. The qualities associated with men – the rational, impartial, deliberative and judicial – were the qualities necessary for public life and political participation. Virtue was thus gendered and as a result morality was

fragmented into a 'division of moral labour' along the lines of gender, the rationale for which is rooted in historical developments pertaining to family, state, and economy. The tasks of governing, regulating social order, and managing other 'public' institutions have been monopolized by men as their privileged domain, and the tasks of sustaining personal relationships have been imposed on, or left to, women. The genders have thus been conceived in terms of special and distinctive moral projects. Justice and rights have structured male moral norms, values, and virtues, while care and responsibilities have defined female moral norms, values and virtues. (Friedman, 1993, p. 261)

This division of moral labour functioned to keep men and women in their socially defined domains, and to justify women's exclusion from public life with the implicit recognition of the superiority of the male domain and their forms of reasoning. Liberal feminists attacked this traditional idea of specifically female characteristics and virtues, and made use of the idea of rational moral behaviour to demand equal rights for women and to justify their entry into the public domain. But some contemporary feminists are attracted to the idea that there are specifically female virtues and ways of reasoning about moral issues. They claim that these highlight the inadequacies of the male model; that they can generate different social priorities as a corrective to the destructive values of male centred activity; that they are a resource for a critique of the values and priorities of contemporary life, and that these new feminist

conceptions of the good should be extended to the public sphere
(Ruddick, 1980, 1990; Gilligan, 1982, 1983, 1986; Held, 1984a;
Noddings, 1984; Tronto, 1993).

Most of these developments are derived from Gilligan's theory of
male and female reasoning. Gilligan devised her theory in response
to Kohlberg's psychology of moral development. Kohlberg claimed
that the highest stage of moral development is when moral
orientation is characterized by impartiality, impersonality and
universalization, and by appeal to rules and principles. Gilligan
argues that Kohlberg's theory is based on male norms that describe
typically male patterns of reasoning. According to Gilligan, men
conceive of morality as constituted by obligations, rights, fairness
and impartiality, whereas women's moral reasoning arises from
considering particular needs in the context of particular relationships. Women argue in a 'different voice' which she claims is 'ethic
of care' as opposed to a male-orientated 'ethic of justice'. In an 'ethic
of care',

> the moral problem arises from conflicting responsibilities rather than from
> competing rights and requires for its resolution a mode of thinking that is
> contextual and narrative rather than formal and abstract. This conception of
> morality as concerned with the activity of care centers moral development
> around the understanding of responsibility and relationships, just as the
> conception of morality as fairness ties moral development to the under-
> standing of rights and rules. (Gilligan, 1982, p. 19)

Gilligan argues that her studies confirm the ethic of care and the
ethic of justice as two distinct orientations that organize thinking,
and that the focus on care is a characteristically female phenomenon
(1986, p. 209). The ethic of justice and its concern with impartiality,
formal rationality and universal principle is the dominant conception of morality in western thought, particularly in Kantian ethics
and strands of utilitarian and consequentialist thought. The study of
women's moral thinking challenges this prevalent definition of the
moral realm. Gilligan shifts between saying that the two ethics are
incompatible (1986, p. 238) and that moral maturity involves using
both perspectives (Gilligan et al., 1988, p. xxvi). However, in most
developments of Gilligan's thought, there is an accepted opposition
between justice and care, and a focus on care at the expense of
justice (see Noddings, 1984, p. 5).

There has been much dispute as to whether the different moral voices are correlated with gender. Walker (1993) cites studies which show there are few sex differences in moral reasoning in childhood and adolescence, and that adult differences are correlated with education levels and occupation. Eisenberg and Lennon (1983) argue that though women have a reputation for altruism and empathy, there is little proof that they are more caring in behaviour. Tronto (1993, p. 244) argues that an ethic of care is not exclusively female, but is a feature of all minorities and oppressed groups. However, even if gender differences are not empirically confirmed, there is a real difference in the moral norms and values associated with gender and these differences resonate with women's experience (Friedman, 1993). Moreover, whatever the empirical evidence which correlate different voices with gender, the idea of an ethic of care has significance for moral psychology and moral philosophy in so far as it presents a challenge and an alternative to dominant notions.

In what follows, I will first address the question as to whether a care-based approach is incompatible with, or distinct from, a justice approach. I will then outline the problems with emphasizing care at the expense of justice and the dangers of opposing care to justice. Finally, I will examine the insights of care theories and suggest how these might be developed in order to provide a genuine and an adequate alternative to dominant conceptions of justice.

Is care incompatible with or distinct from justice?

Kymlicka identifies three differences between an ethic of care and an ethic of justice:

1. moral capacities: learning moral principles (justice) versus developing moral dispositions (care);
2. moral reasoning: solving problems by seeking principles that have universal applicability (justice) versus seeking responses that are appropriate to the particular case (care);
3. moral concepts: attending to rights and fairness (justice) versus attending to responsibilities and relationships (care). (Kymlicka, 1990, p. 265)

In this section, I will argue that these three contrasts are overstated by care theorists. The first contrast between the two approaches seems to involve different views of what morality is. Justice approaches are concerned with learning and applying the right principles. Care approaches are aretaic, that is, orientated to the virtues that describe the qualities, capacities and dispositions of a moral person. (McIntyre, 1967). To be moral is not to apply the right principle, but to possess a moral character.

This is a genuine contrast in the sense that prevailing notions of morality deriving from Kant have concentrated on identifying principles and prescribing moral imperatives. They have tended to overlook the importance of the moral capacities and the qualities that a moral person must have to act according to principle, and this is a particularly important insight of care theories. However, the fact that little attention is paid to the psychology of moral actions in theories of justice does not mean that acting according to principle involves only the application of the rational will and that moral sensibilities and inclinations are redundant. Even if the identification and the prescribing of principles are derived from reason, knowing how and when to apply them is not. This is because principles are formal and abstract, they do not tell us what to do in particular situations. They have to be given content and situations have to be seen as relevant to their application. A responsible moral agent is not an automaton, who has internalized principles and who then executes them consistently and dispassionately.

What it takes to bring such principles to bear on individual situations involves qualities of character and sensibilities which are themselves moral, and which go beyond the straightforward process of consulting a principle and then conforming one's will and action to it. (Blum, 1993, p. 59)

Knowing that a particular situation calls for a particular principle and knowing how to apply principles involves sensitivity and attentiveness to the situation. That is, the 'process of application itself draws on moral capacities not accounted for by impartialism alone' (Blum, 1993, p. 61). Thus, while justice perspectives do not highlight moral capacities nor consider how these might be developed, the dispositions a moral person has are crucial to their ability to act on principle.

The second contrast between an ethic of justice and an ethic of care concerns moral reasoning. Justice is supposedly concerned with solving problems by seeking principles that have universal application, whereas care is concerned with seeking responses that are appropriate to a particular case. However, moral reasoning in an ethic of justice is not limited to asserting, applying and universalizing principles in abstraction from the particularities of a situation, as care theorists suggest. Situation-specific knowledge and response to contextual detail are not the exclusive preserve of an ethic of care. For, again, applying principles and making moral judgements requires attention to the features of a particular situation. In order to know what course of action will be morally right, we have to know and make judgements on which features of the situation are relevant to the moral decision in question. In utilitarian ethics, we have to imagine the consequences of that particular decision. In Kantian ethics, we have to reflect on whether we can characterize the proposed specific action in such a way that we can consistently will that it be universally done. All this requires orientation to the complexities of a particular situation.

In contrasting justice as universal and impartial with care as concerned with particular relationships, care theorists seem to suggest that justice perspectives are committed to the principle of universality and care perspectives are not. If this is the case, it would be both a distinct advantage for a theory of justice and a genuine difference between the two perspectives. But Gilligan intends that the ethic of care be extended to all human beings, not just those with whom we have close, intimate relationships. This can only mean that whatever informs caring must be universalizable from particular individuals to generalized others by virtue of something all human beings have in common. Broughton writes, 'Gilligan and her subjects seem to presuppose something like "the right of all to respect as a person", "the right to be treated sympathetically and as an equal" and "the right to respect and not to hurt others"' (Broughton, 1993, p. 122). If care is meant to apply to all people regardless of our particular relationships with them, then the contrast between the universal and the particular cannot be the basis for the contrast between justice and care. It is, however, a contrast that Gilligan and her followers want to make to show that care responds to our concrete differences, distinct individuality and concrete identity in the context of interpersonal relationships, whereas justice is applied to abstract individuals and generalized others. Justice responds to individuals only in so far as they are instances of rational beings of equal moral worth. Moral dignity lies in what we have in common at an abstract level. However, as we have seen, not only must an ethic of care appeal to common human characteristics at an abstract level in order to generalize from particular relationships, but also that an ethic of justice is not abstract in application and must be concerned with concrete others and their distinct individuality. Care, like justice, is meant to be universalized; justice, like care, is concerned with concrete individuals.

The final contrast between an ethic of justice and an ethic of care is that the former emphasizes claiming rights against individuals, whereas the latter is concerned with promoting responsibilities to care for others. The rights approach is limited to respecting others by leaving them alone and disregards the moral value of positive interaction, connectedness and commitment. (Gilligan, 1982, pp. 22, 136, 147). But theories of justice are only vulnerable to this charge if they advocate rights only as reciprocal non-interference. Not all justice perspectives focus exclusively on negative rights, but some endorse positive duties to protect and aid others. Therefore, they do impose responsibilities and care for the welfare of others.

So far, I have argued that the supposed differences between justice and care approaches do not show that they are distinct orientations. Theories of justice incorporate elements of care. Moral dispositions and capacities are relevant to justice perspectives; the application of moral principles and universalizability is compatible with orientation to particular situations and consideration of concrete others and vice versa; and focus on rights and rules does not necessarily involve ignoring responsibilities and relationships.

Care without justice: care versus justice

Next, I will address the problems with over-emphasizing care at the expense of justice and the dangers of opposing care to justice. First, if an ethic of care focuses exclusively on moral capacities and not moral principles, then we have no way of distinguishing between the qualities that are needed for moral action and moral action itself. Moral actions are reduced to those performed by a caring person. Morality, then, simply becomes a matter of having a contingent set of personality traits. If morality is only a way of behaving that is responsive to concrete needs and sensitive to particular situations, then morality is hopelessly context and situation-relative and as diverse as the different situations in which it is applied (Frankena, 1973). This rules out the possibility of a rational defence of moral action independent of feelings and responses to different situations. Relevant differences in a situation might alter how we apply but not how we define the moral good. Second, in order to know how to respond to a situation in a caring and sensitive way, it is necessary to know what features of the situation are relevant and need a response. And as Kymlicka argues,

> In making moral decisions, we do not simply attend to the different features of the situation, we also judge their relative significance. And while we want people to be good at attending to the complexity of the situation, we also want them to be good at identifying which features of the situation are the morally significant ones. And this seems to raise questions of principle rather than sensitivity. (Kymlicka, 1990, p. 267)

Furthermore, if we dispense with moral principles, then we have no way of ordering priorities when faced with conflicting demands in a particular situation.

Third, as we have seen, though care theorists are critical of universalizability because this overrides distinct individuality, they need at least to assume a principle of something like equal moral worth in order to avoid the conservative implications of advocating commitments to particular others. Otherwise an ethic of care may mean that care is limited to one's family, friends or intimates and not to those most in need, and if care is applied to the public realm it could degenerate into special pleading, nepotism and partisanship. This is obviously not the intention of care theorists who want to include all in the web of relationships, but in order to do so, they must have some way of reconciling commitment to particular others with universal concern. It is not clear how they propose to do this nor is it clear that they can do this. If care is based on relationships, how can it be applied outside the web to situations where relationships with others do not exist? In traditional theories this is usually where notions of justice as universal and impartial moral principles come in to save the day and to bridge the gap between particular and general interests. In a sense then, 'While justice requires abstraction, it is intended as the abstract form that caring takes when respect is maintained and responsibility assumed for people whom one does not know personally and may never come to know' (Broughton, 1993, p. 123). Other problems arise with focusing on caring within existing relationships. If morality is caring within existing relationships, then there is no room for judgements about whether these relationships are good, healthy or worth preserving (Tronto, 1993, p. 250). What is lacking is a careful analysis of the differences between good and morally problematic or even corrupt kinds of care. Care can be corrupt either because of qualitative features of the caring relationship (e.g., based on insincerity or coercion) or because of the relationships content (e.g., the parties have bad aspirations for each other or give sensitive attention to meeting each other's corrupt needs and desires. (Flanagan and Jackson, 1993, p. 75)

The lack of analysis between different kinds of care ignores the relevance of the ideals of justice and fairness within interpersonal relations. If all that is morally required is care and attention to other people's needs within relationships, then this hides the oppressive nature of some of those relationships and the unequal care-taking responsibilities within them, and will justify self-sacrifice to the needs of the dominant partner. Gilligan recognizes this problem to some extent and claims that a morally mature person will understand the balance between caring for the self and others (Gilligan, 1983, pp. 41–5). That is, they will make the transition from a 'self-sacrifice' to an 'interdependent' morality. However, since according to Gilligan, care orientations are typically female, the fact that morally mature women recognize that the 'self and others are equal' will not guarantee that men who are not oriented to care at all, mature or immature, will reciprocate. The assumption that harmonious self–other equality will be recognized precludes an analysis of unequal power relations (which mitigate against equal caring) and denies the role of distributive and corrective justice for determining the balance of benefits and burdens, and for the rectification of the abuse of care within relationships.

It seems, then, that caring on its own cannot be the basis for an adequate moral theory for either the public or the private realm. Gilligan, however, has suggested that women's morality should be seen as a corrective but not an alternative to the dominant model and that it plays a part in public and private morality (Gilligan, 1983, 1986), but the interaction of the two theories and between the public and private is unclear in her work. In fact, the emphasis on the differences between care and justice orientations of men and women tends to entrench the oppositions feminists have challenged. It runs the risk of reinstating old and oppressive dichotomies between reason and emotion, the universal and the particular, the public and the private, men and women, with the danger that female morality is devalued rather than incorporated as a corrective or seen as a viable alternative to male perspectives.

Tronto argues that emphasizing differences is strategically dangerous, 'because in a social context that identifies the male as normal
contains an implication of the inferiority of the distinctly female'
(Tronto, 1993, p. 241). Articulating differences could mean that
women's voices will remain where they have always been –
confined to and seen as appropriate to the domestic sphere, relevant
only for intimate relationships between family and friends,
irrelevant to wider public concerns.

Insights derived from an ethic of care

All this might seem that the idea of an ethic of care ought to be
abandoned. However, emphasis on care not only highlights the
inadequacies of prevailing conceptions of justice, but also provides
insights into the requirements of an alternative theory.

I have argued that justice perspectives incorporate considerations
of care, so that the differences between the perspectives are not as
diametrically opposed as care theorists have claimed. However,
theories of justice also neglect aspects of caring that have moral
significance. For instance, although moral capacities are relevant to
justice perspectives in that they are important for having a sense
of justice and necessary for the application of principles, theories
of justice give no moral recognition to how these capacities are
developed and sustained. This is a significant omission since, as
Baier argues, the stability of these theories depends on people giving
and experiencing care. She argues that theories of justice, including
Rawls's, assume there will be loving parents in order to maintain a
just society and to ensure the development of a sense of justice.

Rawls' theory, like so many other theories of obligation, in the end must
take out a loan not only on the natural duty of parents to care for children
…, but on the natural *virtue* of parental love … The virtue of being a *loving*
parent must supplement the natural duties and the obligations of justice, if
the just society is to last beyond the first generation. (Baier, 1993, p. 23)

If the experience of care and caring has a role in founding an ethical
sense, and if moral dispositions to be just presuppose experiences
of care, then how care is fostered is morally significant. Baier's point
is that 'a decent morality will *not* depend for its stability on forces to
which it gives no moral recognition' (Baier, 1993, p. 25). Given the
importance of care within the family, this also implies that

principles of justice should be applied to the family to ensure that it is an appropriate organization for facilitating care amongst its members. Theories of justice have notoriously neglected the role of care and justice in the distribution of care within the family. In so far as this mitigates against other values they promote, this is a serious shortcoming.

I have argued against care theory, that justice perspectives do involve attention to concrete rather than generalized others. However, this does not amount to caring for them, as defenders of the justice perspective suggest. For example, Okin claims that her understanding of Rawls's original position collapses the distinction between an ethic of care and an ethic of justice. She argues that the original position need not be understood abstractly as rational choice. The principles of justice are founded not on distance and detachment, but on empathy and concern for others. This is because the original position forces us to be empathetic. As contractors we are deprived of knowledge of our own identities and place in society, therefore we are required to 'consider the identities, aims and attachments of every other person however different they may be from ourselves, as of equal concern with our own'. Choosers are required to think from the position of *everybody*, in the sense of each in turn. The original position is not an abstraction from difference, but is rooted in 'an appreciation and concern for social and other human differences'. She concludes that 'the only coherent way in which a party in the original position can think about justice is through empathy with persons of all kinds in all different positions in society, but especially with the least well-off in various respects' (Okin, 1990c, pp. 31–4).

This defence of Rawlsian justice as collapsing the distinction between justice and care, is wide off the mark. The original position may indeed require us to consider concrete others, and to attend to their different identities, aims and attachments, but we do this not because they are of equal concern, or because we care about them, but in case we *are* one of them (in particular, one of the disadvantaged). The requirement to consider everyone equally is not an exercise of empathy, but an exercise of rational self-interest. We are not concerned with the well-being of others, we are concerned with our own. And we are not concerned about other people because the contracting parties are mutually disinterested. This is the case, precisely to ensure that the principles of justice will not depend on 'extensive ties of natural sentiment' (Rawls, 1971,

p. 129) and will apply to everyone whether or not we care about them.

Now this assumption of rationality and self-interest creates further problems for theories of justice in general which care theory highlights. For Rawls in particular, the problem is this: if the parties to the contract are mutually disinterested and consider others from a rational self-interested point of view, that is, in case we are one of the others, then once the veil of ignorance has been removed, why should we continue to consider others at all? Now we know who we are, and if we are not 'one of them', why should we consider their interests at all or abide by the principles? Since care is not part of our motivations, it might not be in our rational self-interest to do so. Even if rational self-interest can do the work of setting up the principles, it cannot, on its own, give us reasons for abiding by them. Similarly, justice perspectives in general suffer from the problem of relying on rationality to tell us what is the right thing to do, and then giving us no independent motivation for doing what reason prescribes. Perhaps care theory could help here.

Care theorists claim that morality is not about individual rational beings legislating and obeying principles generated from within themselves. Morality is about moral dispositions, capacities and sensibilities. To the extent that theories of justice overlook the role of the latter in moral motivations, they create insolvable problems for themselves (see Chapter 1). Kant regarded morality as a matter of reason alone. He assumed that recognition of the rationality of the categorical imperative would be sufficient to motivate people to act morally. Utilitarians assume that we will act in the general interest because it is rational to treat others' interests as no more important than our own. Both theories tell us why it is rational to act according to the principles they advance, but neither tell us why we should want to be rational. They give us no psychological or social reasons for doing what reason prescribes.

An ethic of care with its emphasis on moral capacities and dispositions can give us an account of the genesis of moral motivation and can give us an insight into the social conditions necessary to develop these motivational forces. That is, empathy, love, care and a sense of responsibility are necessary for moral motivation, to *want* to act morally; and we are motivated to act with care and concern because of our social experiences of relationships and ties to other people. Care theorists' rejection of the abstract individual and the rational, autonomous agent of justice perspectives suggests that social bonds create identification with others and that this gives rise to caring, responsible and co-operative behaviour. If this is the case, people's motivation to care derives in part from the social relations in which they stand to one another.

Care theories' account of empathy and care is similar to Hume's on sympathy. Sympathy, according to Hume, is the natural tendency of human beings to share the feelings of others (Hume, 1888, pp. 294–5). Although Hume thought that sympathy was a natural fact of human psychology, his arguments also suggest that sympathy is part of our social nature as it depends on people's relationships and involvements with one another which facilitate sympathetic identification. However, for Hume, sympathy was limited according to the strengths of the relationships and their degree of proximity in time and place. The problem then arises of how to bridge the gap between limited and universal sympathy. This parallels the problem in the ethic of care, of how to extend the web of relations between family, friends and intimates to people in general. Hume's answer is that partial feelings of sympathy can be corrected by the adoption of moral rules which we abide by because it is in our self-interest to do so. However, invoking general rules coupled with self-interest will not solve the problems as to why human beings, who are self-interested and who have limited sympathies, should make moral judgements from an impersonal and impartial point of view, rather than at best from restricted benevolence. Sympathy, as a device to bridge the gap between the self and others, remains confined to and can only be effective within a limited circle. Perhaps an ethic of care could help us to break out of this circle without relying solely on the rationality of the adoption of general rules or principles. Hume's characterization of sympathy, like the ethic of care, shows that the possibility of care, empathy, responsibility and concern for others depends on the social relations people have with each other. Therefore, an adequate theory of justice needs to provide an account of the social relations and conditions necessary for the expansion of moral rather than simply prudential reasons to be just. That is, an account which gives reasons beyond self-interest and beyond impartial reason for the general adherence to moral rules.

Conclusion

If empathy and care are a consequence of our social nature, then we need an account of the social and interdependent individual as opposed to the atomised individual of liberal theory, in order to generate reasons for acting morally, based on interaction, connection and commitment. If sympathy and care are developed because of social bonds, then we need an account of the social conditions and relations which facilitate their development and expression, and their expansion beyond family, friends and intimates. We need to explore the social and political implications of the idea that acting morally depends on the existence of social bonds and intersubjective interests, and that it is only within a co-operative community where all share a common enterprise that motivation for reciprocal care can flourish.

So far, I have argued that an ethic of care can indicate a starting-point for an analysis of the psychological and social basis of moral development and moral behaviour which is lacking in justice perspectives. There is another possibility that emerges from an ethic of care. Because an ethic of care focuses on perceiving and responding to people's different needs in particular contexts, this could be seen as an embryonic theory of justice informed by the principle, 'to each according to his needs' and so could be a defence of an alternative to liberal theories of justice. This could be the basis not just for criticizing the orientation of justice perspectives, and their foci on principles, rules and rights, but a basis for criticizing the content of the principles, rights and rules in different theories of distributive justice. However, the problem with an ethic of care, as it stands, is that it is not clear which needs could provide the basis for such a challenge. Gilligan says, 'Within the context of relationships, the self as moral agent perceives and responds to perceptions of need' (Gilligan, 1987, p. 23). This suggests the needs that should be attended to are felt or perceived needs and it is these subjective desires which form the basis of our moral claims and corresponding responsibilities. This is a problem, because it is not obvious that we have moral obligations to attend to the subjective desires of others or that subjective desires carry moral weight. We need to make distinctions between desires, between those that are subjectively valuable and those that are objectively important, between what is desired and what is worth desiring and worthy of satisfaction. For this, an adequate theory of justice must distinguish between wants and needs and defend the satisfaction of the latter. Since, in common with an ethic of care, liberal theory stresses the importance of the satisfaction of wants, it is to this distinction that I now turn.

8

Wants and Needs

Throughout this book, it has been argued that one of the central problems of liberal political philosophy is taking as its starting-point the abstract individual and the sovereignty of individual desires. It is this which gives rise to impoverished conceptions of freedom as the absence of impediments to pursue autonomously chosen desires; of equality as equality of opportunity to compete to fulfil self-defined, self-interested desires; of the function of the state as guarantor of negative formal and legal rights, and of its illegitimate role in the private sphere; and of justice as a procedural framework which allows individuals to pursue their own ends, purposes, values and conceptions of the good without adjudicating between them.

Implicit in these criticisms is the view that an adequate defence of politics and political morality must begin by rejecting the liberal concept of the abstract individual and the autonomy, rationality and sovereignty of expressed desires. Such a defence involves distinguishing between actual desires and objectively important needs, judging and evaluating subjective desires and distinguishing between those ends, purposes and interests which are of fundamental importance and those which are not. It also involves rejecting the liberal aim of political and moral neutrality which makes liberals both sceptical of and unable to justify any substantive conceptions of human well-being or fulfilment. For the authority and rationality of individual conceptions of the good cannot be brought into question without commitment to some objective and substantive notion of human good that political organization should promote and seek to satisfy. That is, the arguments threading through this book presuppose that an objective account of the nature and claims of need can be given. In this chapter, I will attempt to provide such an account. I will begin by outlining the reasons for the liberal hostility to and suspicion of attempts to defend needs as a moral basis for politics. I will then clarify the concept of need and distinguish this from the concept of felt needs, wants and preferences in order to answer liberal objections.

Liberal Objections to the Concept of Needs

Liberal theorists, utilitarians, orthodox economists and political scientists object to definitions of objective needs and question the moral acceptability of need as a principle of distribution. They stress instead the function of government and the effectiveness of the market for enabling individuals to pursue their own goals and for satisfying felt needs, expressed wants or preferences. This is consistent with both the freedom of the individual and the pluralism of modern liberal society. The advantages claimed for policies and institutions committed to preference and want satisfaction are allegedly epistemological, moral and empirical.

First, it is claimed that theories of objective need are under-pinned by ontological assumptions. They are metaphysical constructs and presuppose a metaphysic. Need theorists talk about needs as though they were facts, as if they related to some objective and impersonal standard. If this is so, then we can be said to have needs which we do not feel and to need what we do not want. Need cannot be established from subjective avowals. We have to impute needs to people and assume they have needs they do not profess to feel. They have to be hypothetically constructed when not experienced. Whereas, with wants and preferences, these are demonstrable dispositions to desire or prefer something. To identify them, we do not have to make any metaphysical assumptions. To establish the wants of any individual, it is not necessary to impute needs which they may not feel. We can ask them what their preferences are, we can observe their demands or we can read them off from what they actually consume or use. That is, to say someone has a need they do not feel is to make an assumption which cannot be verified empirically. To say someone has a want or preference is to state a fact since wants can be shown to exist. Needs are not objective or universal facts but hypothetical constructs whose existence cannot be proved.

Second, it is argued that need claims are not empirical but normative (Benn and Peters, 1959; Taylor, 1959; Fitzgerald, 1977b, 1977c; Springborg, 1981; Soper, 1981). This is because all needs are instrumental. We can need something only for some future end or purpose. Statements of need are always of the form 'A needs x in order to y'. Frankfurt argues that, 'All necessities are ... conditional: nothing is needed in virtue of being an indispensable condition for the attainment of a certain end' (Frankfurt, 1984, p. 3, cf. Barry, 1965, pp. 47–9; White, 1971, pp. 105–6; Flew, 1977, pp. 213–18; Dearden, 1972, p. 50). If all need statements imply that a need is a means to an end, then what people need is logically related and justified with reference to the end in question. Needs may relate to different ends and purposes. Talk about human needs to achieve certain goals or human excellences or conceptions of the good ignores competing claims as to what these are. Such claims reflect the values of the persons claiming there is a need.

Springborg (1981) and Fitzgerald (1977c) argue that theoretical appeal to needs as necessary conditions to achieve an end, while appearing to be empirical, necessarily presuppose values. Need claims cannot be made empirical, because empirical evidence about means to ends is only relevant after normative assumptions about the ends and purposes to which they relate have been made. Since there is disagreement about values and a plurality of ends and purposes which different people think are important or worthwhile, what constitutes a need will vary in accordance with these.

It seems to follow that if classification of need depends on ends and purposes, and these embody different values, there cannot be an empirical or objective definition of need, since need claims are inevitably value-laden. It also seems that responding to wants and preferences involves no such value judgements and no assumptions about the ends and purposes people do or ought to have. People simply have the desires they can be demonstrably seen to have and these are sovereign. Even if values are embedded in what people want, policies which relate to individual wants make no judgement on these. They acknowledge and conform to existing values because these are the values people have.

Third, opponents of need argue for the political and moral superiority of wants over needs. Emphasis on needs as opposed to wants legitimizes authoritarian and illiberal policies (Fitzgerald, 1977c; Flew, 1977; McInnes, 1977; Heller, 1980). Policies based on need can justify expertise by governments and by those who claim to know what real needs are, and can sanction imposing them over people's actual needs. Policies based on particular normative conceptions of need threaten the freedom of individuals to define needs for themselves. In contrast to this, identifying wants with what people perceive them to be avoids the danger of coercion in the name of real needs or best interests, because political practices and economic institutions seek to satisfy the given wants people have and this is compatible with a free society. Finally, it is argued that allocative priority based on planning to meet need leads to tyranny over wants. In the free market existing needs dictate to political institutions and economic processes. Hence this form of political and economic organization is conducive to the maximum and equitable satisfaction of need.

It is not necessary for critics of the concept of need to hold all these four objections. The first two objections claim that policies cannot be based on need for epistemological reasons connected with the concept of need: because needs presuppose a metaphysic, their existence cannot be proved; because they are hypothetical constructs they cannot be known; because they involve normative assumptions they cannot be made empirical. The latter objections are moral and empirical in that policies based on need threaten individual freedom, and that the market both avoids this danger and is more effective at meeting actual needs since it establishes *ex post* through effective demand what they are. Therefore, the market is a morally superior as well as a more efficient mechanism for allocating resources. In order to defend the concept of need, I will first address the epistemological objections by drawing on arguments that define needs as necessary conditions for moral agency.

Defining needs: needs as conditions for action

Critics of the objectivity of need claimed that needs could not be defined in a neutral, empirical or value-free way because needs are means to ends which relate to disputed values. In order to avoid the relativity and therefore the redundancy of the concept of need for claims to satisfaction, political and moral philosophers have argued that objective needs are those which secure ends that are valuable in some objective way. In this vein various writers have proposed that needs can be defined as the necessary precondition or instruments for the attainment of any or all particular ends anyone might want to pursue. Emphasis is placed not on needs' role as means to ends, but on the wide variety of ends they serve (see, for example, Hart, 1955, on 'natural rights'; Barry, 1965, on 'interests'; Nielsen, 1969, p. 188; Rawls, 1971, on 'primary goods'; Weale, 1978, Ch. 4–5;

Shue, 1980, Ch. 1–2; Gewirth, 1982/1987, on 'rights'; Doyal and Gough, 1984, p. 14, 1991; Daniels, 1985, Ch. 2–3; Plant, 1991, Ch. 5; and Sen, 1985).

Following these attempts, I will argue that needs must be defined empirically and objectively as means to ends any human agent has good reason to pursue, desire or value if they are to act successfully to achieve any end or to realize any values whatever they may be. This claim begins from the objective fact of the existence of empirical agents who have ends and goals that they want to pursue and who must act to achieve them. In order to act, the agent must have the necessary conditions of action. As we have seen in previous chapters, Gewirth (1987) claims that actions have two generic features and necessary conditions: freedom and well-being. He argues that freedom and well-being are necessary conditions of action which every agent must regard as necessary goods for himself or herself, since he or she could not act without them. Following Gewirth, I have argued elsewhere that the necessary conditions of action are what constitute the fundamental human needs of every actual, prospective or potential agent. Corresponding to Gewirth's notion of 'well-being' I argue that the notions of survival and physical and mental health approximate these conditions (Ramsay, 1992).

Survival is a fundamental human need because it is a necessary condition of any activity. Physical and mental health are fundamental human needs because they are necessary conditions for purposive and successful activity. All persons who want to act to achieve any end have these needs since the conditions for human activity apply universally to all human agents. Freedom is not considered as a separate need since the freedom to act to achieve any end involves fulfilling the needs for survival and health which are means to those ends. Meeting people's needs contributes and is fundamental to their freedom, defined as the ability to achieve ends and purposes.

This objective, instrumental account of fundamental human needs shows that it is a determinable matter of fact what needs a person has, and is compatible with recognizing a plurality of ends. Needs do not relate to any particular conception of the good, but to any ends a person might have. Survival and health needs, then, are objective and universal requirements for achieving any end and do not embody particular values that are not applicable to all human agents.

We can empirically discover what survival and health needs are from facts about our biological and physiological constitutions in given social contexts. Survival and health needs are determined biologically with differences according to age, sex, climatic conditions and physical and mental constitutions. At an abstract level of generality, physical health needs are the needs for air, to live in a safe and unpolluted environment, the need for food, clean water, sleep, rest, protection against the environment and climate (clothing and shelter), exercise and recreation and protection from physical harm (for a defence of abstract psychological needs for security, love and relatedness, esteem and identity and self-realization see Ramsay, 1992, pp. 149–76).

We can postulate the existence of abstract general needs because we have scientific knowledge of what is necessary for survival and health, and causal evidence of the destructive effects if these needs are frustrated. And it is precisely because we have knowledge of the human organism that we can deduce that all human beings have these needs. However, to identify fundamental human needs at an abstract level of generality cannot provide sufficient information to identify actual needs in specific contexts. What changes over time is not fundamental human needs, but the specific socio-historic form these needs take, ways of satisfying them and choice of objects to meet them. Here 'objects' can be people, social relations, states of affairs, physical objects, consumer goods, public services, living and working conditions, material and non-material resources as well as social, environmental and cultural factors. The validity of the classification of any specific socio-historic need as a fundamental human need will depend on whether the former can be cogently derived from the latter. A criterion for inclusion in the list of socially specific needs is the existence of causal connections between the proposed need, its object of satisfaction, and survival or the achievement, restoration or maintenance of health.

Needs and Wants

If needs are objective requirements for survival and health, they can be distinguished from subjectively felt wants and preferences. We ordinarily distinguish between needs and wants by saying we need what we do not want and we want what we do not need. Though, of course, needs and wants can coincide, they differ crucially in the following ways. Both needs and wants are parallel in that they relate to ends needed or wanted, but they differ in the criteria for their justification. They are parallel in that they both fit the formula:

$$A \text{ needs } X \text{ in order to } Y$$
$$A \text{ wants } B \text{ in order to } C$$

In both cases of wanting and needing there is a subject of want or need, an object wanted or needed, and an end, goal or purpose for which the object is wanted or needed. As has been argued, we cannot just want something, we always want it for something. Want claims must be explained with reference to an end or purpose to give that claim meaning and intelligibility (Anscombe, 1957; Taylor, 1959; Norman, 1971). Similarly, need claims are only made intelligible when the end or purpose for which they are needed is specified. This does not mean that all want or need claims must be followed by an 'in order to Y or C' clause. What the object is wanted or needed for might be tacit, understood or obvious given the context of the claim. However, it does mean that unless the 'in order to Y or C' clause is implicit, tacit or understood, it can be added. If not, the want or need claim is unintelligible.

Both wants and needs, then, are parallel in that they require for their intelligibility an end for which they are wanted or needed. However, since there is good reason to suppose that the intelligibility, justification and value of wants and needs cannot exceed the intelligibility, justification and value of the ends they serve, wants and needs differ where questions of justification and value arise precisely because the character of the ends they relate to differ. Wants can relate to any end. It is logically possible to want anything at all and to fervently desire things that are trivial, detrimental or even harmful. The fact that something is wanted *per se* does not guarantee its value or justify its pursuit or satisfaction. The concept of need does not suffer from the same justification problems since needs relate to the objective goals of survival and health. It is the importance of these goals that justifies the satisfaction of needs as a means to achieve them. The justification of want or need satisfaction lies not in the facts of wanting or needing, but in whether the purposes to which they relate can be justified.

For this reason, needs are objectively valuable and wants are subjectively valuable. Needs are valuable whether we know or experience them, choose them, want them, act on them or appreciate their importance. This is because they are the practical means to attaining the universally important goals of survival and health. They are valuable, whether or not they are subjectively valuable. Wants are what *we* value; we know them, we experience them directly and believe them to be important. They are subjectively valued, even if they are not objectively valuable.

Fundamental human needs may not be known to us or experienced by us in the direct way felt needs, wants and preferences generally are. If needs are objective requirements, then we may be mistaken or ignorant about our needs. We may be in need of something without being aware that we need it, we may not know what we need. We may be ignorant or mistaken about what we need, or think that we need something. In contrast to this, we do know what we feel our needs to be and our wants are subjectively experienced by us. Hence, there is a difference in the evidence for the existence of needs and wants. Though, of course, needs can be felt, feeling a need is not a necessary or sufficient criterion for having a need or part of what it means to need something. Needs are not dependent on the subject experiencing them, therefore they cannot be inferred from what people say they need or from what people actually do. This does not mean, however, that there is no behavioural or empirical evidence relevant to identifying needs.

Their existence can be verified by causal explanations, which, with reference to biological and psychological theories, demonstrate the effects on survival and health if needs are inadequately satisfied or not met all. Wants are characteristically something felt. They are mind-dependent and attributable to the subject of experience. Since felt needs and wants are subjectively experienced, evidence for them comes from what people say they need or want, and wants can be inferred from intentional behaviour and observing what people do.

Wants, however, with the exception of cravings, impulses and instinctive reactions are not just brute psychological facts or mental states. They are intentional and require objects wanted. They are consequently dependent on beliefs about the desirability and availability of wanted objects which are conditioned by social contexts and circumstances within them. In contrast to this, fundamental human needs are independent of feelings and beliefs. What I feel the need for and what I want may be the object of belief, but what I *do* need is not. Because wants and preferences are belief-dependent, subjective experience of wanting in conjunction with a particular belief can lead me to feeling that I want almost anything. However, I cannot really need 'just anything'. What I need is restricted by natural necessity and depends on the properties of the object needed. I can only need something if it is essential to survival and health, not because I believe it is or want it. If I need something, it must have certain characteristics and properties that *are* essential to survival and health.

I can want X without X satisfying my desire, but I can only need X *if* it satisfies that need. For this reason, wants involve choice and needs do not. Choice and deliberation are involved in the formulation of many desires and preferences and there is a sense in which desiring and preferring are themselves acts of choice. To want or prefer something is to choose that it should come about. When A prefers X to Y, A prefers that X should come about, and in this sense chooses X rather than Y. In some cases effectively desiring X involves an act of choosing X. Having a need is not an act of choice. We are not free to choose our needs because what our needs are is determined and limited by our biological and psychological constitutions. The range of our socially specific derived needs may alter over time and place, but objects to meet them must have certain satisfier characteristics, the properties of which we are not free to choose. Likewise, having need is not an act of choice in the way having a want is, since we may be aware of our needs and the means to satisfy them and choose not to seek to satisfy them.

'Need' is not an intentional verb or motivationally connected with action in the way that 'desire' is. We can know what we need and not want it. However, needs are reasons for action, in the sense that we have good reason to act to satisfy them, regardless of whether we desire to do so. The fact that X is not desired does not make it undesirable. Conversely, desires are part of my reason for acting to achieve them but the fact that I desire something does not make it desirable in itself. Reasons for acting are not provided by the fact that X is desired, but by something in virtue of which X is worth desiring. Desires are *my* reason for acting to get what I want. Needs are objective reasons for acting to get what we need.

The definition of needs defended here and their differences to the concept of wants provide the basis for answering epistemological objections to the concept of need and expose some of the disadvantages of basing political morality and policy on the concept of felt needs, wants or preferences. It has been shown that needs as the necessary requirements for survival and health are not metaphysical constructs, but are empirically discoverable means to ends any human being has good reason to pursue, desire or value. The fact that they may not be felt or experienced, does not mean that they do not exist. Their existence can be verified by causal explanations which demonstrate the effect on survival and health if these needs are not met. Needs can be made empirical and are objectively valuable because they are the practical means necessary to act to achieve any other end or value people may have. No matter what different ends or purposes people have, there are some conditions necessary to attain these and therefore they are objective and universal goods. Liberal claims for the advantages of the concept of wants are either invalid or can be outweighed by other considerations.

The liberal view that the notions of felt needs, wants or preferences require no assumptions about 'real' need or raise no ontological issues is mistaken. Want theories only appear to raise no ontological issues because real needs are defined as equivalent to those which are felt, articulated or identified in consumption. But, here, ontology is conflated with epistemology. What *is*, is identified with what we *know*, and what we can know is limited to what we directly experience. Assumptions about needs are not avoided, needs are reduced to what we feel them to be or what we want. Want theory does not escape assumptions about an ontology of real need. The theory has not avoided metaphysics, but merely made different assumptions about what can be known and what real needs are. Moreover, these assumptions are false, because what people want and feel the need for does not always correspond to what they do in fact need. Policies which correspond to wants will then have the harmful consequences of not acknowledging or seeking to satisfy those needs that are not directly manifest as subjective avowals or effective demands.

Though it is claimed that wants are knowable because they are directly manifest, their alleged transparency and the advantages of responding to wants are disputable. Establishing wants is not always straightforward. We may have unconscious or subconscious wants that are not articulated. It is not always obvious to us what we want and which object will satisfy the wants we have. Most of us have unspecified longings and dissatisfactions, as well as ambivalence and confusion about what it is we do actually want. Even when we are sure that we want something, the advantages of having policies on these can be overridden for two reasons. The first reason is that since wants are belief-dependent, they may rest on false or superficial beliefs about what is worth desiring or whether the wanted object will satisfy the desire. If this is the case, then the advantage of being able to identify wants from subjective experience is outweighed by the fact that pursuing or satisfying such a desire is either unimportant, irrational, counterproductive or contrary to our interests. The second reason is seeking to satisfy the given wants people have means endorsing and accepting them, whatever they are and, as it has been argued, the fact that something is wanted and therefore subjectively valuable, cannot by itself make it valuable, worth desiring or having, and therefore is not a sufficient criterion on which to base claims to satisfaction.

For defenders of liberal theory, however, it is precisely this neutrality about other people's wants, preferences, ends, purposes and conceptions of the good that is its advantage over need theory which supposedly presumes and leads to the imposition of partial norms in the guise of universal goals. However, on the one hand, the liberal claim that no judgements are made about which preferences ought to be satisfied, rather than being a virtue of the theory, is a central problem. It renders liberal theory incapable of providing any conception of the good life or a way of identifying genuine needs or significant purposes. On the other hand, liberals do make judgements that wants or preferences rather than needs should be satisfied. The liberal reduction of needs to wants is neither factual nor neutral. They can only be so identified, because the theorist has adopted a particular definition of need which accepts felt needs and desires as the only real needs there are. Aiming to satisfy the given wants that people have has normative implications. It suggests that wants and preferences are the proper criteria for the allocation of resources and has the effect of positively evaluating and endorsing the existing pattern of wants and consumer satisfactions. Value judgements about the appropriateness, desirability and satisfaction of wants are inescapable if wants as a criterion for distribution is to be justified.

Liberals claim to avoid value judgements by simply taking as a starting-point the values embedded in the wants people have, by accepting existing values as facts without endorsing or condemning them, because this happens to be what people want. However, if what people want is accepted as a starting-point simply because they want it, the unquestioned premise of the argument is that it is good for people to have what they want and this is what the good life consists of. Here want is appealed to as an ultimate value and hence emphasis on wants cannot escape presumption of norms.

What has been established so far is a theoretical defence of the concept of needs in relation to wants. Needs can be made empirical and are objectively valuable, wants do not avoid metaphysical or normative assumptions. Given what has been established about objective values and the belief and mind dependency of wants, it can no longer be assumed that it is good for people to have what they want, whereas it seems we can say that it is good for people to have what they need.

This argument suggests that, in principle, policies for the allocation of resources ought to be based on needs rather than wants. Liberals may still make a case for want satisfaction based on moral and empirical claims. These are, first, that identifying wants with what people perceive them to be is morally superior because this respects the freedom of the individual to define wants for themselves and want satisfaction enhances freedom. Second, that market society preserves freedom because the market responds to the given wants people have and it is a more efficient mechanism for meeting needs since it establishes *ex post* what they are. In what follows, I will examine the validity of these claims by examining the extent to which we are free to define, pursue and satisfy our wants in market society.

How free are the wants we have?

Liberals who defend individuals defining, pursuing and satisfying their own wants and preferences because only this is compatible with individual freedom, assume the existence of rational and autonomous individuals who choose their own wants, preferences, ends and values and who are the best judges of their own interests. But once the social conditioning of wants and the limits of individual knowledge and rationality are acknowledged, it is difficult to maintain the assumption of the sovereignty of individual desires and the value and nature of freedom as want satisfaction.

Existing patterns of wants are not expressions of individual autonomous choice, but are the effects of political, patriarchal, economic, social, cultural and commercial forces which shape and limit the kinds of wants and preferences people have. Wants are the product of social conditions. For instance, the private preferences of individuals do not dictate to economic institutions, but rather, what is produced, how it is produced and how it is distributed determines and restricts what individuals want or feel the need for. Wants and preferences are the effects of what is actually around in society – what is produced, consumed and available to individuals given their place in production and in the distribution of wealth and given their access to material and non-material resources. What people feel they want will depend on the kinds of goods produced in a society, will be affected by seeing the consumption of others, and wants expressed in consumption will be limited by what they can afford or what they have access to. Wants and preferences are manipulated indirectly by the process of socialization. Sex-role conditioning in the family and education, gender stereotyping in the media and culture generally affect what women want, what it is appropriate for them to want, what they expect and value.

The social conditioning of wants may be direct. What people want is often the result of conscious intention and deliberate manipulation, the most obvious example being the advertising and marketing policies of commercial institutions which aim to mould consumer choices. They persuade people not just that they want certain products, but these products are presented as symbolic objectifications of a desirable way of life attainable through consumption of the products they promote. Here wants are shaped by deliberately engendering beliefs about the desirable conse-quences of pursuing certain objects of satisfaction. Political institutions, too, directly manipulate the expression of wants and preferences. For instance, governments channel people's desire for security and fears of rising crime and increasing violence into popular support for authoritarian law and order policies, more policing and tougher sentencing. Similarly, people's desires for a decent standard of living, health care, education and housing are translated into valuing the entrepreneurial spirit, individual initiative, self-reliance and personal responsibility which are claimed to be prerequisites for the satisfaction of such preferences, and which government policies on lower rates of taxation, cutting benefits and the minimal welfare state are said to promote. Here, preferences for policies are shaped by beliefs about what are feasible and effective solutions to their satisfaction.

The argument that wants and preferences are constrained and conditioned by social forces tells against the autonomously chosen status claimed for them by liberal theory. The point here is not just that wants and preferences are determined, for what we want will always be shaped by the social circumstances we live in, whatever they are. What is particularly significant is that in a capitalist market economy, wants and preferences are determined by the necessity for the reproduction of individuals within the system, the reproduction of capitalist social relations, the expansion of the capitalist system and the development of a competitive economy. Under patriarchal capitalism, wants and preferences are moulded by class and power relations to suit the interests of the owning classes and power holders whose primary interests may be antithetical to those whose interests they shape.

For these reasons, want satisfaction cannot be equated with freedom. If the wants and preferences a person has are socially conditioned by power relationships, then acting on those wants seems to exemplify lack of freedom and lack of self-determination, rather than freedom and autonomous choice. If the formation and development of our wants are conditioned in ways over which we have little control, then action motivated by them cannot be free activity, even if society is organized in such a way that we are free to pursue and satisfy the wants so formed and developed. Thus, even if market mechanisms did deliver the goods people want, the wants themselves are irreducibly unfree.

Furthermore, if the wants a person has are based on ignorance or misperceptions of what will satisfy, or if they are produced by false beliefs, then acting to satisfy these wants is not compatible with freedom. People may not even formulate or express wants and preferences since their social circumstances structure and restrict their desires so that they no longer feel them. Several sociological studies confirm the ways in which individuals resign themselves to their fate. An attitude survey by Runciman (1966) revealed that the poorest sections of the population were hardly aware of their poverty. Coates and Silburn's (1967) study of poverty in Nottingham concluded that the lower a man's wages, the more deprived he appears to be, the less aggressively he will construe his needs and the less likely he is to respond with vigorous complaints, demands or even active discontent. Unless there is any validity in the counter-intuitive idea that a way of increasing freedom is to restrict desires, then abandoning desires that cannot be satisfied cannot be ignored as a limitation on freedom.

Wants that are felt and expressed may not be compatible with freedom in the sense that they may be based on ignorance of what is available or possible, on false perceptions of what will satisfy and on false beliefs about the consequences of action to achieve them or on mistaken views about what is normal, appropriate or natural and what alternatives are feasible or historically possible. Ignorance and false beliefs restrict the nature of the goals we have as well as action to achieve them, and in so doing limit the autonomy of the individual to define and pursue their own ends and purposes.

These two arguments, that wants are socially conditioned and that they may be the result of ignorance or mistaken beliefs, contradict the liberal assumption that identifying wants with what people perceive them to be respects their freedom.

Want satisfaction and the market

Liberals claim that the market is the mechanism by which freedom and want satisfaction are conjoined. Free market mechanisms distribute resources in accordance with people's needs, wants and preferences. Because the market uses effective demand and actual consumption as the index of what people need or want, then no imposition of one conception of the good and therefore no threat to individual freedom occur in free market exchanges. The market reflects given preferences. The grounds for these claims depend on the validity of the liberal reduction of needs, wants and preferences to effective consumer demands. For, if there are needs and wants that are not gratifiable in consumption or that are not expressed as effective demand, then the claim that the market exemplifies freedom and want satisfaction is seriously compromised.

Now, it is obvious that there are wants and preferences that people have that are not satisfiable by commodity exchange and that these are incompatible with the unfettered operation of the market. People do not just want material goods, they want to develop and use their capacities (creative, moral, intellectual and emotional). They want to engage in relationships and activities not related to contractual exchange or the possession of commodities. They want non-material goods – emotional security and self-esteem, affection, love, a sense of identity and belonging. And although the market attempts to embody the promise of these in the goods it produces, and to persuade that consumerism is the route to all want satisfaction, the market cannot deliver the qualitative non-material satisfiers of these wants and preferences. The market reduces qualitative desires to what is quantifiable, to what can be possessed, consumed, bought or sold. People's wants and preferences are identified with a limited range of material goods which are not autonomously chosen, and satisfaction is seen exclusively as a function of consumption. Even if the market could deliver the goods people demanded, the wants reflected in consumption are merely the wants of human beings as consumers of material utilities. These wants are subject to constraint in the form they take, since individuals can choose as satisfiers only those objects which are imputed to them as consumers.

The market cannot deliver social wants or wants for public services or collective provision, and these wants are undermined by the operation of market principles. If I want a publicly funded, well-resourced comprehensive education system which promotes egalitarian ideas and stimulates self-development, this is incompatible with the function of education in a market economy which requires the majority of the population to do menial, boring work and to be compliant and submissive to authority. It is also incompatible with the co-existence of a private system which ignores the reality of unequal access and which fosters hierarchical and meritocratic values. If I want the collective public provision of services like cheap mass transport or subsidized housing co-operatives, this is ruled out by the privatization of provision in market economies and the necessary emphasis on individual choice and private consumption. If I want to live in a clean and unpolluted environment, how am I going to buy this on the market? How is the market going to guarantee this, when there is good reason to suppose that the market cannot provide the financial incentives for companies concerned with profit to take anti-pollution measures?

It seems, then, that we are only free to satisfy the wants and preferences that can be satisfied on the market. We are not free to satisfy qualitative or social wants, the kinds of preferences that do not register on the market or that are incompatible with its functioning. The market, then, can only respond to a limited range of wants and preferences. However, even if the market were an effective device for satisfying these, their satisfaction would do little to justify the market with respect to freedom. To celebrate the market system because it responds to the wants that it can satisfy overlooks the fact that the market system itself produced these wants. Therefore it is pointless and circular to attempt to justify the system by reference to the freedom of the individual to satisfy those conditioned desires.

This leaves us with the more limited claim that we are free to satisfy the wants we have for market products on the market. It is argued that the market preserves freedom by identifying the needs and wants that people have by their effective demands. The market economy which identifies needs *a posteriori* in actual consumption can respond to changes in effective demands so that goods and services are produced according to preferences. Thus it is claimed that the market is both an efficient distributive mechanism which ensures the satisfaction of needs, desires and preferences, and that the market is consistent with individual freedom and the pluralism of modern liberal society.

Now this view can only have purchase, if we accept a very narrow definition of what it means to have equal freedom to pursue the given wants and preferences we have. And defences of the market are underpinned by such a narrow definition. It is claimed that people are equal in their subjection to the impersonal laws of the market which apply equally to everyone and are placed in a situation of equal opportunity before its laws. Individuals are equally free in the sense that they are free from deliberate interference in pursuit of their own ends. The state regulation of industry and collective welfare provision are to be minimized as they are seen as impediments to liberty and the freedom of the individual to define, pursue and satisfy their own wants and preferences. Public power is to be restricted to maintaining or expanding the framework of private property, competition and trade which guarantee free scope for private enterprise. The implicit normative claims are that in an unfettered market these institutions are self-adjusting leading to an equilibrium of supply and demand, and that they are conducive to maximizing satisfaction. Economists claim that, on the basis of a given distribution of income and resources, the perfect market economy would represent the realization of individual rational choice for goods and services, and would maximize this choice equitably and efficiently.

However, if the satisfaction of need is measured by aggregate effective demand, those individuals with more wealth, income and resources will have more, and will therefore have an unequal say in determining 'efficient' allocation. If there is more effective demand for certain goods and services, then efficiency, on this model, dictates that these demands be met rather than rival demands which lack the money or resources to make them register as effective demands. As a result of the initial inequalities, effective demand is also unequal.

Market arguments can only show at best that the market is the mechanism by which needs, wants and preferences are met in equal proportion to the money and resources any individual has. They cannot show that the market economy enables individuals to freely purchase products or use services to satisfy their needs or wants. Defenders of the market economy can make these claims because they apply an inadequate conception of freedom to the operation of market forces. Only deliberate interference, on this conception, counts as an impediment to freedom and therefore it is argued that all individuals are equally free to do and buy what they want. However, as we saw in Chapter 2, freedom involves more than simply the absence of interference and this narrow definition neglects the possibly unintended, but nevertheless inevitable, effects of social arrangements and capitalist property relations and removes these from critical scrutiny with respect to freedom. It also undermines the rationale for valuing freedom in the first place.

If the absence of interference to buy goods is valued at all, it is because we value the ability to buy them. That is, it is not just a matter of whether we are free from interference, but whether we are free to do and have what we want. If existing social arrangements are not called into question, then it could be argued that we are all equally free from interference in the market place to satisfy our wants and preferences. However, both efficiency arguments which try to show that the market allocates goods according to individual desires, and moral arguments for markets which claim they are freedom-preserving, cannot justifiably begin from the *status quo*. The question is not whether, given the existing distribution of wealth and resources, the market exchange process is efficient or moral because it maximizes negative liberty. What is questionable is the morality of the initial distribution and whether this distribution maximizes the freedom to consume, to do and to buy what we want. Not only do defenders of the market have to morally justify the existing inequalities which result from capitalist property relations from which market trading begins, they also have to show that the unequal resources with which people enter the market do not compromise the value of their freedom.

They can show that those who have resources and those who do not are equally free from interference to pursue their own ends. However, this is not enough, because this freedom is useless and merely a formality for those who are unable to do so. Their ability to do so depends on their access to the means to do what they want. If their income and resources are low, this liberty is pointless. Those with little income and resources are unfree in the sense that they are unable to do what they want, they do not have the necessary means to realize their ends. It is absurd, even on this tradition's own terms, to construe freedom as simply the absence of deliberate interference, for if this is so, there is no point in valuing freedom or in defending the market as the mechanism which uniquely respects it.

Freedom is important in the liberal tradition because it is connected with their view of human beings as purposive beings who seek to fulfil their own ends and purposes. If freedom is disconnected from why freedom is valuable, then why should we care about it or support institutions which demonstrably fail to realize its value?

Two main criticisms have been levelled at the liberal claim that want satisfaction and freedom are inextricably linked. First, the liberal argument that identifying wants with expressed preferences respects the freedom of individuals to define wants for themselves has been shown to be false. Individuals are not free to define their own wants and preferences. These are conditioned by power relations and social forces which shape and constrain them. Even if market society were to satisfy the wants people have, want satisfaction could not be equated with freedom, because the way wants are formed and developed is incompatible with self-determination and the freedom of the individual to pursue their own ends and purposes. Second, the celebration of the market economy because it preserves freedom by responding to the given wants people have, has been challenged. The market leaves many wants and preferences unfulfilled – qualitative and social wants, those not satisfiable in the consumption or through commodity exchange and those not converted into effective demands. The inability to satisfy these wants is a limitation on freedom. If people cannot satisfy their wants because of structural inequalities in access to the means to do so, then they are not free.

Freedom and Needs

Liberals objected to arguments for the objectivity and priority of needs over wants on the grounds that policies informed by needs impose one conception of the good, and are incompatible with the pluralism of modern liberal society. As such, they are a threat to individual freedom. But many arguments have been given to support the counter-claim that allocative priority given to needs enhances freedom and is consistent with the facts of moral pluralism.

Defining needs empirically as necessary conditions for achieving any end is compatible with recognizing a plurality of values, ends and purposes. Needs relate to the necessary conditions of action and, as such, they do not relate to one conception of the good, but to any conceptions which require action to achieve them. Survival and health are objective requirements for acting to achieve any ends. They are the universal means necessary for pursuing a variety of ends and purposes. The claim that we can make valid and objective judgements about which human needs are of fundamental importance supports the argument that need satisfaction has higher priority than want satisfaction and justifies state intervention in production and distribution to meet needs. To do this, it will be necessary to identify the specific satisfiers for these fundamental human needs and for adequate levels of satisfaction. These can be identified by establishing causal connections between satisfiers and the meeting of survival and health needs.

Types of satisfiers and adequate levels of goods, services, actions and relationships to meet needs will vary across time, place, cultures and between different social groups. However, this does not mean that once the concept of need is operationalized in different social settings, it becomes relative and value-laden and hence, once again, vulnerable to liberal objections. Though satisfiers will differ, they must have the characteristics or properties which contribute to the satisfaction of fundamental human needs, and it is in virtue of these characteristics that they are universal across time and place. In this sense, the fact that they are socially relative does not make them relative to particular conceptions of the good. To be derived from a fundamental human need, satisfiers must have universal characteristics which make them valuable to all human beings, whatever else they value.

Given this, it can be seen that meeting fundamental human needs contributes to and is connected with individual freedom defined as the ability to achieve our own ends and purposes. Need satisfaction is important to freedom, since needs are the objectively valuable means to the fulfilment of any ends. Needs are objectively important because we cannot function purposively and successfully to satisfy our desires or achieve any ends if we lack what we need. Theory and practice informed by objective needs are not a threat to freedom, but necessary for freedom, for information about needs, plus the means to achieve them, enhance the freedom of the individual to pursue their own ends and purposes.

Liberals are mistaken in thinking that making judgements about which human needs are of fundamental importance is a threat to freedom and are unjustifiably proud of their neutrality with respect to people's wants, preferences and conceptions of the good. To advocate neutrality between different conceptions of the good gives the misleading impression that there are so many diverse values and views of human flourishing that it is impossible to make valid judgements about the means to realize them without imposing values and threatening individual freedom. However, just what conception of the good could people have that did not require for their satisfaction the meeting of basic needs? What kind of diverse, disconnected creatures would we have to be, if we could not envisage the possibility of consensual agreement through democratic decision-making processes of what would count as adequate levels of satisfaction, or as priorities for meeting these needs?

Liberals premise their arguments for freedom of choice and autonomy on the supposed facts of individual diversity and rationality. It is taken as given that each person has a unique conception of the good life, has different desires and preferences which are rationally chosen. In order not to limit individual liberty by favouring one conception over the other, political action must be neutral between them so that different and competing conceptions can be pursued. These arguments place too much emphasis on diversity, exaggerate the extent to which different conceptions of the good are distinct and competing, over-emphasize individual rational choice and overstate the impossibility of making objective judgements about real human needs and the means to meet them.

While it is true that people have different temperaments, tastes, aspirations, religious and moral beliefs, if we concentrate on similarities rather than differences, we can see that there are some things that we need whatever our diverse views or moral outlooks. And if these are empirically identifiable, the degree to which they are satisfied in any given society can provide a critical standard by which to assess the justice of that society. Liberals talk as if each individual has a conception of the good unique to that individual, that is separate from and in conflict with those of others. This overemphasizes the distinctness and perpetual incompatibility of different conceptions and plans of life. It ignores the fact that human beings are not isolated atoms but social beings.

Marxists, feminists and communitarians have all in different ways drawn attention to the role of social relations, community and historical context in shaping individual beliefs, values, identities and conceptions of the good, and to the interdependence, inter-relatedness and necessary connections between individuals which give rise to intersubjective interests and common purposes. This notion of social and interdependent individuals could provide an alternative starting-point for political theory and practice. One which assumes the possibility of mutual care and interestedness, attachment, community, support, solidarity and co-operation, rather than one which assumes that political theory and practice must take as given individually self-interested, competing and conflicting conceptions of the good and remain neutral between them.

The liberal belief in the importance of individual autonomy and the consequent requirement of neutrality are informed by the belief that ways of life and conceptions of the good are matters of rational choice. Now it seems to me that both the extent to which any individual has a rational life plan and the extent to which beliefs and desires are rationally chosen are grossly overestimated in liberal theorizing. For one thing, liberals seem to imply that individuals deliberate on and choose a coherent, consistent conception of what constitutes the good life for them and then they rationally calculate how to achieve it. Yet surely I would not be alone in being hard pressed to defend or even explain many of my desires, beliefs, actions and decisions as the result of rational choice, let alone as part of a coherent life plan or as exemplifying a systematic and specific conception of the good? Nor would I want to. Some of my desires are whims and fancies, some are reckless, some trivial, counterproductive and contrary to my immediate and long-term interests. Some I wish I did not have.

Even though some of these are strong desires, I certainly do not think society should be organized so that I can pursue them. Moreover, when I make a personal decision I do not always calculate which actions will maximize my own good, still less do I try to abstract from my own interests and generalize the consequences of my actions. And this is probably a good thing, it means I can act unselfishly and non-competitively. It means I can attend to the needs of others, even when there is no obvious benefit to myself. It means that I can make decisions informed by my attachments, relationships, responsibilities, my concern for and my common interests with others. I do not make decisions as a rationally self-interested utility-maximizer separate from, abstracted from and in competition with others. And I am sure I am not alone. I do not know anyone who has anything as grand, as rigid, as abstract, as coherent, as calculating as the liberal notion of a plan of life or a conception of the good that is unique to them as an individual.

Of course, people do have significant beliefs, values and these do differ, but the most important of these are not matters of individual autonomous choice as liberal theory supposes. People do not shop around in a supermarket of cultural, political, religious or moral values and rationally choose which to adopt as personal ideals. They do not examine the labels of ideologies or religions to see how many calories of self-interest they will deliver or how to process them to make them universalizable. These beliefs and values are rarely something we choose. People have little choice about whether to adopt some of their most important defining features – their colour, race, class, gender, sexual orientation or their lifestyles, commitments, moral and religious beliefs.

We learn from Marxists that people find themselves in circumstances not of their own choosing. We learn from communitarians that people's socially assigned roles and relationships, beliefs and values are not things they choose, but attachments they discover. These are not voluntarily entered into, but found in the norms of the community in which they are situated. If people do not autonomously and rationally choose their beliefs and values, if people's choices are socially determined by their material and cultural circumstances, then there is less scope for liberal insistence on the importance of individual choice, for the value of autonomy and for the significance of freedom to pursue these so called 'choices'. The fact that people are less rational, less responsible for their choices than liberals suppose also means that there is more scope for tolerance and compassion than liberals allow with their insistence that people should pay for the costs of their choices or that they should be rewarded because they deserve to benefit from them. It becomes inappropriate to praise or blame, reward or punish people if they do not choose their beliefs and values. We could become more tolerant of people's actions, beliefs and ways of life not because we respect their autonomy or to promote their freedom of choice, but precisely because they are not autonomously chosen.

On the one hand, people are less 'rational' than liberals suppose. They are less self-interested, less calculating, less autonomous, less deserving of praise or blame. On the other hand, they are more 'rational'. Men and women may make history not in circumstances of their own choosing, but they *do make* history. People may find themselves in socially assigned, biologically determined roles. They may be situated in the values of a particular community, but they can and do critically reflect on the values and beliefs imparted by a particular community.

If our desires and preferences, beliefs and values were totally conditioned, all protest regarding their conditioning would be futile, if not impossible. It is precisely because we can examine the conditioning process that our consciousness can cease to be determined by the inevitability of conditioned beliefs. It is precisely because we can judge and evaluate desires, because we can assess the legitimacy of moral values, communal norms and circumstances, that we can cease to be passive victims of the conditioning process. People are rational agents in a more complex way than liberals suppose. They are less rational in the sense that they are less autonomous: they have less choice and they are also less self-interested, less individualistic and less calculating. For these reasons they are more deserving of tolerance and compassion as they are mutually interdependent victims, and they are more capable of co-operation and solidarity as they are inter-related social beings. But people are also more rational, in the sense that their rational agency involves the capacity for judging, evaluating and prioritizing their beliefs and desires, not just validating them because they happen to have them. And the fact that human beings are social and interactive beings means this capacity is not just exercised as a process of individual judgement, but means that human beings are collectively capable of critically reflecting on their different and shared interests, values, desires, preferences and conceptions of the good and adjudicating between them. People are at once more limited, more restricted, more pathetic *and* less accepting, less passive, more determined and more able to shake off their determinations. Given that people's desires and preferences are socially determined, and given that people can recognize these determinations without endorsing them, there seems no value in promoting freedom to satisfy their given desires or in remaining neutral with respect to them.

If we remain neutral with respect to wants, preferences and conceptions of the good, then it is not possible to judge or evaluate these for their importance to freedom. We cannot distinguish between what is desired and what is worth desiring. We cannot distinguish determined choice from voluntary choice, or expressed needs from those genuine needs which must be satisfied in order to make freedom valuable. Once it is recognized that wants are conditioned by social circumstances and not expressions of rational free choice, we can see that our wants may be sources of unfreedom, that some of our desires diminish, restrict or are irrelevant to our freedom. To see this means that moral neutrality with respect to wants, preferences and conceptions of the good must be abandoned and that judgements must be made about which needs and interests are relevant to freedom. And this is possible because human beings are rational in the sense that they have the capacity to individually and collectively criticize, reformulate and prioritize given desires, not just calculate the means to satisfy them.

The fact that something is wanted, the fact that a conception of the good is held, does not guarantee its objective or even its subjective value, does not justify its satisfaction or support the claim that this satisfaction is freedom-enhancing. Whereas, theory and practice based on the conception of objective need are not a threat to freedom, but necessary for freedom. What is needed for survival and health, the necessary conditions of action, are objectively important because we cannot function successfully to achieve our ends if we lack what we need. Part of freedom involves knowledge of this necessity, knowing and being able to determine what we need, as well as the ability, opportunity and resources to satisfy our needs. Policies designed to meet needs are only a threat to freedom if freedom is defined as negative liberty and if this is a valid conception. If freedom means non-interference, then redistributive policies designed to meet needs will restrict the freedom of those who possess more property, power, wealth and resources than others. However, the arguments throughout this book have shown that the concept of freedom as negative liberty is untenable. They have also shown that the loss of negative liberty for the few which results from redistribution is offset by the gain in basic liberties and well-being for the many. Moreover, the individuals affected are not being deprived of their rights. They are not being deprived of anything they have an absolute right to, nor are their civil and political rights affected and they share with others the rights to resources to meet their most important needs and to realize their own ends and purposes.

Needs and Obligations: Rights and Duties

So far this chapter has attempted to establish that the criteria of wants and preferences do not have the epistemological, moral or empirical advantages claimed for them by liberal theorists, and to defend the concept of need as a moral basis for political theory and practice. It has been suggested that needs, because of their objective importance, justify activity aimed at their satisfaction and that they are the appropriate grounds for the just distribution of resources. The arguments in this book also suggest that needs can provide the foundation for rights and obligations or correlative duties to satisfy them. In Chapter 5 it was argued that traditional civil and political rights and social and economic rights aimed at the provision for basic needs, can be derived from the same moral foundation. That is, from the Kantian conception of human beings as ends-in-themselves where rights are seen as the means by which diverse individuals can pursue their own good in their own way. In the liberal tradition, respecting people as ends in themselves justifies a set of negative rights and imposes negative duties on individuals and the state to refrain from interfering with the rights of others. The basis for justifying positive rights and duties to meet needs was that respect for persons to achieve their own ends requires not just the absence of interference but the provision of opportunities and resources to enable individuals to achieve their ends.

Gewirth derived positive and negative rights to freedom and well-being, rights to assistance and provision, as well as rights of non-interference from the same considerations – the fact that freedom and well-being are needs in the sense that they are necessary conditions for action, for the attainment of any human purpose. Adapted and simplified to substitute survival and health for freedom and well-being, Gewirth's argument shows that the practical prescriptive requirement to meet my own needs can lead to moral obligations to meet other peoples (see Gewirth, 1987, pp. 14–18). As a purposive moral agent, I must logically accept that I have rights to survival and health as the necessary conditions of acting to achieve any end, as conditions that I must have. If I deny that I have these rights, then I must accept that others may interfere with my survival and health or refrain from promoting them. This contradicts the belief that I must have survival and health as necessary conditions for any activity. If I accept that my own needs ought to be met because I am a purposive agent and these are the necessary conditions for any activity, then I also must accept that all other prospective, purposive agents have the same rights. If I interfere with their needs or do not help to meet them I deny what before I accepted – that fundamental human needs are necessary conditions for any activity and therefore necessary goods for all agents. Accepting fundamental human needs as necessary conditions for any activity and equally important to all agents, in so far as others are actual or potential recipients of my action, I ought to act in accordance with meeting other people's needs. This requirement is expressed as the general moral principle – the principle of generic consistency 'Act in accordance with the generic rights of your recipients as well as of yourself.' Every agent is logically committed to accepting this principle on pain of contradiction and hence of rationality.

The argument proceeds from my prudential interest in meeting my own needs. I acknowledge other people's needs, on the same grounds that I acknowledge that my own ought to be met. This commits me and every other agent from refraining from interfering in other people's attempts to meet their needs and to assisting them in meeting them. If I do not do so, I deny what I cannot help but acknowledge. In claiming rights for myself, I must acknowledge that all other agents have the same rights that must be respected.

According to Gewirth, then, obligations to meet other people's needs arise from the principle of universalization and non-contradiction. These rights and duties are universal, they relate to all human beings and they are those which everyone must accept merely in virtue of recognizing human beings as moral agents.

As we have seen, these obligations do not fall on everyone equally. For instance, if minimal survival needs generate positive and negative rights to clean air and water, food, clothing, shelter and basic health care, the reciprocal negative and positive duties of forbearance, protection and aid fall on those agencies able to fulfil them. The argument that every individual has a right to the resources necessary for meeting their needs of agency does not impose a burdensome duty on each individual to meet every or any other individual's needs. Needs are the appropriate criterion for the distribution of resources, rather than individual claims against other particular individuals. Duties to avoid, protect and aid fall on social agents, institutions and governments who have the power to use resources and establish policies and priorities to meet needs. Individuals have duties in so far as they are able to support and contribute to this collective endeavour.

Though positive and negative rights can be derived from the needs of moral agency, and though corresponding duties can be established by applying the principles of rationality and universalizability, the discussion in Chapter 7 in relation to an ethic of care cast doubt on whether rationality alone was sufficient to motivate people to act morally or to fulfil these obligations. As a rational being, I can accept that in order to be consistent, I am logically committed to acting in accordance with the needs and interests of everyone. But why should I, and what would make me want to do that which reason prescribes? Even though I must allow that and cannot help but acknowledge that, like me, all prospective purposive agents have the needs for action and have prudential reasons for meeting them, the argument from consistency does not establish why I should or would want to meet the needs of others. In Chapter 7, it was suggested that in order to establish this, we have to look at social relations and the development of moral capacities and dispositions which are necessary for acting according to principle.

Feminists defending an ethic of care argued that morality is not about abstract individuals universalizing principles, but about moral dispositions, capacities and sensibilities and they highlighted the role of these in moral motivations. Care theorists gave an account of the development of moral motivations and provided an insight into the social relations and conditions necessary to foster these. Their arguments implied that the empathy, the care and the responsibility which motivate people to act in accordance with the needs of others spring from the social experience of relationships and ties with other people. Their theorizing, like communitarian critiques of liberal thought, reject the concept of the abstract individual and begin with a conception of the self as constituted by social relations and communal ties.

For feminist theorists, it is these social bonds that create identification with and which generate caring and responsible behaviour towards others. For communitarians, moral obligations that arise from theorizing about what the abstract rational individual ought to accept cannot motivate moral behaviour. This is because the individual is constituted by ends that are not chosen, but that are discovered by virtue of being embedded in some shared social context (Sandel, 1982, pp. 55–9, 152-4). The individual is 'embedded' or 'situated' in an existing social context and social practices. Feminists could be said to be making a point about moral psychology. People's motivation to care and to be responsible for others derives from the nature of the social relations in which they stand to one another. Communitarians go beyond moral psychology and the recognition of social influences on moral behaviour and claim that the shared values embedded in the community of which the individual is part are morally binding or starting-points for moral theorizing and political judgement. Taylor calls communal values 'authoritative horizons' which 'set goals for us' (Taylor, 1990, pp. 157–9).

The first problem with both feminist and communitarian thought in relation to obligations to meet the needs of others is that neither provides grounds for universalizing or generalizing these obligations. In care theory, since morality arises in the context of particular relationships, caring is likely to be limited to attending to, understanding and taking responsibility for meeting the needs of others with whom we have a particular relationship. And though this in itself might highlight the importance (overlooked in impartial ethics) of recognizing that special relationships between family and friends are reasons for special concern, it gives no reason for extending concern outside the web of these particular relationships. In communitarian theory values are relative to a particular community which may or may not be concerned with rights and duties or the obligations to meet the needs of others. This is precisely McIntyre's objection to Gewirth's argument from rational agency to the possession of universal rights. He explains what has gone wrong with Gewirth's argument:

It is of course true that if I claim a right in virtue of my possession of certain characteristics, then I am logically committed to holding that anyone else with the same characteristics also possess this right. But it is just this property of necessary universability that does not belong to claims about either the possession of or the need or desire for a good, even a universal good. One reason why claims about goods necessary for rational agency are so different from claims to the possession of rights is that the latter in fact presuppose, as the former do not, the existence of a socially established set of rules. Such sets of rules only come into existence at particular historical periods under particular social circumstances. They are in no way universal features of the human condition. (McIntyre, 1981, p. 65)

The second problem with feminist and communitarian thought is that in neither theory is there room for a critique of the relationships or the communal values which are the basis of moral behaviour. In care theory there is no analysis of the power relationships within and the quality of existing relationships, or distinctions between expressed needs and genuine needs which ought to be met. In communitarian theory, there is a tendency to endorse existing social practices without evaluating the moral identity conferred by the community or examining the structures of power within them in order to accept or reject the values of that community.

In order to address the problem of why we *ought* to meet the needs of others we must reject the particularist and relativist conclusions of feminist and communitarian thought. We must reject the conservative implications of advocating commitment to particular others and their expressed needs or of endorsing the values of a particular community. To do this, we must defend a theory of universal rights and obligations derived from a transcultural definition of objective fundamental human needs. At the same time, in order to address the problem of why we *should* meet the needs of others, we must build on the feminist and communitarian insights that moral motivation depends on social relations; that it is only in specific communities with shared values that claims to universal rights and duties make sense. This can be interpreted not as an argument against the possibility of universalism in ethics and politics, but as an argument for the impossibility of universalism in societies where there are no shared values or common interests.

If we do this, we have to see the task of political theory not as defining principles which are rational, impartial and neutral between competing conceptions or the good adhered to because it is rational to do so, nor as explicating the values of a particular community. We have to see the task of political theory as defending a substantive notion of the human good based on universal human needs and as developing an account of the kinds of social relations and conditions which are necessary for people to be motivated to respect these needs-based rights and to fulfil their obligations to satisfy them.

We have to see that acting morally depends not on abstract reasoning about each person's equal claims to consideration, but on their identification with the needs of others because they are bound to them in certain kinds of social relations which foster the expansion of moral motivation. The possibility of giving equal consideration to others is specific to the kinds of social relations where people's needs and interests conjoin in a co-operative community where there is a shared common enterprise. It is only in such communities where people identify with the common good that equal attention to people's needs becomes not just appropriate but practically possible. For political theory to begin this task, it must start with a conception of human beings as social and interdependent beings, with universal and intersubjective needs. Without this there can be no account of the common good, nor can there be a place for altruistic moral motivations. For political practice to implement this task, social conditions, social relations and political organization will have to be radically transformed. Liberal theory only hampers this task with its assumption of the abstract, autonomous, rational, independent, asocial individual and its commitment to neutrality between competing conceptions of the good. Liberal practice only demonstrates how urgent this task is. If acting morally and respecting the rights of others are dependent on social and political organization, the existence of social bonds and intersubjective interests, then it only takes two minutes' thought to see that liberal society characterized by mass poverty, unemployment, exploitation, extreme inequalities in wealth and power, and atomistic and divisive social relations, does not seem a promising place for moral behaviour to take root.

Conclusion

The arguments in this book suggest the problems with the inadequacy of liberal concepts arise from their initial commitment to the view of the abstract individual as rational, autonomous and self-interested. This leads to impoverished concepts of individual freedom, equality, justice and rights; an inappropriate distinction between the public and the private sphere and a narrow focus on the satisfaction of individual wants and preferences.

Implicit in these arguments is the view that liberalism's initial radical conviction of the equal moral worth of each individual can generate richer versions of these concepts. These involve an account of the capacities, opportunities and resources necessary for autonomy, a more substantive view of equality and a belief that social justice requires provision for basic needs. The idea of the equal worth of each individual provides arguments for the justifications of social and economic rights as well as political and civil rights and gives grounds for state intervention to protect and enforce these and their correlative duties.

Within the liberal tradition, too, the idea of the intrinsic value of each individual has given rise to arguments for redistribution, welfare provision and increased intervention. However, there is a limit to which liberalism can extend its basic conceptions. Arguments for economic redistribution can only stretch so far before they create a clash between the priority given by liberals to individual liberty over all other social goals. Arguments for the provision of opportunities and resources involve judgements about what is necessary for human well-being and conflict with the liberal aim of neutrality between competing conceptions of the good; challenge the liberal premise of the sovereignty of individual desire and create difficulties about where to draw the line in justifying the coercive power of the state.

Moreover, because liberals endorse private ownership, the market economy and the competitive capitalist system, richer formulations of liberal concepts cannot be fully implemented in liberal society. Welfare liberals are only concerned to redress the effects of the market and to regulate economic competition. They are not concerned to eliminate the inequalities in social power, ownership of production and property, in opportunities and resources that mitigate against instantiating respect for the equal worth of each individual.

Liberal concepts cannot just be expanded within a liberal theoretical framework and within a liberal social context. There is a point at which they collapse back upon themselves because they are necessarily limited by the concept of the individual and a commitment to individualism that is at the heart of their theorizing. To bring forward the emancipatory project liberalism once embarked upon, we can retain the idea of respect for the equal worth of each individual, but we must jettison the liberal conception of that individual and all that follows from it.

Bibliography

Acton, H.B. (1971), *The Morals of Market: An Ethical Explanation*. London: Longman.

Allen, A. (1988) *Uneasy Access: Privacy for Women in a Free Society*. Totowa, NJ: Rowman and Allanheld.

Anscombe, E. (1957) *Intention*. Oxford: Blackwell.

Arblaster, A. (1984) *The Rise and Decline of Western Liberalism*. Oxford: Blackwell.

Aristotle (1962) *Politics*. trans. T.A. Sinclair. Harmondsworth: Penguin.

Assiter, A. (1989) *Pornography, Feminism and the Individual*. London: Pluto.

Baachi, C. (1990) *Same Difference, Feminism and Sexual Difference*. London: Allen and Unwin.

Baachi, C. (1991) Pregnancy, the law and the meaning of equality. In Meehan, E. and Sevenhuijsen, S. (eds) *Equality, Politics and Gender*. London: Sage.

Baier, A. (1993) What do women want in moral theory? In Larrabee, M.J. (ed.) *An Ethic of Care*. New York and London: Routledge.

Baker, J. (1987) *Arguing for Equality*. London: Verso.

Barber, B. (1975) Justifying justice: problems of pyschology, politics and measurement in Rawls. In Daniels, N. (ed.) *Reading Rawls*. New York: Basic Books.

Barker, D.L. (1978) The regulation of marriage: repressive benevolence. In Littlejohn G. *et al.* (eds) *Power and the State*. London: Croom Helm.

Barry, B. (1965) *Political Argument*. London: Routledge and Kegan Paul.

Benhabib, S. (1987) The generalised and the concrete other. In Benhabib, S. and Cornell, D. (eds) *Feminism as a Critique: On the Politics of Gender*. Minneapolis: University of Minnesota Press.

Benn, S.I. and Peters, R.S. (1959) *Social Principles and the Democratic State*. London: Allen and Unwin.

Bentham, J. (1843) A manual of political economy. In Bowring, J. (ed.) *The Works of Jeremy Bentham*, Vol. iii. Edinburgh: Tait.

Bentham, J. (1967) *Introduction to the Principles of Morality and Legislation*, edited by W. Harrison. Oxford: Blackwell.

Berlin, I. (1969) *Four Essays on Liberty*. Oxford: Oxford University Press.

Blum, L.A. (1993) Gilligan and Kohlberg: implications for moral theory. In

Larrabee, M.J. (ed) *An Ethic of Care*. New York and London: Routledge.

Boxhill, B.R. (1993) Equality, discrimination and preferential treatment. In Singer, P. (ed.) *A Companion to Ethics*. Oxford: Blackwell.

Broughton, J.M. (1993) Women's rationality and men's virtues: a critique of gender dualism in Gilligan's theory of moral development. In Larrabee, M.J. (ed.) *An Ethic of Care*. New York and London: Routledge.

Campbell, T. (1988) *Justice*. London: Macmillan.

Carens, J. (1985) Compensatory justice and social institutions. *Economics and Philosophy*, **1** (1).

Carritt, E.F. (1967) Liberty and equality. In Quinton, A. (ed.) *Political Philosophy*. Oxford: Oxford University Press.

Chodorow, N. (1978) *Reproduction of Mothering: Psychoanalysis and the Sociology of Gender*. Berkeley, Los Angeles and London: University of California Press.

Cixous, H. (1981) The laugh of the Medusa. In Marks, E. and de Courtrivon, I. (eds) *New French Feminisms*. Brighton: Harvester Press.

Coates, K. and Silburn, R. (1967) *St Anne's: Poverty, Deprivation and Morale*. Nottingham: Nottingham University Department of Adult Education.

Cohen, G. (1986) Self-ownership, world-ownership and equality: Part 2. *Social Philosophy and Policy*, **3** (2).

Cohen, M., Nagel, T. and Scanlon, T. (eds) (1976) *Equality and Preferential Treatment*. Princeton: Princeton University Press.

Cranston, M. (1973) *What Are Human Rights?* London: Bodley Head.

Daly, M. (1978) *Gyn/Ecology: The Metaethics of Radical Feminism*. Boston: Beacon Press.

Daniels, N. (1975a) Equal liberty and unequal worth of liberty. In Daniels, N. (ed.) *Reading Rawls*. New York: Basic Books.

Daniels, N. (1975b) (ed.) *Reading Rawls*. New York: Basic Books.

Daniels, N. (1985) *Just Health Care*. Cambridge: Cambridge University Press.

Davis, K. and Moore, W.E. (1967) Some principles of stratification. In Bendix, R. and Lipset, S.M. (eds) *Social Stratification in Comparative Perspective*. London: Routledge.

Day, J.P. (1970) On liberty and the real will. *Philosophy*, **95**.

Day, J.P. (1977) Threats, offers, law, opinion and liberty. *American Philosophical Quarterly*, **14**.

Dearden, R. (1972) 'Needs' in education. In Hirst, P. and Peters, R.S. (eds) *Development of Reason*. London: Routledge and Kegan Paul.

Delphy, C. (1980) A materialist feminism is possible. *Feminist Review*, **4**.

Dinnerstein, D. (1987) *The Rocking of the Cradle and the Ruling of the World*. London: Women's Press.

Doyal, L. and Gough, I. (1984) A theory of human need. *Critical Social Policy*, **4** (1).

Doyal, L. and Gough, I. (1991) *A Theory of Human Need*. London: Macmillan.

Dworkin, R. (1977) *Taking Rights Seriously*. Cambridge, MA: Harvard University Press.

Dworkin, R. (1985) *A Matter of Principle*. Cambridge, MA: Harvard University Press.

Dyer, D.P. (1964) Freedom. *Canadian Journal of Economics and Political Science*, **30**.

Eisenberg, N. and Lennon, R. (1983) Sex differences in empathy and related capacities. *Psychological Bulletin*, **94**.

Eisenstein, Z. (1981) *The Radical Future of Liberal Feminism*. New York: Longman.

Elshtain, J. (1981) *Public Man, Private Woman: Women in Social and Political Thought*. Princeton: Princeton University Press.

Feinberg, J. (1970) Justice and personal desert. Appendix in *Doing and Deserving: Essays in the Theory of Responsibility*. Princeton: Princeton University Press.

Feinberg, J. (1973) *Social Justice*. Englewood Cliffs, NJ: Prentice Hall.

Feinberg, J. (1980) *Rights, Justice and the Bounds of Liberty*. Princeton: Princeton University Press.

Firestone, S. (1979) *The Dialectic of Sex*. London: Women's Press.

Fisk, M. (1975) History and reason in Rawls' moral theory. In Daniels, N. (ed.) *Reading Rawls*. New York: Basic Books.

Fitzgerald, R. (1977a) (ed.) *Human Needs and Politics*. Rushcutters Bay: Pergamon.

Fitzgerald, R. (1977b) Abraham Maslow's hierarchy of needs: an exposition and evaluation. In Fitzgerald, R. (ed.) *Human Needs and Politics*. Rushcutters Bay: Pergamon.

Fitzgerald, R. (1977c) The ambiguity and rhetoric of need. In Fitzgerald, R. (ed.) *Human Needs and Politics*. Rushcutters Bay: Pergamon.

Flanagan, O. and Jackson, K. (1993) Justice, care and gender: the Kohlberg–Gilligan debate revisited. In Larrabee, M.J. (ed.) *An Ethic of Care*. New York and London: Routledge.

Flax, J. (1992) Beyond equality: gender, justice and difference. In Block, G. and James, S. (eds) *Beyond Equality and Difference*. London: Routledge.

Flew, A. (1977) Wants or needs, choices or demand. In Fitzgerald, R. (ed.) *Human Needs and Politics*. Rushcutters Bay: Pergamon.

Foot, P. (1967) The problem of abortion and the doctrine of double effect. *The Oxford Review*, **5**.

Frankena, W. (1973) *Ethics*. Englewood Cliffs, NJ: Prentice Hall.

Frankfurt, H. (1984) Necessity and desire. *Philosophy and Phenomenological Research*, **45**.

Franklin, B. (1986) Children's political rights. In Franklin, B. (ed.) *The Rights of Children*. Oxford: Blackwell.

Freeman, M.D.A. (1983) *The Rights and Wrongs of Children*. London: Pinter.

Fried, C. (1978) *Right and Wrong*. Cambridge, MA: Harvard University Press.

Friedman, M. (1962) *Capitalism and Freedom*. Chicago and London: University of Chicago Press.

Friedman, M. (1993) Beyond caring: the demoralization of gender. In Larrabee, M.J. (ed.) *An Ethic of Care*. New York and London: Routledge.

George, S. (1976) *How the Other Half Dies*. Harmondsworth: Penguin.

Gewirth, A. (1982) *Human Rights: Essays in Justification and Application*. Chicago: University of Chicago Press.

Gewirth, A. (1987) Private philanthropy and positive rights. In Frankel Paul, E., Miller Jnr, F.D. and Ahrens, J. (eds) *Beneficience, Philanthropy and the Public Good*. Oxford: Blackwell.

Gilligan, C. (1982) *In a Different Voice: Psychological Theory and Women's Development*. Cambridge, MA and London: Harvard University Press.

Gilligan, C. (1983) Do the social sciences have an adequate theory of moral development? In Haan, N. *et al.* (eds) *Social Science as Moral Inquiry*. New York: Columbia University Press.

Gilligan, C. (1986) Remapping the moral domain. In Heller, T. *et al.* (eds) *Reconstructing Individualism*. Stanford: Stanford University Press.

Gilligan C. (1987) Moral orientation and moral development. In Kittay, E. and Meyers, D. (eds) *Women and Moral Theory*. Totowa, NJ: Rowman and Littlefield.

Gilligan, C., Ward, J. and Taylor, J. (eds) (1988) *Mapping the Moral Domain*. Cambridge, MA: Harvard University Press.

Glover, J. (1977) *Causing Death and Saving Lives*. Harmondsworth: Penguin.

Grey, T.C. (1973) The first virtue. *Stanford Law Review*, **25**.

Griffin, S. (1984) *Women and Nature: The Roaring Inside Her*. London: Women's Press.

Hare, R.M. (1975) Rawls' theory of justice. In Daniels, N. (ed.) *Reading Rawls*. New York: Basic Books.

Harris, J. (1980) *Violence and Responsibility*. London: Routledge and Kegan Paul.

Harris, J. (1982) The political status of children. In Graham, K. (ed.) *Contemporary Political Philosophy*. Cambridge: Cambridge University Press.

Hart, H.L.A. (1955) Are there any natural rights? *Philosophical Review*, **64**.

Hayek, F.A. (1949) *Individualism and Economic Order*. London: Routledge.

Hayek, F.A. (1955) *The Counter-Revolution of Science*. London: Collier-Macmillan.

Hayek, F.A. (1960) *The Constitution of Liberty*. London: Routledge and Kegan Paul.

Hayek, F.A. (1976) *Law, Legislation and Liberty, Vol II: The Mirage of Social Justice*: London: Routledge and Kegan Paul.

Hayek, F. (1991) Freedom and coercion. In Miller, D. (ed.) *Liberty*. Oxford: Oxford University Press.

Held, V. (1984a) The obligation of mothers and fathers. In Trebilcot, J. (ed.)

Mothering: Essays in Feminist Theory. Totowa, NJ: Rowman and Allanheld.

Held, V. (1984b) *Rights and Goods*. New York: Free Press/Macmillan.

Heller, A. (1980) Can 'True' and 'False' needs be posited? In Lederer, K. (ed.) *Human Needs*. Cambridge, MA: Oelgeschlager, Gunn and Hain.

Holt, J. (1975) *Escape from Childhood*. Harmondsworth: Penguin.

Honderich, T. (1980) *Violence for Equality*. Harmondsworth: Penguin.

Hume, D. (1888) *Treatise on Human Nature*. Edited by L.A. Selby-Bigge. Oxford: Clarendon Press.

Irigaray, L. (1991) This sex which is not one. In Gunew, S. (ed.) *A Reader in Feminist Knowledge*. London: Routledge.

Jarvis Thompson, J. (1973) Preferential hiring. *Philosophy and Public Affairs*, **2** (4).

Kennedy, E. and Mendus, S. (1987) *Women in Western Political Philosophy*. Brighton: Wheatsheaf Books.

Kristeva, J. (1981) Woman can never be defined. In Marks, E. and de Courtrivan, I. (eds) *New French Feminisms*. Brighton: Harvester Press.

Krouse, R. and McPherson, M. (1988) Capitalism, 'property-owning democracy', and the welfare state. In Gutmann, A. (ed.) *Democracy and the Welfare State*. Princeton: Princeton University Press.

Kymlicka, W. (1990) *Contemporary Political Philosophy*. Oxford: Clarendon Press.

Lappe, F.M. and Collins, J. (1977) *Food First: Beyond the Myth of Scarcity*. Boston: Houghton Mifflin.

Larrabee, M.J. (ed.) (1993) *An Ethic of Care*. New York and London: Routledge.

Leontief, W., Carter, A.P. and Petri, P.A. (1977) *The Future of the World Economy: A United Nations Study*. New York and Oxford: Oxford University Press.

Lindley, R. (1986) *Autonomy*. London: Macmillan.

Locke, J. (1967) *Two Treatises on Government*. 2nd edn, edited by P. Laslett. Cambridge: Cambridge University Press.

Lucas, J.R. (1977) Against equality again. *Philosphy*, **52**.

Lukes, S. (1978a) *Essays in Social Theory*. London: Macmillan.

Lukes, S. (1978b) No Archimedean point. In Lukes, S. *Essays in Social Theory*. London: Macmillan.

Lyons, D. (1975) Nature and soundness of the contract and coherence arguments. In Daniels, N. (ed.) *Reading Rawls*. New York: Basic Books.

MacCallum, G.C. (1991) Negative and positive liberty. In Miller, D. (ed.) *Liberty*. Oxford: Oxford University Press.

McInnes, N. (1977) The politics of needs and who needs politics. In Fitzgerald, R. (ed.) *Human Needs and Politics*. Rushcutters Bay: Pergamon.

MacIntyre, A. (1967) *A Short History of Ethics*. London: Routledge and Kegan Paul.

MacIntyre, A. (1981) *After Virtue*. London: Duckworth.

MacIntyre, A. (1988) *Whose Justice? Which Rationality?* London: Duckworth.

MacIntyre, A. (1990) *Three Rival Versions of Moral Enquiry*. Oxford: Blackwell.

MacKinnon, C. (1987) *Feminism Unmodified: Discourses on Life and Law*. Cambridge, MA: Harvard University Press.

Macpherson, C.B. (1964) *The Political Theory of Possessive Individualism*. Oxford: Oxford University Press.

Macpherson, C.B (1973) *Democratic Theory*. Oxford: Oxford University Press.

Mandeville, R. (1705) *The Fable of the Bees*, edited by F.B. Kaye (1924). London: Oxford University Press.

Mapel, D. (1989) *Social Justice Reconsidered*. Urbana, II: University of Illinois Press.

Marks, E. and de Courtrivon, I. (1981) *New French Feminisms*. Brighton: Harvester Press.

Marx, K. (1968) *Selected Works*. New York: International Publishers.

Marx, K. (1973) *Grundrisse*. Harmondsworth: Penguin.

Marx, K. (1978) On the Jewish question. In Tucker, R.C. (ed.) *The Marx–Engels Reader*. New York: W.W. Norton.

Mill, J.S. (1875) *A System of Logic*. London: Longman.

Mill, J.S. (1900) *The Principles of Political Economy*. London: Longmans Green.

Mill, J.S. (1962a) Essay on liberty. In Warnock, M. (ed.) *Utilitarianism*. London: Collins.

Mill, J.S. (1962b) Utilitarianism. In Warnock, M. (ed.) *Utilitarianism*. London: Collins.

Mill, J.S. (1989) The subjection of women. In *Liberty and Other Writings*, edited by S. Collini. Cambridge: Cambridge University Press.

Miller, D. (1976) *Social Justice*. Oxford: Clarendon Press.

Miller, D. (1983/4) Constraints on freedom. *Ethics*, **94**.

Miller, D. (1991) *Liberty*. Oxford: Oxford University Press.

Millett, K. (1985) *Sexual Politics*. London: Virago.

Molesworth, W. (1839) *The English Works of Thomas Hobbes* (11 vols). London: John Bohm.

Moore, G.E. (1959) *Principia Ethica*. Cambridge: Cambridge University Press.

Mulhall, B. and Swift, A. (1992) *Liberals and Communitarians*. Oxford: Blackwell.

Nagel, T. (1975) Rawls on justice. In Daniels, N. (ed.) *Reading Rawls*. New York: Basic Books.

Nagel, T. (1979) *Mortal Questions*. Cambridge: Cambridge University Press.

Nagel, T. (1982) Libertarianism without foundations. In Paul, J. (ed.) *Reading Nozick*. Oxford: Blackwell.

Narveson, J.F. (1976) A puzzle about economic justice in Rawls. *Social Theory and Practice*, **4**.

Narveson, J.F. (1978) Rawls on equal distribution of wealth. *Philosophia*, 7.

Nicholson, L.J. (1986) *Gender and History: The Limits of Social Theory in the Age of the Family*. New York: Columbia University Press.

Nielsen, K. (1969) Morality and needs. In MacIntosh, J. and Coval, J. (eds) *The Business of Reason*. London: Routledge and Kegan Paul.

Nielsen, K. (1985) *Equality and Liberty: A Defence of Radical Egalitarianism*. Totowa, NJ: Rowman and Allanheld.

Noddings. N. (1984) *Caring: A Feminine Approach to Ethics and Moral Education*. Berkeley: University of California Press.

Norman, R. (1971) *Reasons for Action*. Oxford: Blackwell.

Norman, R. (1982) Does equality destroy liberty? In Graham, K. (ed.) *Contemporary Political Philosophy*. Cambridge: Cambridge University Press.

Norman, R. (1987) *Free and Equal*. Oxford: Oxford University Press.

Nozick, R. (1974) *Anarchy, State and Utopia*. Oxford: Blackwell.

Okin, S. (1980) *Women in Western Political Thought*. London: Virago.

Okin, S. (1981) Women and the making of the sentimental family. *Philosophy and Public Affairs*, 11 (1).

Okin, S. (1990a) *Justice, Gender and the Family*. New York: Basic Books.

Okin, S. (1990b) Thinking like a woman. In Rhode, D. (ed.) *Theoretical Perspectives on Sexual Difference*. New Haven, CT: Yale University Press.

Okin, S. (1990c) Reason and feeling in thinking about justice. In Sunstein, C.R. (ed.) *Feminism and Political Theory*. Chicago: University of Chicago Press.

Olsen, E. (1985) The myth of state intervention in the family. *University of Michigan Journal of Law Reform*, 18 (4).

Oppenheim, F. (1973) 'Facts and values' in politics. *Political Theory*, 1 (1).

Oppenheim, F. (1980) *Political Concepts: A Reconstruction*. Chicago: University of Chicago Press.

Paine, T. (1969) *The Rights of Man*. Harmondsworth: Penguin.

Parent, W. A. (1974a) Recent work on the concept of liberty. *American Philosophical Quarterly*, 11.

Parent, W. A. (1974b) Freedom as the non-restriction of options. *Mind*, 83.

Pateman, C. (1987) Feminist critiques of the public/private dichotomy. In Phillips, A. (ed.) *Feminism and Equality*. Oxford: Blackwell.

Pateman, C. (1988) *The Sexual Contract*. Cambridge: Polity Press.

Phillips, A. (ed.) (1987) *Feminism and Equality*. Oxford: Blackwell.

Plant, R. (1991) *Modern Political Philosophy*, Oxford: Blackwell.

Popper, K. (1961) *The Poverty of Historicism*. London: Routledge and Kegan Paul.

Popper, K. (1962) *The Open Society and its Enemies*. London: Routledge and Kegan Paul.

Radcliffe Richards, J. (1980) *The Sceptical Feminist: A Philosophical Enquiry*. London: Routledge and Kegan Paul.

Ramsay, M. (1992) *Human Needs and the Market*. Aldershot: Avebury.

Ramsay, M. (1993) Economic and industrial understanding: the problems, opportunities and challenges. *Early Child Development and Care*, **94**.

Rawls, J. (1971) *A Theory of Justice*. Oxford: Clarendon Press.

Rawls, J. (1980) Kantian constructivism in moral theory. *Journal of Philosophy*, **88**.

Rawls, J. (1985) Justice as fairness: political not metaphysical. *Philosophy and Public Affairs*, **14**.

Rawls, J. (1988) The priority of right and idea of the good. *Philosophy and Public Affairs*, **17**.

Rawls, J. (1993) Distributive justice. In Ryan, A. (ed.) *Justice*. Oxford: Oxford University Press, originally published in Laslett, P. and Runciman, W.G. (eds) (1967) *Philosophy, Politics and Society*. Oxford: Blackwell.

Rhode, D.L. (1989) *Justice and Gender*. Cambridge, MA: Harvard University Press.

Rhode, D.L. (1992) The politics of paradigms: gender difference and gender disadvantage. In Block, G. and James, S. (eds) *Beyond Equality and Difference*. London: Routledge.

Rich, A. (1977) *Of Woman Born: Motherhood as Experience and Institution*. London: Virago.

Rich, A. (1980) Compulsory heterosexuality and lesbian experience. *Signs*, **5** (4).

Rousseau, J.-J. (1975) *The Social Contract*. London: Dent.

Ruddick, S. (1980) Maternal thinking. *Feminist Studies*, **6** (1).

Ruddick, S. (1990) *Maternal Thinking. Towards a Politics of Peace*. London: Women's Press.

Runciman, W. G. (1966) *Relative Deprivation and Social Justice*. London: Routledge and Kegan Paul.

Sandel, M. (1982) *Liberalism and the Limits of Justice*. Cambridge: Cambridge University Press.

Scarre, G. (1980) Children and paternalism. *Philosophy*, **5**.

Schaar, J. H. (1967) Equality of opportunity and beyond. In Pennock, J.R. and Chapman, J.W. (eds) *Equality: Nomos IX*. New York: Atherton Press.

Scheffler, S. (1982) Natural rights, equality and the minimal state. In Paul, J. (ed.) *Reading Nozick*. Oxford: Blackwell.

Schrag, F. (1977) The child in the moral order. *Philosophy*, **52**.

Sen, A.K. (1985) *Commodities and Capabilities*. Amsterdam: Elsevier.

Sher, G. (1979) Justifying reverse discrimination in employment. In Rachels, J. (ed.) *Moral Problems*. New York: Harper and Row.

Shue, H. (1980) *Basic Rights*. Princeton: Princeton University Press.

Smart, J. C. and Williams, B. (1973) *Utilitarianism*. Cambridge: Cambridge University Press.

Soper, K. (1981) *On Human Needs*. Brighton: Harvester.

Springborg, P. (1981) *The Problem of Human Needs and the Critique of Civilisation*. London: Allen and Unwin.

Steiner, H. (1974) Individual liberty. *Proceedings of the Aristotelian Society*, **75**.

Taylor, C. (1982) The diversity of goods. In Sen, A. and Williams, B. (eds) *Utilitarianism and Beyond*. Cambridge: Cambridge University Press.

Taylor, C. (1990) *Sources of the Self*. Cambridge: Cambridge University Press.

Taylor, C. (1991) What's wrong with negative liberty. In Miller, D. (ed.) *Liberty*. Oxford: Oxford University Press.

Taylor, P. (1959) Need statements. *Analysis*, **19** (5).

Tronto, J.C. (1993) Beyond gender difference to a theory of care. In Larrabee, M.J. (ed.) *An Ethic of Care*. New York and London: Routledge.

UN Development Programme (1994) *Human Development Report*. New York and Oxford: Oxford University Press.

Walker, L.J. (1993) Sex differences in the development of moral reasoning: a critical review. In Larrabee, M.J. (ed.) *An Ethic of Care*. New York and London: Routledge.

Waltzer, M. (1981) Philosophy and democracy. *Political Theory*, **9**.

Waltzer, M. (1983) *Spheres of Justice*. New York: Basic Books.

Wasserstrom, R. (1980) On preferential treatment. In Wasserstrom, R. *Philosophy and Social Issues*. Notre Dame, IN: Notre Dame University Press.

Weale, A. (1978) *Equality and Social Policy*. London: Routledge and Kegan Paul.

White, A.R. (1971) *Modal Thinking*. Oxford: Blackwell.

Wilson, E. (1977) *Women and the Welfare State*. London: Tavistock.

Wittgenstein, L. (1958) *Philosophical Investigations*. Oxford: Blackwell.

Woolf, R. P. (1977) *Understanding Rawls*. Princeton: Princeton University Press.

World Health Organization (1995) *Bridging the Gaps*. Geneva: WHO.

Young, I. M. (1990) *Justice and the Politics of Difference*. Princeton: Princeton University Press.

Index

ability 71-3, 89-91
abstract individualism
  communitarian
    critiques 24-7, 115-16,
    249-51
  feminist critiques 27-32,
    196, 198, 207, 219, 221,
    249-51
  inadequacy of 32-7,
    207-8, 222, 242-6
  liberalism and 7-20
  Marxism and 20-4, 205,
    243
Acton, H. 92
acts and ommissions 154-7
agency
  moral 133, 148, 162, 225-6
  needs and 148-50, 225,
    248-9
  rights and 148, 162-3,
    248-9
Allen, A. 197
ambition sensitive 90
Anscombe, E. 26, 228
Arblaster, A. 198
Assiter, A. 198
autonomy 57-60, 61-3, 71-5,
    184-8

Baachi, C. 169-70
Baier, A. 217

Baker, J. 83, 98
Barber, B. 118
Barker, D. 194
Barry, B. 224, 225
benevolence 15, 35, 36
Benhabib, S. 115
Benn, S.I. 223
Bentham, J. 8, 10, 12, 13-16,
    38, 52, 102-4, 107-8, 145
Berlin, I. 18, 38, 48, 50-2,
    55-6, 60-1, 64
Blum, L. 212
Boxhill, B. 173
Broughton, J. 213, 215
Burke, E. 145

Campbell, T. 89
capitalism 8, 22-4, 50, 53,
    138, 141, 165
care, ethic of 209-21
  insights of 217-21
  justice and 211-17
Carens, J. 91
Carritt, E. 97
Children's Act 184
chidren's rights 178-90
  needs of 188-90
  paternalism and 178-9,
    181-2
  political rights 182-4, 187,
    188

rationality and 179-81
Chodorow, N. 31
choice 43-8, 71-4, 89-92,
    118-19, 181, 230, 242
civil rights 146-7, 149-53,
    162-3, 166-7, 188, 247
Cixous, H. 30
Coates, K. 235
coercion 41-2, 46-9, 61-3,
    134-5, 225
Cohen, G. 139, 172
Collins, J. 159
common good 22, 35, 102,
    251-2
communitarianism 24-7,
    115-16, 249-51
compensation 83-5, 172,
    173-4, 177
conceptions of the good 36-7,
    66, 106, 114, 139, 222,
    226, 236, 241-6
contribution principle 70, 71,
    76-8
co-operation 30, 35, 78, 84,
    115, 164, 245
Cranston, M. 150

Daly, M. 30
Daniels, N. 121, 122, 226
Davis, K. 80-1
Day, J. 43, 46
Dearden, R. 224
Delphy, C. 28
desert 68-80, 172, 177-8
desires see wants
difference principle 86-9, 92,
    100, 117, 119-22, 135,
    162
Dinnerstein, D. 31
discrimination 70, 166, 167,
    170, 172, 173

division of labour 23, 170,
    199, 202-4, 206
domestic labour 29, 170, 193,
    194
domestic sphere 192-6,
    203-4, 209
    see also public/private
    distiction
Doyal, L. 226
duties
    negative 146, 149, 150-6,
        161, 189, 247-52
    positive 146, 149, 150-6,
        161, 189, 247-52
Dworkin, R.
    equality and 89-92, 99,
        100
    justice and 125-30
    natural assets and 73,
        89-91
Dyer, D. 148

education 97, 185-7, 188, 191
efficiency 81, 138, 173, 238
effort 73-5
Eisenberg, N. 211
Eisenstein, Z. 198
Elshtain, J. 198
endowment sensitive 90
equal opportunities 70, 73, 89,
    92-4, 166, 173-7, 201,
    206
equality
    desert and 69-80
    Dworkin and 89-92
    Nozick and 92-9
    Rawls and 85-9
    utilitarianism and 80-5
European Convention for the
    Protection of Human
    Rights 146

external preferences *see* preferences

family 28, 29, 192-3, 196-7, 202-4, 217
Feinberg J. 47, 54, 55, 64, 83
feminism
  the abstract individual 27-32, 115-16, 198, 207, 219, 221, 249-51
  ethic of care 209-21, 249, 250
  public/private distinction 192-208
Firestone, S. 29
Fisk, M. 114, 120
Fitzgerald, R. 223, 234
Flanagan, O. 216
Flax, J. 169
Flew, A. 11, 224
Foot, P. 155
Frankena, W. 214
Frankfurt, H. 224
Franklin, B. 180, 183, 184
freedom 38-67
  ability and 41-2, 45
  deliberate impediments to 41, 42, 45-53
  equality and 92-9
  internal obstacles to 53-5
  needs and 240-6
  wants and 233-6
  see also liberty
Fried, C. 150, 151, 156
Friedman, M. 18, 38, 92, 209, 211

gender roles 28, 169-70, 173, 202
George, S. 159
Gewirth, A. 147-9, 226, 247-8, 250
Gilligan, C. 31, 116, 167, 210, 213, 214, 216, 221
Glover, J. 157, 158, 159
good *see* conceptions of the good
goods
  Gewirth's generic 148-9, 226, 248
  Rawls's primary 112, 114, 116-17
Gough, I. 226
Green, T.H. 19, 25, 52
Grey, T. 121
Griffin, S. 167

happiness 102-4, 107, 108
Hare, R. 112
Harris, J. 115, 157-9, 178, 180-5
Hart, H. 147, 225
Hayek, F. 8, 9, 18, 38, 41-2, 92
Held, V. 210
Heller, A. 224
Hobbes, T. 9, 12, 13, 15, 17, 38, 68
Holt, J. 183
Honderich, T. 115, 157
housework *see* domestic labour
Human Development Report 152
human nature
  communitarianism and 24-7, 115-16, 249-51
  feminism and 27-32, 115-16, 196, 198, 217, 249-51
  liberalism and 7-37
  Marxism and 20-4
human rights 146-50
Hume, D. 10, 12, 15, 220

impartiality   31, 36, 110, 114,
    209, 212-13
incentives   81-5, 87-8, 91, 99
intention   49, 156
inviolability   109, 145, 146
Irigaray, L.   30

Jackson, K.   216
Jarvis Thomson, J.   172
justice
    care and   211-17
    Dworkin and   125-30
    family and   194-7, 200-3,
        217-18
    Nozick and   131-41
    Rawls and   109-25
    utility and   105-9

Kant, I.   16, 38, 54, 212
Kantian respect for
        persons   71, 133,
        139-40, 142, 162, 247
Kennedy, E.   199
Kristeva, J.   30
Krouse, R.   91
Kymlicka, W.   89, 192, 196,
    204, 211, 215

Lappe, F.   159
Lennon, R.   211
Leontief, W.   153
liberty
    negative   17-20, 38-55,
        100, 147-9, 197-8, 206,
        239-40
    positive   55-63, 100, 147-9
    see also freedom
Lindley, R.   181, 183, 184, 188
Locke, J.   7, 10, 12, 13, 17, 38,
    68, 143-4, 200
Lockean proviso   134-5, 138-9

Lucas, J.R.   94, 95
Lukes, S.   114, 138
Lyons, D.   113, 121

MacCallum, G.   64
McInnes, N.   224
MacIntyre, A.   105, 115, 212,
    250
MacKinnon, C.   168, 196-7
Macpherson, C.   13, 14, 52, 57,
    61-2, 91
McPherson, H.   91
Mandeville, R.   15
Mapel, D.   91
market, free   10, 77, 105, 135,
    153, 225, 236-40
Marx, K.   20-4, 45-6, 145-6
maximin strategy   117-18
Mendus, S.   199
merit see desert
Mill, J.S.
    On Liberty   17, 19, 38, 54,
        57, 179, 180, 185
    On the Subjection Of
        Women   27, 166, 200-3
    utilitarianism   102-4,
        107-8, 145
Miller, D.   49, 83, 114
Millett, K.   194
Molesworth, W.   9, 12, 13, 17
Moore, G.E.   104-5
Moore, W.   80-1
moral agency see agency
moral arbitrariness   86, 89,
    100, 120
morality   14, 16, 31, 148,
    209-20, 249
Mulhall, B.   25

Nagel, T.   120, 139, 172, 178
Narveson, J.   121

natural rights   7-8, 68, 107-8, 144-6
needs   222-52
    as conditions of action   225-7, 241
    freedom and   240-6
    liberal objections to   223-5
    obligations and   247-52
    rights and   247-52
    wants and   227-33
negative liberty see liberty
neutrality   66, 106, 114, 128-30, 222, 242-6, 251-2
Nicholson, L.J.   194
Nielson, K.   96, 98, 225
Noddings, N.   31, 167, 210
Norman, R.   26, 83, 88, 96-7, 228
Nozick, R.
    arguments against equality   92-9
    arguments against redistribution   135-7
    problems for   137-42

obligations see duties
Okin, S.   199, 202-3, 218
Olsen, E.   194
Oppenheim, F.   40-1, 43
original position   16, 110-16, 118, 124, 218-19

Paine, T.   144
Parent, W.   43, 45, 46
Pateman, C.   116, 192, 195-6, 199
paternalism   178, 185, 189
patriarchy   28, 193, 194, 200-4
Peters, R.   223
Phillips, A.   192-3, 195

plans of life see conceptions of the good
Plant, R.   48-9, 139, 156-7, 226
pluralism   223, 238, 240-1
political rights   146, 149-53, 162-3, 166-7, 181-4, 187-9, 247
Popper, K.   8, 9
positive liberty see liberty
poverty   50-2, 158-60, 187, 189, 235
preferences
    external   127-9
    personal   127-9
    see also wants
primary goods   112, 114, 116-17
privacy
    rights to   192, 196-8
property rights   134, 135, 136, 137, 140-1
public/private
    distinction   192-221
    characteristic of liberalism   198-208
    domestic/public distinction   192-4
    public and private virtues   209-21
    state/society distinction   195-6

Radcliffe Richards, J.   176
Ramsay, M.   187, 226, 227
rationality
    critique of   27, 30-1, 36-7, 207, 212-13, 219
    impartiality and   15-17, 219-20
    self-interest and   14, 15-17, 218-20

Rawls, J.
    original position   16,
        110-16, 124, 218-19
    the two principles   85-9,
        117-23
reason *see* rationality
rectification   134, 135, 141,
    172
redistribution   65, 89-92, 97,
    99, 135-7, 163
reflective equilibrium   110-13
responsibility
    for choices   71-5, 89-92
    in care ethic   210, 220, 249
reverse discrimination   171-8
Rhode, D.L.   169, 170
Rich, A.   29, 167
rights
    children's   178-90
    civil and political   146-6,
        149-53, 162-3, 166-7,
        181-4, 187-9, 247
    human   146-50
    Kantian basis for   68, 132,
        139, 147-50, 162-4, 247
    natural   7, 68, 107-8,
        144-6
    needs and   247-52
    social and economic   146-
        7, 149, 150, 152-3, 247,
        353
    women's   166-78
risk aversion   118
Ruddick, S.   31, 167
Runciman, W.G.   235

Sandel, M.   25, 115
Scarre, G.   180, 181
Schaar, J.   93-4
Scheffler, S.   139
Schrag, F.   180, 181

self-determination   19, 40,
    56-8, 139, 163, 235
self-interest   12-14, 23, 30, 35,
    164, 219-20, 243-5
self-ownership   136-8
self-respect   94-5
Sen, A.   226
separateness of persons   133,
    139-40
sexual equality   167-78, 199,
    203, 204, 206
sexual violence   29, 161, 194
sexuality   28-9, 191, 194,
    203-4
shared values *see* conceptions of
    the good
Sher, G.   173
Shue, H.   151-2, 226
Silburn, R.   235
Smart, J.   109
Smith, A.   10, 15, 38, 52
socio-economic rights   147,
    149, 152-3, 162-3, 247,
    253
Soper, K.   223
Springborg, P.   223, 224
state
    mimimal state   18, 131-5,
        141, 164
    welfare state   19, 91, 131,
        135, 194
Steiner, H.   43, 45, 46-7
sympathy   220-1

taxation   63, 118, 132, 135,
    140, 151
Taylor, C.   25, 40, 44-5, 53-5,
    57-8, 115, 228, 250
Taylor, P.   223
tolerance   244, 245
Tronto, J.   210, 215, 217

UN Convention of Economic,
    Social and Cultural
    Rights   146
UN Convention on the Rights of
    the Child   184, 188
UN Declaration of Human
    Rights   146
universalizability   31, 116, 124,
    213, 248, 251
utilitarianism   80-5, 101-9,
    118, 125-8, 130-2
  act utilitarianism   108-9
  rule utilitarianism   108-9,
    225
utility
  inequality and   80-5
  justice and   101-9, 125-7
  rights and   125-7, 130, 145

veil of ignorance   111, 118-19,
    122

Walker, C.   211

Walzer, M.   25, 115
wants
  freedom and   43-4, 233-6
  market and   44-5, 236-40
  needs and   9-12, 26-7,
    227-33
Wasserstrom, R.   175
Weale, A.   225
welfare   19-20, 65-7, 131,
    135, 164, 194
White, A.   224
WHO Report, Bridging the
    Gaps   189
Williams, B.   109
Wilson, E.   194
Wittgenstein, L.   25
women
  equal rights and   166-9
  special rights and
    169-71
Woolf, R.P.   25, 115

Young, I,   168, 170